W9-ASR-732

More Praise For *When Can You Trust the Experts?*

"As a parent, when it was time for my daughter to start school I was overwhelmed by all the claims made about education and then appalled by the level of pseudoscience in the various claims and theories about the best educational method. I didn't know where to turn because the experts seemed to contradict one another. I wish I had Daniel Willingham's guide for the educationally perplexed—*When Can You Trust the Experts?*—when I was trying to sort through the maze of ideas. He has succinctly cut through the obfuscating jargon to reveal what we know and do not know about education. A must-read for parents, educators, and policy makers alike."—Michael Shermer, publisher, *Skeptic* magazine; monthly columnist for *Scientific American*; author, *The Believing Brain*

"There are a lot of proposals on how to improve education, but too often the current heated debate is fueled by preconceived opinions rather than hard evidence about what actually works. Dan Willingham is determined to change that. In this carefully reasoned, important book, he teaches us how to thoughtfully evaluate educational research in the sincere belief that the debate will benefit from more light and less heat."—Joel Klein, CEO Education Division, News Corporation; former chancellor, NYC public schools

"The phrase 'the research says...' gets used to justify just about every practice in contemporary education, including those for which there's very little real empirical evidence. So those who want classroom practice to be informed and improved by data may find themselves asking, 'What does the best research really tell us?' and, 'How do you differentiate the real thing from pseudo-science?' Fortunately, Dan Willingham—for my money the most insightful and readable cognitive scientist in the field—has written a book that can help teachers, and just about everyone, understand the difference."—Doug Lemov, author, *Teach Like a Champion*

"Willingham's latest book offers a vital contribution to our stale school debates. In a clear, step-by-step fashion, he teaches us how to use evidence and reason to understand what is good educational research, how to spot the snake-oil salesmen, and ways to separate fact from fantasy. It is a must-read for policy makers, practitioners, and parents."—Tony Wagner, author, *The Global Achievement Gap* and *Creating Innovators*

"This is a wise, engagingly written book on an important topic. If you see education as an evidence-based field, it would be worthwhile for you to read it. If you see education as an art not amenable to science, it is essential that you read it." —Russ Whitehurst, director, Brown Center on Education Policy, The Brookings Institution

WHEN CAN
YOU
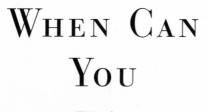
THE EXPERTS?

DANIEL T.
WILLINGHAM

When Can
You
Trust
the Experts?

HOW TO TELL GOOD SCIENCE FROM
BAD IN EDUCATION

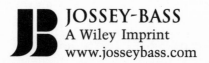

JOSSEY-BASS
A Wiley Imprint
www.josseybass.com

Published by Jossey-Bass
A Wiley Imprint
One Montgomery Street, Suite 1200, San Francisco, CA 94104-4594
www.josseybass.com

Pages 253–255 constitute a continuation of the copyright page.

Jacket design by Jeff Puda. Cover Illustrations © istock RF.

Jossey-Bass books and products are available through most bookstores. To contact Jossey-Bass directly call our Customer Care Department within the U.S. at 800-956-7739, outside the U.S. at 317-572-3986, or fax 317-572-4002.

Wiley publishes in a variety of print and electronic formats and by print-on-demand. Some material included with standard print versions of this book may not be included in e-books or in print-on-demand. If this book refers to media such as a CD or DVD that is not included in the version you purchased, you may download this material at http://booksupport.wiley.com. For more information about Wiley products, visit www.wiley.com.

Library of Congress Cataloging-in-Publication Data
    Willingham, Daniel T.
    When can you trust the experts? : how to tell good science from bad in education / Daniel T. Willingham. — First edition.
        pages   cm
    Includes bibliographical references and index.
    ISBN 978-1-118-13027-8 (hardcover); ISBN 978-1-118-22569-1 (ebk.);
    ISBN 9781-1-182-3327-6 (ebk.); ISBN 978-1-118-26310-5 (ebk.)
        1. Education—Research.   I. Title.
  LB1028.W519175 2012
  370.72—dc23   2012010764

Printed in the United States of America

FIRST EDITION
HB Printing   10   9   8   7   6   5   4   3   2   1

This book is dedicated to my children.

If a man will begin with certainties, he shall end in doubts; but if he will be content to begin with doubts he shall end in certainties.
—Francis Bacon

Contents

About the Author xi

Acknowledgments. xii

Introduction: What Are You to Believe? 1

PART ONE

Why We So Easily Believe Bad Science

CHAPTER 1

Why Smart People Believe
Dumb Things. 31

CHAPTER 2

Science and Belief:
A Nervous Romance. 57

CHAPTER 3

What Scientists Call Good Science. 81

CHAPTER 4

How to Use Science. 107

PART TWO
The Shortcut Solution

CHAPTER 5
Step One: Strip It and Flip It 135

CHAPTER 6
Step Two: Trace It. 167

CHAPTER 7
Step Three: Analyze It. 183

CHAPTER 8
Step Four: Should I Do It?. 207

Endnotes 223
Name Index 237
Subject Index. 243

About the Author

Daniel T. Willingham earned his B.A. degree in psychology from Duke University in 1983 and his Ph.D. degree in cognitive psychology from Harvard University in 1990. He is currently professor of psychology at the University of Virginia, where he has taught since 1992. Until about 2000, his research focused solely on the brain basis of learning and memory. Today, all of his research concerns the application of cognitive psychology to K–12 education. He writes the "Ask the Cognitive Scientist" column for *American Educator* magazine and is the author of *Why Don't Students Like School?* (Jossey-Bass, 2009). His writing on education has been translated into ten languages. His website is http://www.danielwillingham.com.

Acknowledgments

My thanks to Dimi Berkner, Wendy Fisher, Tracy Gallagher, Jonathan Haidt, Lisa Hansel, Joe Hartley, Robin Lloyd, Margie McAneny, Jason Millard, Brian Nosek, Denny Proffitt, Samantha Rubenstein, Abe Witonsky, and three anonymous reviewers. My particular thanks to Esmond Harmsworth.

WHEN CAN YOU *Trust* THE EXPERTS?

Introduction:
What Are You to Believe?

> Before obtaining certainty we must often be satisfied
> with a more or less plausible guess.
>
> —*George Polya*[1]

Try this sometime. Ask a friend, "Why do you believe what
you believe? What sort of evidence persuades you that someone is right or that a product is good?" This question seldom elicits a careful, thoughtful response. Rather, it elicits silence
and narrowed eyes. Most people think that their beliefs are shaped
by logic and reason. Your friend will likely detect a whiff of insult
in the question.

But our beliefs are fueled by much more than reason and fact. Yes,
we are persuaded by solid evidence assembled into arguments that
conform to principles of logic. But that's true only for the messages that we examine, and we don't have the time to audit every
advertisement we hear and blog posting we read. We are pelted
by information almost constantly. Just think of the ubiquity of
screens. At airport gates, in restaurants, in waiting rooms, in the
post office, even in hotel elevators. If a location provides a captive
human audience, there is likely to be a screen, flashing updates from
Afghanistan, coverage of a golf tournament, or an advertisement
for Claritin. Much of this information is not neutral. It is meant to

persuade us of something. Yet we don't have the time or the mental energy to think through every message that comes our way.

Are we influenced by messages that we ignore? I stand in line at my bank and notice a large television behind the teller, displaying a channel exclusive to my bank. An advertisement appears, showing a sedan wending along a New England country road, scattering autumn leaves. I go into a reverie, thinking of the Berkshire mountains. I haven't consciously noticed the make of the car . . . but am I nevertheless influenced? When I next need a car, even if it's four years from now, perhaps I'll be a bit more likely to buy this model because I was exposed to this ad. Will I be more likely to apply for a car loan at this bank, rather than shopping around for the best rate? *Is it possible for attitudes to change outside my awareness?* Although it makes us uncomfortable to contemplate it, psychological research from the last fifty years indicates that the answer is yes.

Sometimes, of course, I do pay attention to these messages, and I don't fully trust what I'm hearing. For example, when I read *Mother Jones* or the *Weekly Standard*, I am aware that each has a political point of view, and I try to remember that information may be omitted or the interpretation of facts stretched to be consistent with that view. When I hear the president of Iran give a speech, I recall that he has denied that the Holocaust took place, so I am wary of any claim he makes. *When I listen carefully to messages, am I able to account for the bias or trustworthiness of the source?* To some extent, yes, but not completely.

I am making it sound as though we all are buffeted about—no, worse, systematically manipulated—by forces that operate outside our awareness or, even if we are aware of them, outside our control. Putting it that way is a bit dramatic, but it's not far from the truth.

This book will tell you how to evaluate new ideas—in particular, those related to education—so that you are less likely to be persuaded by bad evidence.

The Golden Ratio

Forewarned is forearmed. The first step in defending yourself from hidden persuaders is identifying them. I begin with what is perhaps the strangest example. The very *shape* that carries information to you has an impact on whether or not you believe this information. This story is a bit complex, although the mathematics behind it is relatively simple.

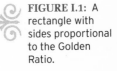

You and I have a number in common, a number that influences what we consider beautiful and worthy of our sustained attention: 1.618. (Actually, it's 1.6180339887, but I'll use the truncated version.) It's important not as a number but as a ratio, and the simplest way to understand it is to consider the rectangle shown in Figure I.1.

FIGURE I.1: A rectangle with sides proportional to the Golden Ratio.

The ratio of the length of side b to side a is 1.618, and people find rectangles of this proportion more aesthetically pleasing than other rectangles. Confronted with, say, thirty rectangles of various proportions, most people pick this one as the most attractive. Because of its importance in aesthetics, 1.618 is called the Golden Ratio.

Researchers have observed this ratio in classical architecture. For example, the width and height of the façade of the Parthenon in Greece respects the Golden Ratio. It is also observed in the great pyramid of Giza.

FIGURE I.2: Classic works of architecture such as the Parthenon (or the reproduction in Nashville, Tennessee, shown here) and the Great Pyramid of Giza have the Golden Ratio embedded in their proportions.

If one forms a triangle as shown, the ratio of the length of one face to half the length of the base is within 1 percent of the Golden Ratio (Figure I.2).

1   .618   1

FIGURE I.3: Iconic works of Western art that show the Golden Ratio in their proportions.

The Golden Ratio is observed in smaller-scale works of art as well, including the placement of figures in paintings by da Vinci and the elements of a Stradivarius violin (Figure I.3).

Why would this ratio be aesthetically pleasing across cultures and across centuries? A reasonable suggestion is that it is commonly observed in nature. Indeed, the Golden Ratio is found in proportions

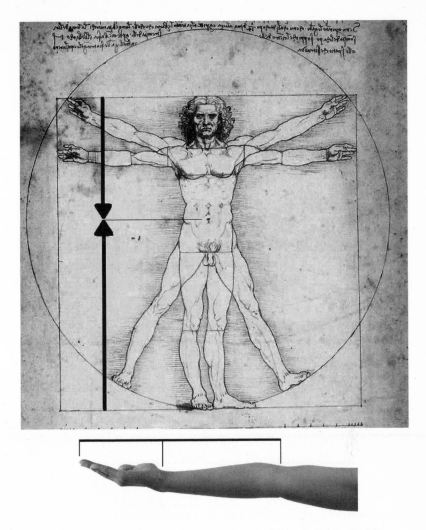

FIGURE I.4: Ratios of body parts also show the Golden Ratio. See text for description.

of the human body (Figure I.4) and the human face, especially faces that others find attractive.

If the distance between the navel and the foot is taken as 1 unit, the height of a human being is typically equivalent to 1.618. Some other golden proportions in the average human body are

- The distance between the finger tip and the elbow/distance between the wrist and the elbow

- The distance between the shoulder line and the top of the head/head length
- The distance between the navel and the top of the head/distance between the shoulder line and the top of the head
- The distance between the navel and the knee/distance between the knee and the end of the foot

Naturally, there is variation across individuals in these proportions. The Golden Ratio is observed when we take averages across many individuals, and individuals with the "ideal proportions" are judged by others as having well-proportioned bodies.

The same is true for faces, and here the relationship to attractiveness is easy to appreciate. Faces are attractive not only because the eyes and the mouth are well shaped. The proportions of the face must be right. If a person's eyes are too close together or too far apart, he or she is not attractive. The actress Jessica Alba, commonly considered to be very attractive, not only has a dazzling smile and beautiful eyes, but the distances between her features match the Golden Ratio perfectly (Figure I.5).

The Golden Ratio is observed elsewhere in nature as a spiral. To understand how, you need a basic understanding of the underlying mathematics. The Golden Ratio was first described by twelfth-century mathematician Leonardo Fibonacci. Perhaps you've heard of the Fibonacci sequence: I begin with the numbers 0 and 1, and then add the last two numbers in the sequence to generate the next number. That is, $0 + 1 = 1$, so the sequence begins 0, 1, 1. To obtain the next number, I add the final two in the sequence thus far, hence, $1 + 1 = 2$. So now the sequence is 0, 1, 1, 2. Continuing, the sequence is: 0, 1, 1, 2, 3, 5, 8, 13, 21, 34, 55, 89, 144, and so on. If I take the ratio of successive numbers, the values converge on the Golden Ratio (Table I.1).

Now suppose that I create squares, each with sides equivalent to the numbers in the Fibonacci sequence (that is, I create squares whose sides are of lengths 1, 1, 2, 3, 5, and so on). Each square I create is added to the others so that they form a rectangle (Figure I.6). I can create an arc by connecting opposite corners of the squares.

This is called a Fibonacci arc, and it too is observed in nature—for example, in the shape of seashells like the nautilus, and in the pattern

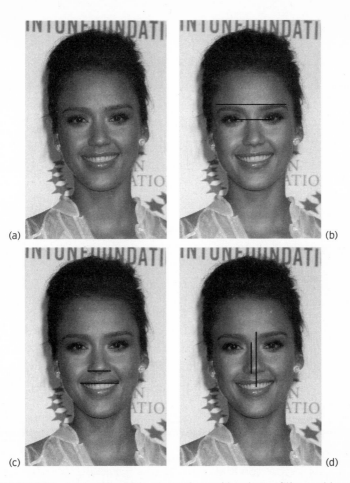

FIGURE I.5: Jessica Alba (a) is commonly considered one of the most beautiful women in Hollywood. These photos show some of the Golden Ratios observed in the proportion of features observed in the ideal human face: (b) distance between pupils / distance between eyebrows; (c) width of mouth / width of nose; and (d) distance between lips and where eyebrows meet / length of nose.

TABLE I.1: The ratio of neighboring numbers in the Fibonacci sequence converge on the Golden Ratio.

Ratio	Value
3 to 2	1.5000
8 to 5	1.6000
21 to 13	1.6154
55 to 34	1.6176
144 to 89	1.6179

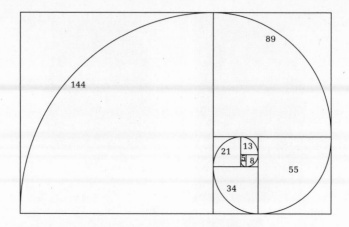

 FIGURE I.6: A Fibonacci arc. See text for description.

of the seeds of flowers (such as the sunflower and daisy, as shown in Figure I.7). Spirals are observed in other plants as well—for example, the cauliflower, although easier to see in the Romanesco (a kind of broccoli-cauliflower hybrid).

Fibonacci sequences are also present, though more subtly so, in the arrangement of leaves of many plants.

For example, in the rubber plant shown in Figure I.8, starting from the top we have three clockwise rotations before we meet another leaf directly below the first, passing five leaves on the way. If we go counterclockwise, we need just two rotations. Note that 2, 3, and 5 are consecutive Fibonacci numbers. This ratio of rotations to leaves is commonly observed.

The interpretation of the aesthetic value of the Golden Ratio would seem to be clear: we are naturally drawn to objects showing the Golden Ratio because this ratio is found throughout nature.

But what is the connection of the Golden Ratio to persuasion? The great nineteenth-century British poet John Keats ended "Ode on a Grecian Urn" with these words: "Beauty is truth, truth beauty. That is all ye know on earth, and all ye need to know." Keats, it turns out, was an excellent psychologist. We associate beauty and truth. When we see something that is physically beautiful, we assume that it has other good qualities, including truthfulness.

FIGURE I.7: Examples of Fibonacci arcs observed in nature.

In semiotics (the study of symbols) one would call this a "sign." Just as red means "hot" and blue means "cold," beauty means "truth." But the significance of red and blue to temperature is a cultural convention, and one that each of us must learn. The connection of beauty and truth is made across cultures, and need not be learned. It seems to be a natural part of the human makeup.

People are more likely to believe the contents of a book or magazine if its dimensions correspond to the Golden

FIGURE I.8: The leaves of many plants grow in a Fibonacci spiral, centered on the stem.

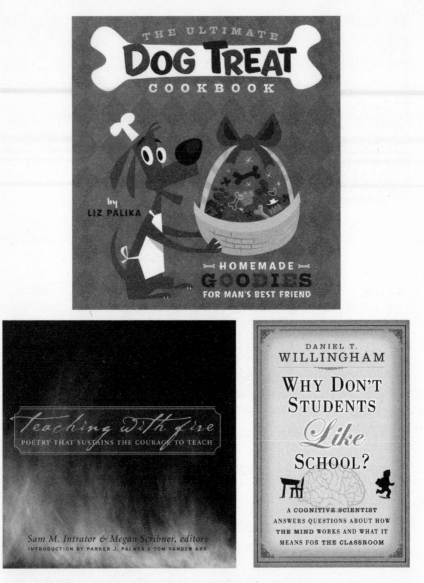

FIGURE I.9: A surprisingly high percentage of nonfiction books use page formats corresponding to the Golden Ratio, but only those that seek to persuade.

Ratio. Children's books might be square, and so might art or cook-books, but something like 95 percent of the nonfiction books that seek to persuade are sold in dimensions within 2 percent of the Golden Ratio (Figure I.9). The figure for magazines is over 90 percent.

The Golden Ratio does exert a powerful and powerfully subtle influence on persuasion. Or it would, if not for a small problem: the Golden Ratio theory is bunk.

Some of the statistics I've cited here are just plain inaccuracies. Studies have been conducted in which people (ordinary people[2] or professional artists and designers[3]) are shown a large selection of rectangles and are asked which they find most attractive. It's *not* the case that people select the Golden Ratio rectangles. Another study examined the dimensions of 565 rectangular paintings by famous artists. Artists showed no predilection for canvas sizes that respected the Golden Ratio; the mean ratio was 1.34.[4] And natural objects like the human body, faces, and seashells show lots of variability. It's not the case that the most attractive show the Golden Ratio.[5] The statistics about the dimensions of books and magazines are complete fabrications.

Some of the Golden Ratio phenomena are accurate but trivial— trivial because examples that fit the Golden Ratio are empha- sized, and examples that do not fit are ignored. Why evaluate the Parthenon and not the Pantheon? Why the pyramid of Giza and not the pyramid of Khafre? For that matter, why not the Roman Colosseum, the Taj Mahal, the Alhambra, or the Eiffel Tower? Then, too, a complex figure like the Parthenon or *The Last Supper* has many measurable features; that makes it too easy to pick and choose measurements that yield the desired ratio.[6]

I apologize for beginning this book with a sucker punch. (Maybe some part of me wanted company. I fell for the Golden Ratio hook, line, and sinker when I first heard it.*) The Golden Ratio is not interesting because it's true. It's interesting because the idea sur- vives and continues to attract believers even though it is *known* to be wrong. In that way, it's an object lesson for this book. Knowing what to believe is a problem.

---

*I was in graduate school. A professor laid out the evidence for the Golden Ratio with a straight face, and I was not merely interested: I was agape. I was sure that God himself had placed this number in nature as some sort of code for us to decipher. When the professor pointed out all the flaws in the Golden Ratio argument, I felt cheated.

The Problem

People believe lots of things for which the scientific evidence is absent: that a special coin brings them luck, that aliens visit Earth regularly, or that astrological predictions are better than chance.[†] Many such beliefs, though unfounded, are harmless. Maybe they cost us a little time or money, but we find them fun or interesting, and we don't take them all that seriously anyway.

But unfounded beliefs related to schooling are of greater concern. The costs in time and money can be substantial; worse, faulty beliefs about learning can potentially cost kids their education. Scientific tools can be a real help in sorting out which methods and materials truly help students learn and which do not. We cannot afford to let educational practice be guided by hunch or hope if better information is available. But even though scientific tools are routinely applied, the product is often ignored, or else it's twisted by people with dollars on their minds.

Consider learning styles theories. These theories maintain that different people have different ways of learning, and that we can identify an individual's style, tune our teaching to that style, and make learning easier or more effective. For example, the most popular theory of learning styles holds that some people learn best by seeing things (visual learners), some by hearing things (auditory learners), and some by manipulating objects (kinesthetic learners). This theory has been around for at least twenty-five years, and it has been tested in scientific experiments. In fact, testing the theory is quite straightforward.

1. Take one hundred people and identify them as visual or auditory learners. (Let's skip kinesthetic learners for the sake of simplicity.)
2. Devise comparable visual and auditory materials to learn. For example, people might listen to a story (auditory) or watch a silent slide show depicting the same story (visual).

[†]If you believe any of these things, please don't be insulted by my cavalier dismissal. I'm not here to tell you what to believe. But I will state flatly that there is no scientific evidence supporting these beliefs.

3. Have fifty people experience the story in their preferred way, and fifty people experience the story in their nonpreferred way.

4. The next day, test everyone's memory for the story. If the learning styles theory is true, people who experienced the story in their preferred way ought to remember it better.

Experiments like this have been conducted, and there is no support for the learning styles idea.[7] Not for visual, auditory, or kinesthetic learners, nor for linear or holistic learners, nor for any of the other learners described by learning styles theories.

Yet if you search for "learning styles" on the Internet, you will not find a brief, academic obituary for this interesting idea that turned out to be wrong. You'll find almost two million hits. You'll find almost two thousand books on Amazon. You'll find the term mentioned on the syllabi of thousands of college courses. And you'll find lots and lots of products that promise improved educational outcomes once you know students' learning styles . . . although knowing a child's learning style often requires buying the book they want to sell you, or attending a workshop they are conducting.

The main cost of learning styles seems to be wasted time and money, and some worry on the part of teachers who feel that they *ought* to be paying more attention to learning styles, for it appears that most teachers don't do much with them. The cost of other scientifically inaccurate beliefs has been more substantial. Consider this example. Before about 1920, the way to teach children to read seemed obvious. You start by teaching them the sound associated with each letter or letter combination (Figure I.10).

In the first quarter of the twentieth century, another theory of reading rose to prominence.[8] In essence, it argued that children should be taught to read the way adults read. Adults seem to read entire words or even phrases all at once. (Watch the eyes of someone reading, and you'll see that they do not dwell on each word, but rather stop a few times as they scan each line.) Adults read silently, which is much faster than reading aloud. And adults read what interests them. Children, in contrast, are taught to read sound by sound (not whole words), aloud (not silently), and out of boring primers (not engaging material).

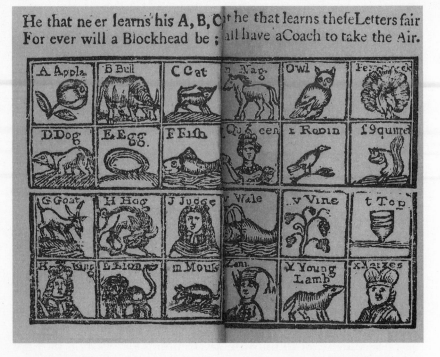

FIGURE I.10: For many years, students learning to read were first taught to associate the shape of letters with associated sounds, as in this image, reproduced from the *New England Primer*, published around 1760.

In what became known at the look-say or whole-word method, children were encouraged to memorize entire words. Books for reading instruction used a limited set of words so as to make memorization possible.[9] Students were encouraged to guess at a word based on the surrounding context and pictures if they did not recognize it. This method also emphasized that phonics drills—memorizing letters and their associated sounds—are boring and that using them was likely to make children hate reading. Instead, the whole-word method suggested that children be surrounded by real books, not drill materials, and that the stories be ones that they can understand and identify with. The whole-word method became dominant in American education during the 1930s and 1940s.[10]

Two factors might have tipped off educators that this approach to reading instruction was suspect. First, written language is a sound-based system, not a meaning-based system. Seeing the three letters *d, o,* and *g* doesn't tell you meaning. Letters signify *sounds.* If that weren't true, then when I showed you an unfamiliar word—for example, "mielesta"—you wouldn't just be uncertain of its meaning; you would also have no idea of how to pronounce it. Given that writing is sound based, teaching reading with a method that ignores sound seems risky.

Second, the theory encourages the teaching of reading based on the way adults read. On the one hand, you can see the logic: if you want to learn something, find someone who is good at it and then try to do what he or she does. On the other hand, there's no guarantee that the expert did it that way when he or she was a beginner. An expert basketball player no longer needs to think about the basics of ball handling and footwork because that has been so extensively practiced. The expert thinks about play making and strategy, but the beginner needs to think about fundamentals. Copying an expert reader is not necessarily a good strategy for beginning readers.

In 1955, the book *Why Johnny Can't Read* was published.[11] It argued that if the direct teaching of the sounds that go with letters were omitted, reading was not being taught. The book was a strident, take-no-prisoners invective, and it became a best seller. The book was negatively reviewed by many education professionals, however.[12] Professors who studied reading argued that the book was ill-informed and that the author was simply wrong. Over the next several years, arguments over how to teach reading raged, later dubbed "the Reading Wars."

In 1961, the Carnegie Corporation sought a scholar to comb through all of the scientific studies and to draw a conclusion: Was phonics-based or whole-word instruction superior? Jeanne Chall, a professor at the Harvard Graduate School of Education, was selected to conduct the review. In her 1967 book, she said that the relevant research showed that the phonics method was superior.[13]

That sounds clear enough, right? Education rides off the rails briefly (well, actually for thirty years or so), but science comes to the rescue. So we would expect that post-1967, the whole-word approach to reading instruction would be relegated to the dustbin. Well, we'd be wrong. The basic idea behind whole-word reading resurfaced in the mid-1980s.[14] Renamed "whole language," the pitch was familiar: phonics instruction deadens interest and is unnecessary. Learning to read is as natural as learning to speak. Just surround kids with authentic materials, and they will learn to read on their own. The Reading Wars began again. Some districts and even entire states (notably California) adopted curricula based on the whole-language method of teaching reading.

In 1997, Congress asked the Department of Education to draw together a panel of reading experts to sort through the scientific research on reading instruction. Their conclusion, published in 2000, matched that of Chall in 1967.[15] Phonics instruction is a critical part of learning to read. In its absence, some kids figure out on their own the sounds that go with letters and letter combinations. But some don't. And those kids will end up disliking reading, and some of them will end up being labeled as dyslexic.

The first phase of the Reading Wars was understandable. Someone had an ill-conceived theory about reading instruction. It sounded good, so people tried it. It's somewhat more difficult to understand why it took as long as it did—some thirty years—for the scientific evidence to influence public opinion and public policy. It is nearly inconceivable that the same mistake was made again twenty years later, sparking the second phase of the Reading Wars.‡

When science is brought to bear on education problems carelessly or underhandedly, perhaps the worst damage is inflicted on kids with disabilities. (As the parent of a child with Edwards' syndrome—also called Trisomy 18—I have personal experience here.) Many developmental disabilities do not have effective treatments, and parents are desperate. They are willing, even eager, to try unproven alternative treatments—anything that *might* work, anything that holds out some hope. Furthermore, there are a lot of disabled kids in this country—estimates are that about 13 percent of kids have some

---

‡At least one historian (D. Ravitch, 2000, *Left back* [New York: Simon & Schuster]) argues that the whole-language method caught on because phonics instruction was taken up with too much zest; reading instruction had become boring for kids through the overuse of worksheets and the like. My emphasis on the importance of phonics instruction doesn't mean that there is no value in any aspect of the whole-word or whole-language approaches. Advocates certainly got right the importance of the child's interest. But teaching phonics is not negotiable.

disability, ranging from very mild speech impairments to chromosome disorders that affect nearly every aspect of intellectual and physical development.[16]

Scam artists go where the money is, and the parents of kids with autism spectrum disorder (ASD) are some of their preferred targets because there are a lot of them. Kids with ASD show a fairly broad range of characteristic behaviors, but they tend to have these in common: (1) difficulty with communication, both verbal and nonverbal (that is, pointing, gesturing); (2) problems in social relations, especially in perceiving the emotions and thinking of others; and (3) repetitive behaviors, such as following a strict routine or repeating words or actions again and again. Rates of autism have skyrocketed since 1994 (probably due to changes in diagnostic criteria[17]) so that now approximately 1 in 110 American kids is diagnosed.[18]

Treatment options are limited. The most reliable are behavioral therapies. These boil down to trying to teach the child which behavior is appropriate in a given situation—for example, to make eye contact and to respond when a cashier says "thank you." If he knows which behavior is appropriate but usually doesn't do it, the focus is on increasing the frequency with which the child does it.

Behavioral therapy for ASD is frustrating for everyone involved. It's slow and painstaking, and it must feel to parents like a Band-Aid. It doesn't address the underlying problem, just the symptoms. The underlying problem is certainly not behavioral; kids don't have ASD because of something their parents did or didn't do. ASD has a biological basis. So it seems that the treatment ought to be biological.[§]

Hucksters offer a bazaar of dubious biological therapies for ASD, none of them approved by the Food and Drug Administration, and all of them seeming to offer the promise of getting at the root cause. The least expensive and safest (but certainly inconvenient to follow) include vitamins and supplements or special diets. Other therapies can be wildly expensive—for example, hyperbaric oxygen therapy. Here the child is put in a sealed environment of enriched oxygen

[§]Medications developed for other problems (for example, selective serotonin reuptake inhibitors) are sometimes prescribed for people with ASD. Some medications help with symptoms for some people, but there is not a medication that provides a full-blown cure.

at a pressure greater than atmospheric pressure, which helps the blood carry more oxygen to the organs. Treatments might cost several thousand dollars each month. Another unproven ASD treatment is immunoglobulin (antibodies approved for leukemia and AIDS), which runs about $10,000. Much worse than the costs are the potential side effects. Hyperbaric oxygen therapy can put stress on the lungs, heart, and other organs. Immunoglobulin can cause fever, headache, meningitis, or anaphylactic shock.[19]

What are these parents thinking? Why would they subject their children to unproven therapies? As is so often the case, treatments that initially sound bizarre *do* have a certain logic, once you scratch a bit beneath the surface. There *are* data showing evidence of inflammation in the brains of autistic children. These data come from a study published in the prestigious scientific journal *Annals of Neurology*, by a research team at Johns Hopkins University.[20] The claimed benefit of hyperbaric oxygen therapy and of immunoglobulin is the reduction of inflammation. So there is a rationale for the treatment.

If you were a parent listening to someone trying to sell you one of these treatments, the odds are good that you would be told about the study showing inflammation in the brains of kids with ASD. What you would *not* be told is that the researchers anticipated that quacks would rush to use their research as the basis for ASD "remedies." So on their Web site they published a plain-language explanation of the findings, along with a strongly worded warning against using these findings: "THERE IS NO indication for using anti-inflammatory medications in patients with autism."[21] The Web site mentions immunoglobulin in particular as unlikely to have a significant effect because of the mechanism by which it reduces inflammation.

When we read about fringe ASD treatments, there is a strong temptation to think, "I'm no sucker. I wouldn't believe something for which there is no evidence." Other parents, teachers, and administrators aren't stupid either. As I note, the treatments they believe will work do have a certain logic behind them. Whole-language advocates were correct in criticizing many phonics drills as boring, and the idea of following the methods used by more expert readers has a surface plausibility. The purveyors of unproven ASD therapies can point to reputable scientific studies as their backing, and it would take some scientific sophistication to know that the studies were being misinterpreted. Digging deep enough to spot the misinterpretation may be tougher than you'd think.

Why the Obvious Solution Doesn't Work

Suppose you're a parent looking for supplementary support for your child with dyslexia, or a teacher curious about your district's plan to put a new math program in place, or an educational administrator who has been asked by a superintendent to attend a weekend seminar on team building. In each case, you are assured that the program is "research based."

If you want to know whether something is *really* research based, how could you know? Well, "research based" means that someone has done some formal scientific studies to evaluate whether or not the program, therapy, or gadget really does what it's purported to do. Such research will be published in specialty journals that are devoted to this sort of thing, so that's where you will have to look for it. The simple act of trying to locate scientific studies of a practice may tell you that such studies haven't been done. That alone is useful, and, happily, merely finding out whether the studies have been done is now fairly easy using the Internet. I'll have more to say about this in Chapter Seven.

But knowing whether or not relevant research exists is usually not enough. We saw this in the case of hyperbaric oxygen therapy for ASD. There is bona fide, high-quality evidence for inflammation in the brains of kids with ASD. There is bona fide, high-quality evidence that immunoglobulin can reduce inflammation. But to understand why the therapy is unlikely to work, you need a finer grain of detailed knowledge than most of us have; I'm dimly aware that there are multiple mechanisms by which brain tissue can become inflamed, but I really doubt I would have thought to wonder about that. I also would not have known that inflammation is not always a bad thing; it turns out that inflammation is sometimes a sign that the brain is trying to repair itself. I also probably would not have thought of the possibility that there is some other factor, call it X, that causes ASD *and* causes inflammation as a by-product. Treating the inflammation would be like treating the fever you get when you have the flu. It doesn't make the virus go away, because fever is a symptom, not a cause.

Here's another example of the need for deep knowledge when trying to evaluate whether something is research based. When I search "secretin autism" in Google Scholar (a database of scholarly research), I get 2,010 hits.[22] (Secretin is a hormone that is important in digestion.) The first article is titled "Lack of Benefit of a Single Dose of Synthetic Human Secretin in the Treatment of Autism and Pervasive Developmental Disorder." The second article is titled "Improved Social and Language Skills After Secretin Administration in Patients with Autistic Spectrum Disorders." Hmm. So it seems there's some controversy.[23] Unfortunately, that's typical. Human behavior is not a simple cause-and-effect system. Behaviors (for example, repetitive behaviors in kids with ASD) usually have multiple causes—for example, stress may make symptoms worse. And the problems will vary across kids. So even if secretin has some positive effects, you may see them in some studies and not in others. More important, studies will vary in quality; there are better and worse ways of conducting scientific research, and a study doesn't have to be perfect to be published in a scientific journal. So what you really need to do is look at all the studies that have been done and try to see whether the ones that employ the best methodology are also the ones that show positive effects for secretin.

That sounds hard enough to do, but the problem is still one step more difficult than that. It's not easy to know what constitutes a "good" study. Obviously, there are principles that guide research design and the use of statistics. Practice in thinking about those is certainly a help. But evaluating research quality also requires knowing the relevant *scientific content*. That's because the content affects your interpretation of whether or not the study was well done. Here's a simple example. Let's say you read a study of the effect of secretin on the behavior of kids with ASD. The study reports that secretin didn't help. You happen to notice that the study didn't test boys and girls separately. All the kids with ASD were considered one big group. Does that make it a bad study? It depends. If previous research had shown that gender was an important variable in the way secretin works, that might mean this was a bad study.

Or if there was reason to think that gender mattered in ASD, either in its symptomology or its treatment, then researchers probably should look at the effect of secretin separately on boys and girls. For any study, you can usually think up dozens of distinctions—right- or left-handedness, time of day, other medications taken, diet, gene markers—that *might* make a difference. And if we know that a factor has been important in prior work and the researcher ignored it, that's a valid criticism.

Or suppose that the results of a study seemed to directly conflict with the results of previous research. The author ought to at least discuss the possible reasons for the conflict, if not pursue the issue in a new study. Or suppose that prior research has shown that the statistical method one might typically use in a given situation doesn't work in this specialized case. Statistical techniques always rely on assumptions about the data, and let's say it's known that an important assumption doesn't hold for a particular reading test when kids under the age of twelve take it with a time limit. It's hard to be an intelligent reader of scientific articles if you are not already fairly well versed in the content.

All of the details I'm listing here are simply to emphasize that (1) saying "the research supports it" ought to mean that the research was conducted in the right way, and (2) knowing whether or not the research was conducted in the right way is no small matter. That's not to say that only professional researchers can assess scientific quality. I've met people who became expert on one topic or another and were sophisticated consumers of research. But it took them a long time to get that way. Research expertise is just like any other type of expertise—developing it takes a lot of hard work and practice. Most people who have families, jobs, and other responsibilities cannot put in that sort of time. Is there a way to evaluate research that does not require becoming an expert?

We undertake other tasks that, if done properly, would be terribly complex and time consuming. The typical solution is not to invest the time and energy into doing a foolproof job. Rather, we find shortcuts that, although imperfect, get the job done. Consider the process of buying a car. It's a big purchase, and you want to be sure that you get the most for your money, right? If you really want to

TABLE I.2: An example of a "logical" way to select an automobile for purchase.

	Importance	Ford Taurus	Porsche 911	Dodge Ram Pickup
Headroom	.2	7	2	8
Sound system	.4	5	9	4
Reliability	.8	6	6	5
Gas mileage	.5	6	3	2
Trunk space	.2	5	1	10
Traction in snow	.3	3	2	8
Style	.8	2	10	4
TOTAL (desirability)		13.89	19.10	15.8

optimize this decision, here's what you ought to do. First, rate the importance to you of all of the features of an automobile from, say, 0 to 1.0. Hence, you might give "reliability" a 0.8, but "heated seats" just a 0.2. Second, rate every model of automobile for each of these features, using a 1–10 scale. The Porsche 911 gets a 10 for style, the Taurus gets a 3, and so forth. Third, for each car, multiply the ratings from step 2 and the importance values from step 1, and add the products. Now you have an overall value for each car that represents how much you like it. An example for a small set of features and for three vehicles is shown in Table I.2.

Now that you know the desirability of each car, you need to factor in cost. In step 3, you would research the maintenance costs for each car, as well as depreciation. In step 4, you would visit every car dealership and negotiate a price for every model that they carry. In step 5, you would repeat steps 1 through 4 for used cars. In step 6, you would combine all of your information about desirability and cost to select the optimal car.

Obviously, no one picks a car this way. It's too time consuming. We are confronted by many tasks with similar properties: there is a way to do the task that might be optimal, but we lack the time or knowledge to complete the task that way. So what do we do instead? We use an imperfect method called a *heuristic*. A heuristic is a shortcut. It's not the *best* way to do something, but it yields a solution that's usually pretty good, and it has the great benefit of practicality: it's easy to calculate. When I last bought a car, my heuristic was *Buy the first car you see that is fairly reliable, has four doors, a big trunk, room for two car seats in back, and costs less than $18,000.* I may not end up with the optimal car, but by putting up front the characteristics I know I care about a great deal, I'll probably end up satisfied. And I've made the problem manageable.

Evaluating research is like buying a car. There's an optimal solution to the problem, which is to read and digest all of the relevant research, but most of us don't have time to execute the optimal solution. The epigraph to this chapter says, "Before obtaining certainty we must often be satisfied with a more or less plausible guess." Indeed, when certainty is not available, a plausible guess is the best we're going to do. What we need is a good shortcut.

The Shortcut Solution

Our education system has multiple levels. The federal government attempts to influence the education policy of state governments. There are some thirteen thousand local school districts,[24] each with its own administration, making decisions within the framework set by the states. School principals run their schools within the framework set by the district administration, and teachers run their classrooms within the framework set by the principal. If kids aren't learning enough in those classrooms, parents try to supplement what they learn.

At every level of this system, people—motivated by politics, money, or altruism—try to influence what happens. And one of the most frequently used persuasive techniques is to figuratively don the white lab coat of science and intone, "The research says . . ." I've said that a shortcut is the best way to judge whether or not a claim really is scientifically supported, but before I introduce the shortcut, I need to persuade you that it makes sense. The reasoning behind the shortcut I described for buying a car is pretty transparent: cars have so many features that you can't possibly evaluate all of them, so instead you pay attention only to the most important. For the research shortcut to look logical, we need to get a few issues straight.

First, we need to understand what sorts of things people find persuasive. I've already said that the people who try seemingly odd educational remedies—those who put their children in oxygen pressure tanks or who figure that kids will learn to read by memorizing what words look like—are not crazy, and they are not stupid. People were aware that the stakes were high as they made these decisions, and I'm more than ready to give them the benefit of the doubt that they made them thoughtfully. Nevertheless, people were persuaded that an educational intervention was scientifically backed when they should not have been so persuaded. What goes into a decision to believe or to disbelieve? In Chapter One, I'll summarize some fifty years of research on this topic, and we'll see that the mind actually comes pre-equipped with shortcuts. Certain features of messages are treated as signals of truth. For example, long messages are deemed more believable than short ones. You may not be aware of the message features your mind focuses on, but salespeople, politicians, and savvy social manipulators are. It's time you knew about them too, and I'll describe them in Chapter One.

Second, we need to understand how laypeople—not scientists—think about scientific evidence. Surveys show that scientists are trusted more than people in almost any other profession, and people believe that scientific research is the most reliable type of evidence. Why? Why this implicit trust in science? This story starts in sixteenth-century Europe, a time and place in which observing the world—the cornerstone of science—was considered the *least* persuasive type of evidence. The most persuasive was authority. If the Bible (or ancient thinkers, especially Aristotle) said it, it had to be right. The next hundred years saw a complete reversal of this attitude, with observation—especially controlled observation as found in experiments—held in the highest esteem. The change in the weighing of evidence was due primarily to the wild success of the method in explaining the world and improving the human condition. Science came to influence—and, usually, to improve—virtually every aspect of human affairs. This means that the simple veneer of scientific evidence is an important persuader. This type of evidence is so powerful that in other fields (for example, medicine and engineering) we have strong institutions that monitor and control its use. It's illegal to say that a medicine has been scientifically tested if it has not. Education has no such constraints. Anyone can say that an educational nostrum is "research based,"

INTRODUCTION   **25**

and that's why salespeople repeat the phrase like parrots. And that's why the research shortcut is needed. In Chapter Two, we'll look at how the situation reached this point.

Third, if we're to have a research shortcut, we need to understand the path that we're cutting short. The shortcut is meant to provide easy passage to the goal we would reach if we took the long route. The goal is "good science." What does that look like? Interestingly enough, good science turns out to be as difficult to describe as pornography, but we cannot, as Supreme Court Justice Potter Steward famously did, satisfy ourselves by saying, "I know it when I see it." In Chapter Three, I'll describe seven principles that most experts would agree are scientific essentials.

Chapter Three will describe what good science looks like, but not how to use it. That's the subject of Chapter Four, which describes the distinction between basic sciences (for example, chemistry, biology, psychology) and disciplines like education that *use* findings from the basic sciences. For example, if psychologists learn a new fact about how children think, is that new fact ready to be used in the classroom? I'll outline two ways that scientific findings can be used in education. The first method is rather painstaking and expensive, but yields quite reliable knowledge. The second is inexpensive and is still painstaking when done well, but is also easy to do sloppily. It produces knowledge of educational practice that ought to be considered tentative. As I'll show, the difficult, expensive method is a rarity in American education. The cheap, sloppy method is commonplace. Part of the shortcut is to recognize the difference.

In Part One, I argue that people are persuaded by poor arguments (Chapter One) and especially by arguments that appear to be scientific (Chapter Two). Unfortunately, people are unable to distinguish between good and bad science (Chapter Three), and they are usually unclear on how scientific findings can be brought to bear on education problems (Chapter Four). Part Two offers the shortcut, composed of four processes to be applied to the candidate educational program: strip it and flip it; trace it; and analyze it; in the fourth step, you make your decision about whether to adopt it.

"Strip it" means to lay the claim bare, devoid of the emotional language and other ornamentation that people use to cloak the actual scientific claim. Examining the claim in its simplest form can make many problems plain to you: the claim is true but self-evident, or the promised outcome is vague, or no one specifies the connection between what you're supposed to do and what is supposed to improve. "Flip it" addresses the way that promised outcomes are sensitive to the description provided; for example, saying that ham is "90 percent fat free!" sounds quite different from saying it is "10 percent fat!" We'll examine different ways that people try to make education products sound good, and how you can see past those claims.

"Trace it" is applied not to the educational program but to its inventor. Most of us use this step already and, in fact, overuse it. It means to pay attention to the qualifications and motivations of the person trying to persuade us. We are most convinced by people who are knowledgeable and impartial. Unfortunately, it's hard to judge whether or not someone is knowledgeable about a subject unless we ourselves have some expertise. We tend, therefore, to rely on credentials. We believe doctors when they speak about medicine, and electricians when they talk about our fuse box. Naturally, credentials can be faked, but I'll argue that even when they are genuine, credentials are not a reliable guide to believability in education. In fact, this most commonly used earmark of credibility is the *least* useful.

"Analyze it," the third step of the shortcut, means to consider why you are being asked to believe something. We'll take up two topics: how to use (and not to use) your own experience, and simple methods of evaluating research. I will argue that your experience does count: if the claims about an education product fly in the face of what you know to be true, there is a problem. At the same time, your experience is not an infallible guide. If it were, there would be no need for scientific research. So once we agree that your prior beliefs matter but are not definitive, we need to sort out the circumstances under which they are trustworthy and when they are likely to lead you astray. "Analyze it" also means to apply some simple guidelines to evaluate research claims. The point of the shortcut is to save you from having to evaluate research, so we're not going to get too technical here. But there are some useful rules of thumb to apply.

After evaluating an idea's scientific merit, you need to decide whether or not it should be adopted. Although I'm advocating for a shortcut here, I'm not advocating that a decision be rash. Nor am I saying that one should never adopt an educational program that lacks scientific support; as we'll see, most lack such support. What I'm arguing for is adopting a program only when you have all of the relevant information before you. And that's the final step—gathering what you know in one place at one time so that you can put it together.

This book will be especially useful in two situations. In the first, someone else has made a decision, and you're affected by it. A superintendent has decided to adopt a reading program, and you're a teacher who must implement it, or you are the parent of a child in the district. Or perhaps you're a principal in the district who has just been told to bring the news to parents at the next PTA meeting. In each case, someone else has decided that an educational program is a good idea. This book can guide questions that you might pose to the decision maker. Decision makers often respond to any question by saying, "All the research supports it." Or "This program was designed by Professor So-and-So at [fill in the name of prestigious university here]." This book will show you why these responses are inadequate, and will offer better questions to ask.

In the second situation, you yourself are the decision maker. You're a parent looking for supplemental educational services for your child who is struggling in math. You're a teacher who has been asked to recommend a software product for interactive whiteboards, to be used schoolwide. You're a principal considering whether it's worth using half of a teacher workday for a program on bullying recommended by a principal at another school. You're a school board member wondering whether it's worth sending all the principals in your district to a national conference. In each case, there is a product for sale, and you're wondering about its educational value. This book will help you know which questions to ask, and what a good answer looks like.

This book will not turn you into a research expert. Indeed, the point of the book is to obviate the need for expertise. And the method I offer is imperfect, like all heuristics. You might apply these methods and still draw the wrong conclusion.

But I can promise this. Whatever your current level of research sophistication, this book will help you ask better questions about the research base behind a product, and it will help you think through the wisdom of purchasing and using a product in your classroom, school district, or home.

Part One

*Why We So Easily Believe
Bad Science*

1

Why Smart People Believe Dumb Things

> It is useless to attempt to reason a man out of a thing he was never reasoned into.
>
> —*Jonathan Swift*

Suppose you're in a library, and you need to photocopy some pages from a book. You find the copy machine, and happily you discover that you have some quarters. You're about to drop a coin in the slot when a stranger approaches you. He asks whether he can use the photocopier. Would you let the stranger use the machine, or would you politely decline, given that, after all, you were there first?

In this chapter, we will be less interested in whether or not you would comply with this request, and more interested in whether or not you would *think* before answering. It would seem that a social interaction—deciding whether or not to grant a small favor— would require thought. But it doesn't, according to a landmark study conducted by Ellen Langer.[1] An experimenter approached individuals just as they were about to use a coin-operated copy machine, with one of three requests:

1. Excuse me, I have five pages. May I use the Xerox machine?
2. Excuse me, I have five pages. May I use the Xerox machine, because I'm in a rush?
3. Excuse me, I have five pages. May I use the Xerox machine, because I have to make copies?

The first request offers no reason, whereas the second offers a socially acceptable reason. The third request is odd. It offers a reason that is not a reason—if you're asking to use the photocopier, then obviously you have to make copies.

The surprising finding was that people found this nonreason persuasive. Sixty percent of people complied with the request when no reason was offered, but 93 percent complied when the nonsensical "reason" was added—about the same percentage as when the bona fide reason was added. What's going on?

Langer argued that people are not thinking during this seemingly complex interchange. People are willing to do small favors for strangers, especially if the stranger makes the request politely and if the stranger offers some reason for the imposition. What the experiment seems to show is that the person hears the word "because" in the request and thus knows that a reason has been offered, *but the person doesn't take the trouble to evaluate the quality of the reason.*

The idea that we are on autopilot even when we engage in complex behaviors is familiar to most of us. Obviously, you don't need to consciously guide the movements of your hands as you button your shirt in the morning or tie your shoes; you *did* consciously control those movements at age two or three, but now they have become automatic. And routinized behaviors can be more complex than simple movements like shoe tying. You've probably found yourself pulling your car into your driveway and realizing that you had daydreamed the whole way home—stewed about a problem or fantasized about a vacation—and all the while obeyed traffic laws, braked for pedestrians, made the correct turns, and so on. It's as though there is a computer program in your mind that you initiate when you climb in the car, and the "drive home" program runs without your supervision, leaving you free to think about other things.

An autopilot program is especially noticeable if it plays at a moment you wish it wouldn't. If you want to stop at the supermarket on the way home, you may well find yourself in your driveway without having made the stop. The "drive home" program dictates a left turn at Elm Street, and you didn't interrupt it to make sure that you took a right to go to the market. Or, to use the example offered by the great nineteenth-century psychologist William James, "Very absent-minded persons in going to their bedrooms to dress for dinner have been known to take off one garment after another and finally to get into bed, merely because that was the habitual issue of the first few movements when performed at a later hour."[2]

This phenomenon—that consciousness may contribute little or nothing to the initiation of complex behaviors and the making of complex decisions—has created something of a revolution in social psychology. Researchers have discovered that more and more of the thought that drives our social lives happens outside of awareness.[*]

Here's another example. When you speak with someone who has an accent, have you ever noticed yourself slipping into the accent yourself, without quite noticing that you're doing so?[†] This is an instance of a more general phenomenon: humans imitate each other during social interactions.[3] In one experiment demonstrating this phenomenon, subjects were paired with someone they thought was another subject, but who was actually a research assistant. The pair was to describe the contents of ambiguous photographs. During the task, the research assistant engaged in one of two nervous habits—either shaking her foot or touching her face. The subjects unconsciously mimicked the behavior of the research assistant.

---

[*]Ap Dijksterhuis, a leading social psychologist from Holland, put it this way: "If [an] editor would have asked us to write about automaticity in social behavior 25 years ago, he would have been met with a blank stare. . . The whole concept of automatic or unconscious behavior would have struck anyone as odd at that time. . . [Today] if we wanted to write a short chapter, perhaps we should have asked the editor to assign us a chapter on conscious processes in social behavior." Dijksterhuis, A., Chartrand, T. L., & Aarts, H. (2007). Effects of priming and perception on social behavior and goal pursuit. In J. A. Bargh (Ed.), *Social psychology and the unconscious: The automaticity of higher mental processes* (pp. 50–131). New York: Psychology Press.

[†]Some studies show that if you're having trouble understanding someone who speaks with a strong accent, imitating it can actually improve comprehension. Adank, P., Hagoort, P., & Bekkering, H. (2010). Imitation improves language comprehension. *Psychological Science, 21,* 1903–1909.

Why do we mimic? Mimicry breeds liking. We like people who are similar to us. In First Corinthians, Paul says, "To the Jews I became like a Jew, to win the Jews. To those under the law, I became like one under the law to win those under the law. To the weak, I became weak, to win the weak."[4] Similarity aids persuasion even when based on something as trivial as having the same nervous tic or taking an ice cream sample of similar size.[5] We unconsciously imitate each other to smooth social interactions.

The emerging picture is that we have two modes of social interaction. One is conscious and involves the logical integration of evidence. For example, a waiter puts the check down on the table and says to me, "I hope you enjoyed your meal!" I think to myself that the steak was a bit tough, but the salad was expertly prepared. Consciously weighing the good and the bad, I offer the waiter a measured comment like "Yeah, it was pretty good." In the other, automatic mode, I merely detect certain cues or signals that mark the waiter's comment to me as belonging to a category of social interactions—in this case, "social pleasantry." Other categories might be "acquaintance asks a small favor" or "perform a task with a stranger." Once I've identified the category, I can act appropriately to the situation (grant the favor, mimic the stranger) with little or no conscious thought. Sometimes this mental process goes wrong. We miscategorize what someone has said, or the automatically generated behavior doesn't quite fit. More than once, a waiter has set a check on my table and said with a farewell intonation, "Enjoy the rest of your dessert!" and I've responded "Thanks, you too." My unconscious mind coded the waiter's comment as a social pleasantry and then my unconscious mind generated a response that typically works, but in this case was inappropriate.

Unconscious Persuasion

If indeed we have two modes of social thought—conscious and unconscious—is each mode capable of evaluating persuasive messages? Can persuasion happen outside awareness or, at least, with little thought? The answer is an emphatic yes.[6]

First, let's be clear what unconscious persuasion does *not* mean. You may have heard about subliminal (that is, unconscious) persuasion effects in advertisements. The idea is that advertisers embed messages in their ads that are not consciously perceived but will nonetheless affect behavior. For example, the words EAT POPCORN might appear in a single frame of a movie, too briefly for the conscious mind to perceive. Or a stylized sexual image might be worked into a product photograph—for example, a swirl of butter that, if you squint, looks a bit like a woman's breast. The theory is that the hidden message or drawing will still be perceived unconsciously, leaving the moviegoer with a yen for popcorn and the magazine reader thinking that a particular brand of butter is somehow strangely appealing.

This idea has been around since the 1950s[7] and seems to be perennial,[8] probably because it's such a fascinating, if chilling, possibility. Researchers have found it interesting as well, and lots of evidence compiled in the last few decades shows that this sort of subliminal persuasion doesn't work.[‡] There *are* some circumstances in which stimuli you don't consciously see can influence your behavior, but the behaviors subject to this influence are pretty low-level laboratory tasks that wouldn't have much impact in your daily life, such as how rapidly you can verify that a string of letters forms a word ("bread") rather than a nonword ("plonch"). You can't get people to buy popcorn or other products with this method.

The real concern is not that you are persuaded by things outside your awareness. The real concern arises when you're aware of these messages but don't recognize that they persuade you. Subjects who surrendered the copier were aware of the request, but surely did not notice that their response was prompted by the phantom "reason" given by the experimenter. The cue "reason offered" tells our inattentive mind to accede to an innocuous request from a stranger. What are the cues that tell our inattentive mind "This message is probably true"?

---

‡The idea is easy to test. One way is to show a group of people an ad for butter and ask them to rate how attractive they find it, whether they think the ad makes them a little more likely to buy the brand, and so forth. Show a second group of people the same ad with the erotic picture subtly airbrushed into the photo and compare the ratings. For a review of such research, see Theus, K. T. (1994). Subliminal advertising and the psychology of processing unconscious stimuli: A review. *Psychology and Marketing, 11,* 271–290.

Familiar Ideas Are More Believable

One such cue is familiarity. Things that are familiar seem reliable, safe, likable, and believable.[9] In a typical experiment investigating this phenomenon, subjects heard a series of statements presented as little-known facts—for example, that comedian Bob Hope's father was a fireman or that the right arm of the Statue of Liberty is forty-two feet long.[10] (The "facts" were fabricated, to be certain that subjects could not have known any of them before the experiment.) Later, subjects were presented with a set of trivia statements of the same sort, and they were asked to judge the likelihood that each is true. Some of the statements were repetitions of the prior set, and these statements were judged as more likely to be true. The effect is just as large if you tell subjects which statements were presented earlier and warn them that "these statements might feel true just because you heard them recently."[11]

Even more remarkable, familiarity affects credibility *even if people know they shouldn't believe the source at the time.* In one experiment, subjects were told who made each statement—for example, "John Yates says that three hundred thousand pencils can be made from the average cedar tree."[12] Subjects were told that statements from males were always accurate and that statements from females were always inaccurate. (Half of the subjects were told the opposite gender-truth relationship.) Later, subjects read a list of statements, with the instruction to judge the credibility of each. They were told that they had heard some of the statements earlier in the experiment, and they were reminded that some of them were false. So what happened?

Familiar statements were *still* judged as more likely to be true. Why? Well, during the trivia test when a subject reads, "Eighteen new-born possums can be placed in a teaspoon," she might say to herself, "Hmm . . . that seems familiar. Did I hear that during the experiment, or is it just one of those odd facts you pick up somewhere?" If she doesn't remember hearing it during the experiment, she will judge that it's true. But even if she remembers hearing it during the experiment, she still might not remember who said it—a member of the lying or truth-telling gender.

In general, source information (where and when we heard something, and who told us) is more fragile than content information (what we heard). For example, think how often it happens that you remember something but can't remember who mentioned it: "Oh, *someone* told me that movie was terrible." Much less frequently does the opposite happen: "Sam told me he saw that movie, and I know he had an opinion . . . now what in the world was it?"

This type of result gives us insight into why propaganda works. We might hear information from a source that we know to be unreliable—the propaganda minister of a totalitarian government, for example—and we discount the truth of the information at the time. But later, there's some chance that we'll remember the content and forget that it came from an unreliable source.

We Believe Things That Others Believe

Another aspect of familiarity is knowing that something is familiar—and accepted—by others. This is often called "social proof"—you see that others find something credible. The logic of using social proof is easy to appreciate in purchasing decisions. For example, one of the drains in my house becomes clogged perhaps once every two years. So I'm an occasional buyer of drain cleaner. When I'm in the store, confronted by half a dozen brands, how am I supposed to choose? I could pick the cheapest one, but a clogged drain is such a nuisance that I don't want to risk buying an inferior product. Ah, there's Liquid-Plumr, a familiar brand. I've seen ads for it since I was a kid. It's not only familiar, but I can infer that people must use it. At the very least, it can't be terrible—if the stuff didn't work, surely the company would have gone out of business. So instead of buying the brand I've never heard of (which probably works just fine), I pay more for Liquid-Plumr.

Social proof can become a real problem if an inaccurate belief becomes widely accepted. For example, I mentioned in the Introduction that something like 90 percent of American adults believe that people differ in their learning styles.[§] There's actually

---

[§]The idea behind learning styles is not that people vary in mental ability—it's that two people with the same ability have preferences about which way is easiest for them to understand and learn, and that these preferences have an impact on the efficacy of learning. For more on learning styles, see Riener, C., & Willingham, D. T. (2010). The myth of learning styles. *Change, 42,* 32–35.

no laboratory evidence that people learn in fundamentally different ways. But there is surprisingly little doubt among Americans. I don't think it occurs to most people that the truth of the learning style idea is open to doubt. It's like doubting atomic theory—it's just one of those things that "they" have figured out to be true. If everyone knows it, it must be true.

We Believe Attractive People

It is also the case that liking—that is, liking a person—makes what the person says seem more credible. Even our snap impression of a stranger influences how believable we find him. There must be a reason that advertisers use attractive people in their ads. Indeed, there are a couple of reasons. First—surprise, surprise—people shown ads for fictitious products in a laboratory setting are more likely to say they would be willing to buy a product if the person in the ad is attractive than if they are ordinary looking.[13] (My colleague David Daniel notes that it's easy to separate bona fide scientists who seek to apply research to K–12 education from charlatans: charlatans are more attractive and have beautifully coiffed hair. Being bald myself, I thought this comment showed great insight.)

The second way that attractiveness persuades you may take much longer to develop, but it's also more powerful. Sometimes the attractive person is not there to give us a message at all—he or she is there simply to look attractive (Figure 1.1). How might an attractive woman help sell

FIGURE 1.1: Many advertisers use attractive models in an overt way to sell products. Although we think it has no impact on us, it does make us regard their products more favorably.

FIGURE 1.2: The Honda 600 Coupe, which most would see as lacking sex appeal.

a car? Consider the case of the Honda 600 Coupe (Figure 1.2), an inexpensive, rather boxy little car sold in the early 1970s. About the last thing you'd call this car is sexy.

Honda came up with a clever advertisement, highlighting the car's low price. The image showed eight attractive women standing behind the car. The text implied that by spending less on his car, a guy would have more money to date these beautiful women.

Step 1: Food → Salivation

Step 2: Bell → Food (repeated)

Step 3: Bell → Salivation

FIGURE 1.3: The three steps of learning via classical conditioning.

Most people think that advertisements have little impact on them . . . although they think they *do* affect other people.[14] The Honda ad may not convince readers via the soundness of the suggested dating-investment strategy—in fact, I'm guessing most guys would dismiss it—but it might work by classical conditioning—the same type of learning that made Pavlov's dog salivate when it heard the bell (Figure 1.3).

Step 1: Attractive Women → Positive Emotion

Step 2: Car → Attractive Women (repeated)

Step 3: Car → Positive Emotion

FIGURE 1.4: Emotional responses–such as the positive emotion of seeing attractive women–can be classically conditioned as easily as salivation can.

Before Pavlov began the experiment, there was a natural association in his dog between food and salivating: if you put food in a dog's mouth, it will produce saliva as part of the digestive process. The experiment really begins with step 2, in which Pavlov repeatedly presents the bell and the food together. With enough repetitions, these two become associated, and the bell is enough to elicit salivation, shown as step 3.

Advertisers are not interested in getting you to salivate, but they are interested in changing your emotional response to their products, and that can be done with classical conditioning. A Honda 600 Coupe can be made to seem sexy if it is associated with something that people already think is sexy (Figure 1.4).

Step 1 represents a preexisting response—in this case, the positive emotion that the magazine reader feels when seeing attractive women. In step 2, the sight of the Honda 600 Coupe is paired with the sight of the attractive women. If this step is repeated enough (that is, the person sees the Honda 600 Coupe advertisement repeatedly), eventually the sight of the car will come to elicit the emotional response elicited by the attractive women.** So you don't need to believe the overt content of advertisements for them to have an effect on you.[15] The point of the ad was probably not to entice young men who could afford a 1972 Ford Mustang (about $3,000) to buy a Honda (about $1,700) so that they could use the extra money to attract and date beautiful women. That's a tough sell. The point was to make the Honda seem like a little bit less of a dud, to make the emotional reaction to it a little more positive, so that someone with only $2,000 to spend would prefer the Honda to the Volkswagen Beetle.

**The response that comes from conditioning is seldom as robust as the response to the real stimulus. That is, the dog doesn't salivate as much in response to the bell as it does in response to the food, and the positive feeling from seeing the Honda is not the same as it is from seeing the attractive women. But there is an effect.

Perhaps the best example of the impact of emotional conditioning comes from a famous blunder: the introduction of New Coke. The early 1980s was a difficult time for Coca-Cola. The brand, which had long dominated its closest competitor, Pepsi, was losing market share. Pepsi ran a series of effective advertisements showing hidden-camera accounts of dedicated Coke drinkers comparing Coke and Pepsi in blind taste tests and preferring Pepsi. And Pepsi claimed that such taste tests had been conducted in a rigorous fashion and that more than half of avowed Coke drinkers actually preferred the taste of Pepsi.

In a move that in retrospect looks panicky, executives at Coke decided to change the taste of their flagship product. New Coke was introduced in 1985, and consumers hated it immediately, thoroughly, and with finality. Attention has been drawn to the fact that the famous Pepsi taste tests didn't match the way people actually use the products. After all, you don't take a few sips of a cola; you typically drink eight ounces or more. The argument goes that Pepsi tastes good initially because it's a little sweeter than Coke, but after a few ounces, people prefer Coke. That may be true, but that can't explain the emotional outrage that followed the introduction of New Coke. A consumer hotline at the company was receiving eight thousand calls per day, virtually all of them complaints. When New Coke ads appeared on screens at sporting events, crowds booed.[16]

People were angry about the disappearance of Coke not simply because they thought it tasted better. People had an emotional attachment to Coke. The Coca-Cola corporation had spent decades and untold millions of dollars building an association in people's minds between Coke and patriotism, Coke and Santa Claus, Coke and young love, and so on. Then the corporation took all of that away, offering the promise that New Coke tasted better. It's as though I went to a teenager's house and said, "You know how your mom is always nagging you and won't get you the cool cell phone you want and embarrasses you in public? I found someone who won't do those things. Here's New Mom!" New Mom might have objective features that Old Mom didn't, but the emotional attachment to Old Mom is not so easily replaced.

We Believe People Who Are Like Us

We like (and therefore believe) not only people who are attractive but also people whom we perceive to be similar to us. The classic experiment studying this phenomenon was conducted in the spring of 1954, just before the Supreme Court decision on school desegregation. Black college freshmen were asked to listen to a radio broadcast during which a guest argued that if the Supreme Court ruled segregation unconstitutional, it would still be desirable to maintain some private black colleges as all black, in order to preserve black culture, history, and tradition. It was known that a large majority of the subjects opposed that idea. Yet they found the communication fairly persuasive when the speaker was presented as similar to them; he was described as the president of the student council at a leading black university. Black students were much less persuaded when the speaker was described as a white adult.[17]

People who are like us seem more trustworthy, less likely to steer us wrong. But of course, they are not always more likely to be knowledgeable. On occasion they are, as when a teacher finds a message about classroom practice more believable because it is delivered by another teacher. In that case, the teacher finds the message more believable not only because he can identify with the teacher but also because the teacher has expertise that's relevant to the message. That expertise effect still applies when the similar-to-me effect is absent. In short, people figure that experts know what they are talking about.[18] This seems only logical; shouldn't I believe my pediatrician rather than my friend the graphic designer when each makes a different recommendation for treating my child's rasping cough? Sure, but as we'll see in Chapter Six, the issue of expertise is more complex than you might guess.

Let's take a step back to remind ourselves of the big picture. We're talking about why people believe what they believe, and in particular how they evaluate new information. I've suggested that we are often on autopilot, even when exposed to messages that are meant to persuade us. Rather than carefully evaluating the factual basis of the message and the logic of the argument, we rely on what are often called *peripheral* features of the message (in contrast to the facts and logic, which would be the central features). Peripheral features include things like the familiarity of the message, how it makes us feel, the attractiveness of the source of the message, whether we identify with him, and his apparent expertise.

But surely we think *some* of the time? Okay, I probably won't think too carefully about the car advertisement as I stand in line at the bank. But what if I'm in the market for a car? Won't I pay more attention to the advertisement? Won't I evaluate the meaning of "it has the best repair record of any American car in its class" and whether the car really is the "quintessence of luxury"?

Yes. We are much more likely to snap out of autopilot and really evaluate persuasive messages when we perceive the stakes to be high. The stakes are high when the persuasive message is personally relevant (as when we're in the market for a car) or when we think we might be called on to describe the pros and cons of the argument (for example, when we make a decision at work and the boss asks for an explanation).

But wanting to evaluate a message is not the same as evaluating it. And evaluating it is not the same as evaluating it effectively.

"I'm Trying to Think, but Nothing Happens"[19]

Unfortunately, we still make plenty of mistakes when we evaluate arguments, even when we are not on autopilot, when we're really doing our best to think things through. Why?

Two things must be in place for us to evaluate an argument successfully. We must be motivated to do so—as mentioned, that usually happens when we have some personal stake in the argument or when we think we might be called upon later to summarize it or explain a decision. But in addition to being willing to evaluate the argument, we must also be *able* to do so, and here we may encounter significant stumbling blocks.

The first of these is attention. Suppose I'm a teacher, and I'm required to attend a presentation by a district official who will describe a new scheduling scheme for my school. But I didn't sleep much the night before, and it's warm in the auditorium. I try to keep my mind on what the speaker is saying, but my wife's birthday is the next day, and I haven't planned any sort of celebration, and ideas of what I might pick up on the way home keep popping in my head. In short, I *want* to listen, but I'm tired and distracted, and I can't really think through the speaker's argument as to why this change is going to save money and benefit students, yet will call for no extra work by staff.

Evaluating the strength of her argument and judging the truth of the facts she's citing might be hard when I'm tired and distracted, but picking up on the peripheral cues of the message is not demanding at all. I can do that even when I'm tired and distracted. I notice that the speaker is attractive, and her manner is warm and sincere. She mentions several times her own experiences in the classroom, so I know she's a teacher, like me. And even though I'm not really following the argument, she seems quite confident, and she seems to be listing a lot of reasons that this is a good idea, including citations from some research experts.

When someone presents an argument and we're too tired to really figure out what she's saying, most of us don't withhold judgment, even though we know that's probably the smartest thing to do. We're likely to use peripheral cues. I won't leave the auditorium as a cheerleader for the new plan, but I might very well leave with a vague sense that it's going to be all right.

Now suppose I'm not tired and distracted. The district official is giving her talk, and I'm giving her my full attention. But I'm still not getting it. She's explaining how the schedule change saves money, but it doesn't make any sense to me. She emphasizes that everyone will work the same hours at the same salary, and when it comes to the savings part, she uses some accounting jargon that I don't know. The same thing happens when she talks about research that is supposed to show that this new schedule helps students. She doesn't just say, "The research shows it works"; she's actually describing the research in detail, which I appreciate . . . but it's too *much* detail. She's talking as if we're all researchers, and again, I'm not really following it. At the end of the presentation, a friend who I know is quite sharp on business matters asks a question about the details of the accounting, and the speaker answers promptly. My friend nods, apparently satisfied. A little later, someone I don't know very well asks a question about the research studies, and again she answers promptly, and the questioner seems to think the answer was okay.

Just as you do when you're tired, if the argument is too technical to follow, you use peripheral cues:[20] the speaker's attractiveness and likeability, the fact that you identify with her and that she seems well informed, and the social proof that others at the presentation seem to be persuaded. So the first challenge to critically evaluating scientific research in education is pretty obvious. We're talking about technical information that is hard to evaluate. And you know that a speaker can twist results or cite only the studies that support her case and omit the ones that don't, and will likely get away with it, unless you know the research literature quite well.

You might think that people surely would refrain from using peripheral cues when the stakes are high. But they don't. Even when we're picking a president, we care very much about the candidate's attractiveness and how he or she makes us *feel*—more than we care about his or her ideas.[21] Another example comes from higher education. Selecting a college is certainly a high-stakes decision, and presumably it's one that people would consider carefully. But comparing candidate colleges is complicated, so parents and kids use peripheral cues: some global sense of "reputation" (which is just another name for social proof) and, curiously enough, price. When we are unsure of the quality of a product, we use price as a guide: if it's expensive, surely it's good. Traditional economic theory would indicate that raising tuition would decrease the number of people wanting to go to a college. In fact, the opposite is true. Raising tuition *increases* the number of applicants.[22]

Another stumbling block in trying to evaluate the strength of an argument is perhaps the most troubling. Each of us is pretty reluctant to change our beliefs. We like to imagine ourselves as impartial judges, rationally weighing evidence and ready to accept any conclusion to which the facts point. We're not. An enormous amount of research shows that we are biased to conclude that new evidence supports what we already believe. To extend the metaphor, we are not judges weighing evidence: we are attorneys building a case, and we build the case, not to convince a jury, but ourselves. We seek to persuade ourselves that our beliefs have always been correct and that the new information before us merely confirms what we already knew. This tendency is called the *confirmation bias*, and it affects all stages of thinking: what information we seek, how we interpret information when we find it, and how we remember it later.

Here's a simple example of our bias when we're gathering information. Suppose I challenge you to guess the number I have in mind. I tell you that it's between one and ten, but rather than have you guess outright, I ask you to pose yes-no questions to deduce the number. Suppose you know that I think seven is my lucky number, so you're guessing I picked seven. You have a hypothesis, and now you must gather some information to test whether it's true. Consider this: you could ask me, "Is the number odd?" or you could just as well ask, "Is the number even?" The confirmation bias refers to our tendency to seek information that confirms our hypothesis—if you hypothesize that the number is odd, you're more likely to ask "Is the number odd?" than "Is the number even?"[23]

A bias in playing a guessing game is harmless, but seeking only confirming information in other contexts can lead to trouble. Your hypothesis can be wrong—even very wrong—but you still might find a few positive examples, and they will make you think you're correct. Suppose I'm a job interviewer, and I'm interviewing an applicant who is an acquaintance of someone in my office. My coworker tells me that the applicant is quite introverted. The confirmation bias will make me more likely to pose questions that *assume* the applicant is an introvert, and the person will come off looking like one.[24] Worse yet, suppose I'm a physician, and a few symptoms lead me to suspect that a patient has a particular disease. Might not the confirmation bias lead me to order tests that might confirm my diagnosis, instead of other tests? The answer is yes,[25] although more experienced doctors may be better at resisting this tendency.[26]

The confirmation bias is not restricted to how we seek out information. We're more likely to *notice* confirming evidence and to ignore or discount disconfirming evidence. This phenomenon was first demonstrated in a clever experiment using college classrooms.[27] An experimenter appeared in a college course and told students that their regular professor was out of town and that a substitute would be arriving soon. The regular professor had given him (the experimenter) permission to collect the students' opinions of this substitute as part of an ongoing research study. To provide a bit of background information, the experimenter said that each student could read a brief biography of the substitute. Each student received a written paragraph. The biographies were all identical, with one crucial exception: half of the students saw this sentence as part of the biography: "People who know him consider him to be a rather cold person, industrious, critical, practical, and determined." For the other students, the words "rather cold" were replaced by "very warm." Naturally, the substitute professor had no idea which students had seen which description. But after the class, people who had expected to see a warm person felt that they had seen one. They rated the substitute as more considerate, more good-natured, and funnier than the students who expected the substitute to be a cold fish.

We see what we think we'll see. This helps us understand how stereotypes can be maintained. The bigot who thinks, for example, that African Americans are lazy will tend to notice and remember any instance of laziness he observes in African Americans. Hence, the bigot will note (and remember) an encounter with a lackadaisical store clerk who is black, but the same interaction with a white clerk will go unnoticed, or the bigot will assume that the clerk has a valid excuse for being a little slow.[28]

The confirmation bias also applies to how we interpret ambiguous information: it's interpreted as being consistent with our beliefs. For example, in one study, subjects were presented with true facts about politicians that showed them as contradicting themselves. Thus subjects read that in 1996, John Kerry had said that the Social Security system had to be overhauled, including cutting benefits and raising the retirement age. Subjects were then told that during the 2004 presidential campaign, Kerry had promised that he would never cut Social Security benefits or raise the retirement age. When subjects were asked what they thought of this, virtually all faulted Kerry for the contradiction. Not too surprising. But the really interesting part of the experiment came next. Subjects were given a potential explanation for Kerry's contradiction; they were told that in 1996, economists had thought that the Social Security system would run out of money in 2020, and that urgent action was needed to save it. But at the time of his campaign statement, economists had reversed their opinion, and it seemed that the system was no longer in imminent danger. This third statement renders Kerry's apparent turnaround ambiguous: Did he rationally respond to changing economic conditions, or did he go back on his word so that he could appeal to an important political constituency? Once the information was ambiguous, the confirmation bias came out in full flower. Subjects who identified themselves as Democrats thought Kerry's change of heart was perfectly justified, whereas Republicans thought that Kerry was using economic forecasts as an excuse and was obviously dishonest.[29]

Even if we are *forced* to acknowledge that some evidence goes against our beliefs, and even if this evidence cannot be twisted in our minds so that it seems ambiguous, we *still* have another way to maintain our beliefs: we set a higher standard for disconfirming evidence than for confirming evidence.[30] In one study, the subjects' attitudes on two controversial issues—gun control and affirmative action—were measured.[31] Then they read arguments on both sides of each issue and were asked to rate the strength of the arguments. Subjects were urged to set any personal opinions aside and to try to be as objective as possible. And subjects believed that they were doing so . . . but—you guessed it—their ratings were influenced by their beliefs. People who favored gun control thought that the pro–gun control arguments were very strong and that the anti–gun control arguments were weak. People who did not favor gun control showed the opposite pattern of ratings. It seems that when we encounter a conclusion we disagree with, our minds spring into action, looking for flaws in the argument. But if we agree with someone, we're more likely to say to ourselves, "Yes, yes, I already know this. I'm so glad you agree with me."††[32]

---

††Scientists are not immune to this motivated reasoning. When an experiment turns out as we expected, we take the results at face value. But when it turns out other than we expected, we comb over the data to make sure they were recorded correctly, reconsider whether we implemented variables properly, recheck equipment, and so on. We're more critical of disconfirming evidence than of confirming evidence. For examples of the confirmation bias in science, see Koehler, J. J. (1993). The influence of prior beliefs on scientific judgments of evidence quality. *Organizational Behavior and Human Decision Processes, 56,* 28–55; Mahoney, M. J. (1977). Publication prejudices: An experimental study of confirmatory bias in the peer review system. *Cognitive Therapy and Research, 1,* 161–175.

Sometimes the beliefs that we seek to confirm can be more subtle. They do not concern a specific object or fact about the world, but rather constitute a more global sense we have about the nature of things. We might call them meta-beliefs because their generality means that they will influence many other beliefs. One example might be that "natural things are generally good, and are better than similar objects that are artificial." Some confirmation biases would be an obvious consequence of this belief. For example, someone who held this belief might set a low standard for evidence that an artificial sweetener like Aspartame causes cancer. But this meta-belief could have more subtle consequences as well. For example, if you think that natural things are good, you might be open to the idea that humans left in a more natural state are more likely to be healthy, virtuous, and morally upright. It is modern, urban society—an unnatural human construction—that leads to crime, depravity, and wickedness.

Scientists have identified a few meta-beliefs that many of us share. An example is the *just-world belief*, a sense that the world is basically fair. According to this belief, living a moral, just life brings happiness and good fortune, whereas immoral behavior is punished by fate, eventually.[33] The subtlety and importance of this belief to persuasion can be appreciated from this experiment.[34] Researchers first measured college students' knowledge about global warming and their attitudes toward the issue—how real was the danger, what is likely to happen to the climate in the future, and so forth. Next, subjects read an article describing the dangers of global warming, which ended in one of two ways. One version concluded with an apocalyptic warning of terrible danger to future generations. The other ended with similar facts but a more hopeful message about possible solutions through new technologies. Subjects who read the doomsday message became more skeptical about the existence of global warming. Researchers hypothesized that this was a consequence of the just-world belief: if the world is just, innocent people do not deserve to die as a consequence of global warming, so it is deemed less likely to be a problem.

The confirmation bias sounds . . . well . . . stupid. Confronted by evidence that we're wrong, we put all our cognitive energy into figuring out why we must be right. It doesn't seem very adaptive.

But when you think about it, it's not quite as dumb as it seems. It would be disruptive indeed if you changed your beliefs every time you encountered a new bit of evidence. I say "disruptive" because very few of our beliefs are wholly isolated. For example, my belief that global warming is a serious problem is connected to my belief that I was smart and virtuous to buy a hybrid car. It's also connected to my dislike for my coworker who is full of loud scorn for global warming. So if I change my belief about global warming, that affects my belief about my car (I was a sucker to pay extra for a "green" car) and about my coworker (that loudmouth was right all along).[35]

A useful metaphor is to think of belief as a web, with each fact we believe varying in its interconnectedness to other facts.[36] The greater this interconnectedness, the more we can expect that I will struggle to maintain this belief, because changing it will have far-reaching consequences throughout my web of belief. Beliefs that are newly acquired have not had much time to be thoroughly incorporated into the web, so are relatively isolated from other beliefs. These I can change without disrupting other beliefs, so I'll be more ready to do so. As he so often did, Tolstoy captured this human truth in vivid terms: "The most difficult subjects can be explained to the most slow-witted man if he has not formed any idea of them already; but the simplest thing cannot be made clear to the most intelligent man if he is firmly persuaded that he knows already, without a shadow of doubt, what is laid before him."[37]

Beliefs are not simply matters of fact. Emotion is intertwined with belief, a factor that we have until now ignored and to which we must now turn.

We're Not That Cool

I've made it sound as though people are both ruled by logic and completely illogical. On the one hand, I've said that sometimes we don't bother to think logically, and even when we try to do so, we are nevertheless influenced by peripheral cues like a speaker's attractiveness, and we stack the evidence in such a way as to maintain our current beliefs. On the other hand, I've made it sound as though the only acceptable motivation for belief is accuracy, that all we ought to care about in choosing what to believe or not to believe is whether the belief is aligned with the real world.

People *do* care about accuracy.[38] But we're not so coolheaded that we care about accuracy to the exclusion of all else. People have other motivations for believing or disbelieving:

> Our beliefs help maintain our self-identity.
> Our beliefs help protect our values.
> Our beliefs help maintain social ties.
> Our beliefs help us manage our emotions.

Our Beliefs Help Maintain Our Self-Identity

Some beliefs may be linked to important aspects of our identity, our self-concept. For example, suppose that you see yourself as politically liberal. You conscientiously recycle, you contribute to progressive political candidates, you believe that the government plays an important and effective role in righting social wrongs, and you are somewhat distrustful of large corporations. You think corporations put profit above human values and that executives in large corporations inevitably do likewise. What's more, you think of liberal values as an important part of who you are. When asked "Tell me about yourself," it comes up early in your description.

Now imagine that your school district is considering hiring a superintendent who has no experience in education, but has worked for the last thirty years as a high-level manager in the corporate world. You decide to look at published research on the track records of business leaders who have run school districts with no prior education experience. Here's a case where you have two motivations for belief. On the one hand, you are motivated to be accurate in assessing how likely the candidate will be to succeed. On the other hand, you are motivated to believe that he will not succeed. There's more to it than maintaining your current beliefs. Part of your *self-identity* as a liberal is that you see important differences between yourself and corporate executives; those people do not have the right values nor the right sense of community nor a good understanding of children. To find that corporate executives have made excellent school superintendents would cast doubt on the accuracy of your view of the corporate world, and for you to conclude that the corporate world may not be so bad is threatening to your self-image as a liberal.‡‡ "So now I think that big corporations are just fine and that the vultures who sell us stuff we don't need and pollute our environment and trample the underprivileged should be in charge of our children? Who the heck *am* I, anyway?"

Our Beliefs Help Protect Our Values

A second motivation for belief is to protect values that you see as sacred. Examples might be "I believe that people should be free," or "I believe in the sanctity of human life," or "God's intention is that sex be between a man and a woman." The last of these examples is controversial in American society today, but even beliefs that are not controversial become controversial when we begin to interpret and apply them. Everyone believes that human life is sacred, and everyone believes in freedom; the controversy over abortion is largely due to the pitting of those two values against one another: if an hours-old zygote is a human life, then abortion is unconscionable, but if it's not, than restricting a person's right to abort it is government interference with an individual's liberties. Could scientists provide a definitive answer to whether life does indeed begin at the moment of conception? I doubt it, but even if they could, *most people would not want to hear the answer*. Their position on abortion is not driven by facts but by values.

As with the maintenance of self-concept, the protection of sacred values can have far-flung implications, depending on how the value is interpreted. For example, consider the belief "All people are equal." Most people interpret this idea to mean "equal before the law" and "equal in dignity" and "equally important as living beings." But someone may also have the sense that "equal" extends to abilities. If so, he may be uncomfortable with the idea that apparent differences

---

‡‡I don't mean to suggest that it is only liberals who care to maintain their self-image. The example could have just as easily been of political conservatives who would be motivated to see charter schools succeed because the policies on their governance seem to align with conservative views of the roles of competition.

in intelligence are largely genetic, that some people are just not very bright and there is not much that they can do about it. That would seem to be a cosmic violation of one of his core values. Nature or God seems *not* to intend that people be equal.

So how does he resolve this conflict? One choice is to deny the evidence that intelligence is genetically determined. People start life with roughly equivalent abilities, but some live in poverty or have careless parents or come from crime-ridden neighborhoods. Society makes them unequal. Or he could conclude that, yes, intelligence is largely determined by genes, but when someone is short-changed in intelligence, nature makes up for it by endowing that person with greater emotional sensitivity or athletic ability or some other skill. Drawing either of these conclusions can, in turn, affect one's views on other large-scale policy matters. Consider how your views would differ on funding for public education, on public assistance programs like welfare, on criminal justice policies, depending on whether you think that people are smart or not-so-smart either because of their genes or because society made them that way. My point is not about the scientific support for any of these beliefs.[§§] My point is that the shaping of these beliefs does not depend solely on a hunger for factual accuracy about the nature of the world. People's values shape their beliefs about scientific matters, such as the relative contribution of genes and environment to intelligence. They then interpret data to confirm those beliefs.

Our Beliefs Help Maintain Social Ties

A third reason that we adopt beliefs is that they help build a sense of social identity, of solidarity with a group. Some beliefs and behaviors

---

[§§]If you're curious: the very premise that intelligence is mostly genetic is under assault. Through 1990, most psychologists would have said that perhaps 70 percent of intelligence (as measured by middle-of-the-road intelligence tests) is determined by your genes and perhaps 30 percent by the environment. Today, most would reverse those percentages. For a readable summary, see Nisbett, R. E. (2009). *Intelligence: What it is and how to get it.* New York: Norton. There is no evidence at all for the idea that people who are low in intelligence make up for it with some other ability. In fact, abilities tend to be positively related, and this relationship is stronger for people with lower ability levels; see Detterman, D. K., & Daniel, M. H. (1989). Correlations of mental tests with each other and with cognitive variables are highest for low IQ groups. *Intelligence, 13,* 349–359.

that we adopt for this purpose are quite obvious. When I arrived at college, I had never attended a basketball game. I doubt I knew how the game was played, beyond a crude knowledge of the rules. But I was attending Duke, home of a basketball dynasty, and a school that had the wisdom or foolhardiness to reserve the plum seats of Cameron indoor stadium not for big donors but for undergraduates, affectionately called "Cameron Crazies." Like many fellow students, I waited for hours in foul weather to get tickets, I knew all the statistics, and I shouted myself hoarse at games. I absorbed from my peers not only passion but beliefs: beliefs about the value of big-ticket athletics to campus spirit, for example, and beliefs about the indirect benefits of athletics to the common good of the university through improved fundraising. I developed these beliefs solely because of the social environment and my desire for solidarity with my peers. Had I attended a school with weak athletic teams, my beliefs likely would have been different.

It is hard to be unaffected by one's social group. For example, my social group is composed of college professors, and college professors are, compared to other Americans, politically liberal. Suppose that I start my job with relatively conservative views. My reaction to this strong current of opinion need not be to absorb the opinions of the group, as I did with basketball as a student. That's less likely because my political views are more settled than my views on basketball. But at the very least, I am going to meet a number of nice, helpful people who hold liberal political views. Because I'm surrounded by left-leaning people, I will have greater access to liberal views on current events than I have had in the past. And whether I like it or not, I will absorb the idea that liberal views are part of what it means to be a college professor, just as being a basketball fan was part of what it meant to be an undergraduate at Duke.

Our Beliefs Help Us Manage Our Emotions

A final contributor to my belief may be strongly held emotion. Consider this example. In the summer of 2010, there was an acrimonious national debate over the building of a mosque and cultural center near the site of the September 11 attacks in New York

City. Not all of the information entering this debate was accurate, and one often-repeated rumor was that the imam behind the plan, Feisal Abdul Rauf, was a terrorist sympathizer. Two fact-checking organizations, known and respected for their objectivity (Factcheck.org and Politifact) had investigated this rumor and found it to be false. Yet it was widely believed. Two psychology professors at Ohio State University decided to see if they could persuade people that the rumor was false.[39] It wasn't easy. When people who either believed the rumor or were unsure about it were exposed to the information from the fact-checking organizations, only 25 percent concluded that the rumor was false. Furthermore, the researchers found that it was relatively easy to undo the persuasive power of the facts. If the text were accompanied by a picture of the imam in traditional Arab garb, the percentage of people persuaded dropped, presumably because it made him seem less like an American and perhaps less loyal to his country and less sensitive to American sensibilities.

Note that the researchers weren't trying to convince people that building the mosque was a good idea. They were simply asking them to reevaluate the rumor that the promoter of the idea had been a terrorist sympathizer in the past. If people want their beliefs to be accurate, why wouldn't they change them when confronted with relevant facts? A factor that likely played a role in this case is emotion. For most Americans, any thought connected with the September 11 attacks calls up anger and fear. It is difficult for facts to gain a toehold under those circumstances.

Here's another example. Suppose that I am a bit prudish about all sexual matters, but I find the thought of homosexual acts to be outright disgusting. In fact, the feeling is so strong that I'm reluctant to talk about any aspect of homosexuality at all, because doing so inevitably calls up this strong, unpleasant emotion. Now suppose you are trying to persuade me that there is no harm in an openly gay man teaching mathematics to seventh graders. You may hit me with factual arguments—for example, the lack of evidence that a teacher's sexual orientation influences students. But factual arguments won't do much good, because what's behind my objection is not a fact but an emotion—disgust at the thought of homosexuality.

I'm unlikely to be aware of what's driving my opinion, so I may answer you with facts of my own or with an attempt to discredit your argument. But the whole discussion is actually a red herring.[40]

This chapter has been a parade of disappointing facts, easily summarized: when we don't weigh evidence carefully, we are prone to believing or disbelieving things for trivial reasons; and even when we do weigh evidence carefully, we are still subject to those trivial influences. If we are really interested in maintaining accurate beliefs, and especially in knowing which educational practices or reforms are "scientifically based," what are we to do? Part of the answer is to gain a better understanding of the precise nature of the "trivial influences" to which we are most susceptible, the better to avoid them. That is the subject of Chapter Two.

2

Science and Belief

A Nervous Romance

> But the best demonstration by far is experience.
> —*Francis Bacon[1]*
>
> Sweet is the lore which Nature brings
> Our meddling intellect
> Mis-shapes the beauteous forms of things
> We murder to dissect
> —*William Wordsworth*

In Chapter One, we saw that we believe things (or not) partly due to the presence of peripheral cues—"peripheral" meaning that they are aspects of the situation that are irrelevant to whether or not the message is really true (for example, the attractiveness of the speaker or the length of the message). Although we are seldom aware that they influence us, these cues have an impact even when we consciously try to evaluate the logic and factual basis of a persuasive message. We also saw that we have a broad bias to believe new information if it is consistent with what we already believe, and we criticize new information that is inconsistent with our beliefs. To protect ourselves from believing false things, we need to (1) be aware of the peripheral cues that persuade, so that we can discount them, and (2) be aware of the beliefs we now hold, because they will bias how we evaluate new information.

Naturally, there is a lot of variation in what individuals believe, but in this chapter, I will suggest that there are also important commonalities of thought in the Western mind, expressed in two broad traditions. These traditions constitute meta-beliefs, as I called them in Chapter One—beliefs so general that they influence many other beliefs. They are really assumptions, ways of viewing the world, and they are so pervasive that we rarely think to question them.

The first meta-belief is that **the best way to understand the world is through reason.** It includes a confidence that our world—from the workings of the galaxy to the workings of our bodies—is subject to laws, and that the human mind can discover and describe these laws. According to this meta-belief, the epitome of reasoned thought is the scientific method.

The second meta-belief is that **the best way to understand the world is through personal experience.** According to this view, the scientific tradition overestimates what can be understood by reason, and people who overrely on it miss much of what is important, in particular the individual's emotional responses. According to this view, a true understanding of what is important—especially in appreciating our natural world—means understanding that some things are mysterious and ineffable, and are *not* open to analysis by reason. Reasoning about them not only misses the point but destroys the experience altogether, as Wordsworth says in this chapter's epigraph. By trying to analyze (that is, dissect) these sublime experiences, we destroy them.

The first meta-belief originated during the seventeenth century in conjunction with the development of the modern scientific method. This period is usually called the Enlightenment. The second meta-belief originated during the late eighteenth and early nineteenth centuries, a time usually called the Romantic period. Old though they may be, these meta-beliefs are still very much with us today. When an advertiser has an actor wear a doctor's white lab coat for a cough syrup advertisement, or when a Web site selling educational software describes its impact as the correction of "brain glitches," they are attempting to tap the residue of Enlightenment thinking.

When a book promises to "unleash" hidden learning potential in your child, or when an advertisement for an ADHD treatment emphasizes that it is "drug-free and all-natural," it is attempting to tap the residue of Romantic thinking.

In this chapter, I argue that each meta-belief is typified by certain catchphrases, and these catchphrases are peripheral cues to persuasion. They invite us to conclude that the new information offered to us—about cough syrup or about educational software—is consistent with one of these meta-beliefs, or even both. The catchphrases reassure us that the argument being made—"this cough syrup works"—is consistent with something we already believe, and thus the argument doesn't need to be evaluated all that carefully.

I could simply list the catchphrases with the warning "Be on guard when you see these!" But to fully understand why they might work as peripheral cues (and to recognize others I have missed), you need to understand the meta-beliefs behind them. And to fully understand these meta-beliefs, we need a better understanding of their origins and justification. That takes us to sixteenth-century Europe.

The World Turned Upside Down

It is difficult to recognize our meta-beliefs and their influence exactly because we are immersed in them. Meta-beliefs are tantamount to a worldview, a lens through which all our experiences pass, so asking us to analyze them is like asking a fish to describe water. The best way to appreciate a worldview is to contrast it with another.

One of the most startling aspects of sixteenth-century European culture was people's attitude toward evidence, what they found persuasive. Consider this. Suppose you wanted to persuade me that a husband and wife who don't love one another can nevertheless have a happy marriage. What evidence would you guess I'd find convincing? You might tell me a story about a couple you know; she was a foreigner who wanted citizenship, and he was a businessman who wanted to be married for the sake of his career. They live together like roommates and both are happy enough with the arrangement. In short, you would try to convince me that you have seen the evidence with your own eyes.

FIGURE 2.1: Frescoed ceiling in Camera degli Sposi, the Ducal Palace, Mantua, painted by Andrea Mantegna in 1473. In the late fifteenth century, it was understood that the senses were untrustworthy, and artists well knew how to exploit the foibles of the visual system so as to make a flat ceiling appear to have depth.

In medieval thinking, seeing something with your own eyes was not the best evidence; it was the worst. Perception can deceive. Haven't you noticed that a straight stick looks bent when it's partly submerged in water? Haven't you noticed that a man's voice sounds different when he calls to you from a rapidly approaching horse compared to when the horse is running away? The senses are untrustworthy (Figure 2.1).

In contrast to our untrustworthy senses, we have available to us wisdom that has stood the test of time—most notably, the Christian scriptures. You want to know whether a marriage can be happy if the couple is not in love? The Bible has the answer: "Husbands, love your wives, just as Christ loved the church and gave himself up for her" (Ephesians 5:25). The ideal for marriage includes love.

Scripture was the most potent authority, but ancient Greek philosophers were also important, especially those whose thinking had been integrated into Christian thought. Foremost among these was Aristotle,* and an understanding of his system of physics was essential training in the late medieval period for those embarking on a career in theology, law, or medicine.² Indeed, the thinking of Aristotle had such a profound influence that in 1585, Oxford University passed a decree that read

> all Bachelaurs and Undergraduats in their Disputations should lay aside their various Authors, . . . and only follow Aristotle and those that defend him, and take their Questions from him, and that they exclude from the Schools all steril and inane Questions, disagreeing from the antient and true Philosophy . . .†³

In the fifteenth century, then, the world of ideas was static because one could not entertain ideas that conflicted with the authorities of the past.‡ This view profoundly affected how intellectual energy would be channeled. The goal of investigating nature was to understand the role that each object plays in God's universe. The goal was not to *change* nature. That's a core reason that we study nature

---

*Aristotle's system of physics was integrated with Christian scripture by Thomas Aquinas in the *Summa Theologiae* in the thirteenth century.

†The disputation mentioned in the passage has a formal meaning. Disputations were public debates meant to clarify complex questions, often of a religious nature: what was purgatory like, what is the nature of free will, how is God's grace expressed on Earth, and so forth. Disputations had formal, rigid rules, and the ordering of the weight of evidence I've mentioned is an example: direct quotation of authority first, then logical inference drawn from authority, and finally human experience.

‡As Francis Bacon would say in 1620, the greatest impediment to advances in the sciences "lies in men's lack of hope and in the assumption that it is impossible." Bacon, F. (2000). *The new organon* (Book 1, Aphorism 92; L. Jardine & M. Silverthorne, Eds.). Cambridge: Cambridge Press. (Original work published 1620)

today—to defeat disease, to increase crop yields. But to the medieval mind, God's world was not to be tampered with, but rather to be understood, as a way of contemplating and appreciating God's goodness and wisdom.

Needless to say, these are not the meta-beliefs shared by most Westerners today, nor by most educated Europeans by the end of the seventeenth century. The change was the consequence of an intellectual movement lasting roughly two hundred years from the early seventeenth century through the end of the eighteenth.§ Although Enlightenment thinking touched on all aspects of human affairs—science, government, religion, the arts—I focus here on the change in how educated people thought about knowledge: How is knowledge acquired, and how certain is knowledge? To the medieval mind, authorities had provided things that one *knew* to be true, with certainty. Doubting them was irreligious. Today we hold ancient authorities in much less esteem; we assume that we have benefited from the experience of our forebears and actually know more than they. How did we come to change our beliefs about where knowledge comes from?

Let's begin with the concept of doubt. Why did people in the seventeenth century decide that it was acceptable to doubt things, to ask questions? What shook them out of their fatalism, their unspoken assumption that nothing would ever change? The person most responsible was René Descartes. You've surely heard Descartes' most famous quote: "I think, therefore I am." What does that mean? Descartes was responding to philosophical skepticism, a strain of thought reaching back to the Greeks and popular again in the mid-seventeenth century, which asks, "How can we be certain that anything is true?" Well, to be certain that anything is true, you need to set some criterion of truth. In other words, you say, "If a statement meets these conditions, then I accept it as true." For example, I might say, "If a statement agrees with something I observe with

---

§Although I've been talking about "medieval thought," it is, of course, a caricature. There were many schools of medieval thought, and that's true of the Enlightenment period as well. Then, too, I don't mean to imply that no one used reason prior to the seventeenth century in Europe. I'm really only tracing the current Western attitude that puts reason ahead of other ways of understanding the world.

my own eyes, then I accept the statement is true." But then I might ask, "But how do you know that your criterion of truth is reliable? How do you know that things you see with your own eyes are true?" So in response you provide some reason that this criterion of truth is reliable. For example, you might say, "Things I've seen with my own eyes have almost always proven true in the past." But then I, in turn, might ask, "So that's your *reason* for your criterion of truth; you're saying that there is a history of things you've seen turning out to be true. But how do you know that that *reason* is reliable? How do you know that this history of reliability will continue?" In other words, every time you give me a criterion by which you know that some knowledge is true, I ask for a criterion for that criterion.

Many thinkers had, up to that point, simply scolded skeptics as irreligious. Descartes argued that the skeptic's argument had to be taken seriously, and his statement "I think, therefore I am" was his answer. Descartes' project was to find a criterion of truth that was reliable, a set of rules by which one could *know* something was true, with certainty. Descartes thought that if he could find a statement that could not be doubted, he could then discover *why* it could not be doubted, and then he'd have a criterion of truth—he'd know what characteristics a statement must have for one to be certain of its truth.

"I think, therefore I am" was the indubitable statement. Most any other statement could be doubted. You see something with your eyes, but how do you know it's not a hallucination or a dream? You claim that 2 + 2 is 4, but you can't *really* know that you haven't made an error in calculation. But if I'm thinking, there must be some "me" to be doing the thinking. There's no way around it.

Descartes made people take seriously the question "How do I know that something is true?" And in so doing, he *invited doubt*. He challenged his contemporaries to ask, "How do we know that this is true?" rather than simply accepting it as true because an authority said it.

In contrast to Descartes, who sought certain knowledge, John Locke argued persuasively that some knowledge is always bound to be imperfect. At best, we can say that something is very likely to be true, but never certain. Locke offered two broad reasons that this is so. First, he pointed out that human thinking is frail and subject to error. Our thinking is easily confused, our thoughts are often clouded through the misuse of language, and our memories are limited, so if a long chain of reasoning is necessary to connect two ideas, we're likely to lose track.[4]

The second broad reason that we should consider knowledge at best probable is that it's always possible that we'll gain new knowledge tomorrow which shows that we are in error today. For example, suppose that you observe the Old Faithful geyser in Yellowstone National Park. For well over one hundred years, we have seen it shoot a plume of boiling water over a hundred feet high, with between fifty-five and ninety-five minutes elapsing between eruptions.[5] So will Old Faithful erupt sometime tomorrow? That is certainly likely. But Locke would point out that there might be an earthquake tonight that disrupts the spring feeding the geyser. A diabolic team of anarchists might seek to plug Old Faithful. Improbable? Of course. But we can't *know* that it won't happen.[6] Locke warns that we shouldn't run with this idea and conclude that nothing is knowable, such that we are therefore paralyzed into inaction. ("Why go to work today? How do I know the world won't end in thirty seconds?") Locke says that the best possible knowledge arises when all people have the same experience and agree as to how to interpret it. That's close to certainty, and we should act as though it were certain.

To people of the late eighteenth century, the idea that there was no certain knowledge was radical indeed. The Church certainly argued that there are many things that are known with certainty, and the Church further argued that it, as an institution, knew these Truths. Locke, in contrast, argued that what is known is known by experience, but even that knowledge is imperfect.

Important as Descartes and Locke were, perhaps the most important Enlightenment figure was Francis Bacon.[7] Bacon argued forcefully for what we would today recognize as the scientific method as the royal road to knowledge: Bacon said that rather than taking authoritative sources as true, we must learn about nature by examining nature directly, as described in this chapter's epigraph. By careful observation, we might then derive a generalization or law about the natural phenomena we observe. And Bacon added the crucial, final step: he said that we must test this law by generating new predictions from it, and seeing whether they are true.

So to summarize, Descartes encouraged people to doubt, and prompted them to ask themselves how they were sure they were right about what they thought they knew. Locke persuaded people that knowledge is never certain, but is always a matter of probability. And Bacon argued that the best source for knowledge is one's own experience. The final figure I'll mention provided an amazing example to the public of the success of the scientific way of thinking that these philosophers advocated. Isaac Newton showed that Bacon's method was much more successful in revealing the order underlying God's universe than was the study of scripture.

The most stunning example of this work was Newton's *Principia*, published in 1687, which contained Newton's laws of motion and law of universal gravitation. Johannes Kepler had, in 1609, published his three laws that described how the planets moved. Galileo had, in 1638, published the law relating distance, time, and acceleration of small bodies moving on Earth. Newton brought these observations and many others together into a coherent, mathematical description of our physical world. The implication seemed clear: our world is ruled by mechanistic laws, and humankind is capable of understanding and describing them.

Newton's contribution was seen as dramatic verification of the value of the scientific method. The method was so successful that thinkers tried to apply it to realms other than the natural world. For example, philosopher David Hume's great book *A Treatise of Human Nature* was subtitled *Being an Attempt to Introduce the Experimental Method of Reasoning into Moral Subjects*. Voltaire would later sum up Newton's impact by arguing, in essence, "Newton was right, and so Enlightenment thought, although applied to other realms—political, moral, social—must be right too because we have used Newton's method!"[8]

In the space of two hundred years—from 1600 to 1800—there was a truly remarkable transformation of what we have been calling meta-beliefs—the broad assumptions that one makes about the world. In 1600, Western Europeans viewed the world as static, and ordered by God in a way that was mysterious. Humankind could

FIGURE 2.2: In this print published in 1750, fine ladies and gentlemen peer through the wrong ends of telescopes, while the man in the center "inspects" a model of a celestial sphere with a magnifying glass.[10] Science was fashionable in the eighteenth century, even if many of its advocates were not well versed in its practice.

come to understand some of these mysteries, and in so doing better appreciate God's creation. The way to arrive at this understanding was careful study of received authority. By 1800, Western Europeans viewed the world as dynamic and changeable, but subject to mathematical laws. Humankind could understand these laws, and the purpose of this understanding was not an appreciation of God's majesty but to improve our well-being. The way to come to this knowledge was not to assume that received authority was correct but to observe the world, especially through scientific experimentation.

But how important was all this to the everyday life of average citizens? Isn't this all just so much intellectual gas, so to speak? Initially, yes. But these ideas did filter down to a much broader reading public of lower nobility, doctors, lawyers, and merchants. In the eighteenth century, science became fashionable. England's George III studied botany. Portugal's John V studied astronomy.[9] Lesser lights followed suit, perhaps not always making a substantial contribution to scientific advances (Figure 2.2), but certainly making a contribution to

FIGURE 2.3: *Experiment on a Bird in the Air Pump*, by Joseph Wright of Derby, 1768. In this family scene, a vacuum pump is operated by a traveling demonstrator. The glass bulb at the top contains a fluttering cockatoo, which will expire if the demonstration continues. Note that the evening's entertainment for this eighteenth-century family is *watching a scientific experiment*.

the change in mind-set of the populace (Figure 2.3). Indeed, many of what today are recognized as key texts in the transformation of mind fostered by the Enlightenment were not considered academic tomes at the time—they were best sellers. So the Enlightenment was not merely the province of an intellectual elite.

The Romantic Impulse

By the early decades of the nineteenth century, Enlightenment thought was so pervasive in the West that it could be considered conventional. Romanticism began in no small part in reaction to some Enlightenment views, particularly views of nature and of humankind.

In the Enlightenment view, nature was a mechanism, akin to an enormous, enormously complicated clockworks. Integral to Enlightenment thinking was the idea that nature was governed by laws and that the human mind, by harnessing reason through the method espoused by Bacon, could penetrate those laws. That's what Newton had shown the world. Although the clockwork metaphor makes nature sound rather pedestrian, in fact Enlightenment thinkers conceived of nature as very close to the divine. Many argued that God did not want to make himself known only to those who had access to the Revelation; he would not deprive people in "backward" lands of knowledge of his goodness and his wisdom. Instead, God had made himself obvious to all through the glories of nature.**

Divine nature may have been, but Romantic thinkers were still disgusted by the mechanistic view of the universe. They saw nature as a poet sees it, not as a scientist does, and they thought that the proper response to nature was emotional, not rational. The raw power of nature—for example, the ability of a storm to wreak havoc—ought to fill one with trepidation. The majesty of a fog-wreathed mountain ought to fill one with awe. By trying to reduce nature to a system of mathematical equations, scientists were missing most of what mattered about nature, however close to the divine they might say it was. The Romantic view of nature is plain in paintings from the period (Figure 2.4).

Romantic thinkers were much less enthusiastic about the power of reason than their Enlightenment forebears. Although reason was clearly useful, they saw it as cold and in some way limited. They wanted to validate emotion as a response—or if not pure emotion, at least reason shot through with emotion.[11] The ability to rouse emotion—especially deep emotions like terror—became a primary goal of Romantic art. Romantic poet William Wordsworth said, "Poetry is the spontaneous overflow of powerful feelings."[12] This interest in emotion as a viable human response could be found in other art forms—for example, music (Figure 2.5).

**Deism* is the term for a religious point of view arguing that reason and observation of nature are enough to understand and appreciate God and that organized religion is unnecessary. A number of America's founders, including Jefferson, Madison, and Franklin, are thought to have been Deists. They did not describe themselves as such, and it would have been imprudent for them to do so. The exact nature of their beliefs remains controversial.

FIGURE 2.4: *Kindred Spirits,* by Asher Durand, 1849. As is typical of Romantic artwork, the human figures are depicted as insignificant before the beauty and grandeur of nature–the towering trees and mist-shrouded mountains in the distance. At the same time, the gorge reminds us of the terrible power of nature, capable of tearing rock, and the tree stump reminds us of the frailty of life.

Wordsworth's characterization of poetry as spontaneous is also important. Reason, after all, is time consuming, plodding. Intuition, in contrast, is rapid, spontaneous, unpredictable. In music, this idea was formalized in the nineteenth-century impromptu, a form meaning "offhand" or "spontaneous." An *impromptu* was meant to sound as if the performer were creating the music as he played.

This idea of spontaneity fits too with another theme running through Romantic thought: that of hidden potential, hidden power. Romantic paintings often show a natural, peaceful scene, but one in

FIGURE 2.5: One of Josef Hoffman's sketches for the set design of Richard Wagner's opera *The Ring of the Nibelung*. Note the stark setting–the craggy rocks and storm clouds suggesting the power of nature. Wagner's music is famous for eliciting strong emotion, and the visual experience only increases its power.

which great forces have been at play; we see a mountain or a gorge, and we are left to imagine that great geological forces went into its creation. We see a blackened tree, and we are left to imagine the great storm during which it was shattered by lightning.

These four lines from Wordsworth's "Tables Turned" capture many of Romanticism's themes:

> One impulse from a vernal wood
> May teach more of man,
> Of moral evil and of good,
> Than all the sages can.

Sages who reason are rejected. Matters of importance may be understood by close attention to our personal, spontaneous responses to nature.

Meta-Beliefs in Education Today

Let's take a step back to recall the big picture. Each of us inevitably holds beliefs about the nature of the world and of humankind, and about how people come to know things. I have described two prominent and highly influential sets of such beliefs, one from the Enlightenment and the other from the Romantic era. Naturally, I'm not claiming that these beliefs exclusively dominate the thoughts of everyone today. There are other important meta-beliefs that have their origins elsewhere, most notably religious faith. But when we look about us today, we seldom see people trying to use nineteenth-century American populism or the Great Awakening as intellectual touchstones for educational methods. They frequently, however, base arguments about learning on meta-beliefs from the Enlightenment and Romantic eras. So what do these arguments look like?

The arguments are often indirect, or even telegraphic. The person doing the persuading doesn't want you to think carefully about whether or not the new educational program is a good idea; it's much better from his perspective if he gets you to think that *you already believe it*, because, as described in Chapter One, we are all biased to maintain our beliefs. So rather than provide an elaborate justification, he'll toss out a few pat phrases that draw on Enlightenment or Romantic meta-beliefs. He's gambling that these ideas resonate with the audience. Even though the information provided might be irrelevant, it *feels* right to us because it travels well-worn patterns of thought. We've reasoned using similar lines before ("Science proves the truth"), so thinking about this new claim ("It's true because it's scientific") seems fluent and easy and, therefore, probably correct.[13] The "No Child Left Behind" act of 2002 refers to "scientifically based" research more than one hundred times.††

Enlightenment meta-beliefs dictate that reason is the best way to understand the world and that the scientific method is the best way

---

††The text of No Child Left Behind is available online at http://www2.ed.gov/policy/elsec/leg/esea02/107-110.pdf.

FIGURE 2.6: Images similar to those on a Web site offering a homeopathic remedy for ADHD. The image of the physician and the precision suggested by the eyedropper are meant to make it seem that there is a scientific basis to the product. There isn't.

to deploy reason. Thus people draw on these ideas by claiming that the educational program they advocate is research based. The imagery and authority of science are often invoked. Technical jargon is used to explain why the program will be effective. We are asked to believe authority figures who tell us that it will work, but the authority figures are not from the clergy. They are scientists in white lab coats. Figure 2.6 shows figures similar to those culled from the front page of a Web site that offers homeopathic remedies for ADHD. Homeopathy is a pseudoscientific alternative medical approach that is not supported by the majority of clinical studies.‡‡

---

‡‡In homeopathy, a substance that would typically make you ill is administered as a cure— but the amount is very, very minute. The strategy is to take a solution of the substance and then dilute it. You make it one drop in a hundred. Then you take one drop of that solution and dilute it into ninety-nine drops of pure water. Typically, that dilution process would be conducted a total of thirty times. So what do you end up with? Water. The active ingredient has been diluted so many times that it's not one molecule among a million water molecules or one molecule among a billion molecules. The number of water molecules is one with sixty zeros after it. Meta-analyses indicate that homeopathic remedies are no more effective than sugar pills, which should not be surprising because we would expect water to be about as efficacious as sugar pills in combating disease. James Randi, who has spent decades debunking pseudoscience, has offered a million-dollar prize to anyone who can show that a homeopathic remedy is effective.

Another potent symbol of "science" in education is anything related to the brain. Cynics have labeled this tendency *neurophilia* (from the Greek roots *neur*, meaning "nerve," and *phil*, meaning "love"). Research indicates that people do indeed love the brain. For example, in one study, subjects read descriptions of well-established psychological phenomena.[14] After subjects read a description, they saw one of two explanations of why it happens. One explanation made sense, but the other didn't. In addition, the explanation either included neuroscientific information or didn't—but when present, the neuroscientific information was always irrelevant to the explanation.

Subjects rated explanations as more satisfying when they included the irrelevant neuroscientific evidence. Without the neuro-verbiage, subjects accurately saw that a bad explanation didn't make sense, and rated it as poor. But the neuro-nonsense obscured that, and subjects rated the bad explanation as okay (although not as good as the good explanation).

Even pictures of the brain make information seem more scientific. For example, in one study, researchers had people read a description of a study titled "Watching TV Is Related to Math Ability." The study reported the (fictitious) finding that the same part of the brain is active when people watch TV and when they solve math problems. It concluded that watching TV helps you learn math. Even if the finding were true, the conclusion does not logically follow. Maybe the part of the brain that's active during math and during TV watching is the part of the brain that supports paying attention; you pay attention when you do either task. But the conclusion *seemed* more logical to people when they saw a picture of the brain, as shown in Figure 2.7.[15]

It's no surprise, then, that people trying to sell education products try to capitalize on neurophilia by labeling them "brain based" and using images of the brain. I'll have more to say about how neuroscience relates to education in Chapter Four.

What about Romantic meta-beliefs? These meta-beliefs find expression in a few ways. The first is an emphasis on the natural. Recall that Romantics held an almost religious reverence for nature, and this reverence is seen in American culture today in our regard for natural products. We believe that spring water must be not only clean but also superior to tap water because it comes directly from the Earth

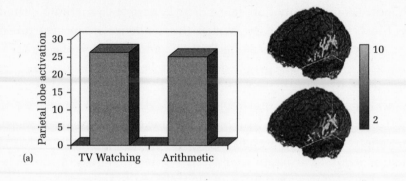

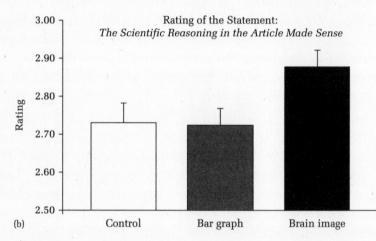

FIGURE 2.7: (a) People read the same description of a fictitious scientific study. Some people also saw a bar graph of the key result–equivalent activation in part of the brain when people watched TV or solved arithmetic problems. Other subjects saw the same data, not in a bar graph, but in a brain activation image. (In the original, the brain activation was shown in red.) Control subjects saw neither. (b) The bar graph at bottom shows that subjects who saw the brain image rated the scientific reasoning in the study more highly than other subjects did.

and is not processed.[16] People believe that herbal remedies are less likely to lead to adverse reactions than manufactured pharmaceuticals[17] and are generally less risky to take.[18] Of course, the fact that something is found in nature doesn't mean it's healthful. Nightshade is perfectly natural, but you'll die if you eat its lovely purple berries.

The meta-belief "natural is good" runs deep in education. For kids who suffer from ADHD or another disorder for which medicines are available, there is a panoply of "natural" treatments: alternative diets, exercises, homeopathy, and others, all of which trumpet their "natural" credentials. Another, more subtle manifestation of Romanticism's reverence for nature is the view that learning is natural, meaning that it is the normal state of affairs for children to be curious and to learn. Think of the natural curiosity of a toddler and compare that to the curiosity of a teen. Doesn't it seem obvious that school deadens a child's natural curiosity? This Romantic meta-belief is tapped by using peripheral cues like the phrases "learn the natural way," and "draws on the child's natural curiosity."

Less often, the negative side of schooling is described: arguing for the unnaturalness of asking children to sit at desks in rows, or likening school to a factory (with students as output) or to a prison with the same deadening routine and lack of freedom. Learning is natural and will occur healthily and bountifully if nature is allowed to take its course. Schooling, as an adult construction, is an encumbrance to this process; school is the problem, not the solution. The nub of the argument is that students should have a good deal of say in what they want to learn. Such arguments have long been the basis for one variety of nontraditional schools. The basic ideas date to eighteenth-century philosophical works, including Rousseau's *Emile* (1762) and Pestalozzi's *Leonard and Gertrude* (1781), but they pop up repeatedly, often with an Enlightenment twist. The idea that children are innately wise and that learning is the mere unfolding of innate abilities is offered as a scientific insight based on recent research, as in the 1960s' *Summerhill* and again in the 1980s' *Teach Your Own*.[19]

This Romantic meta-belief is partly true, but easily twisted out of shape. There are some things that humans are primed to learn, especially how to walk, how to talk, and how to interact socially. Each represents a highly complex skill that most children learn without the benefit of instruction, simply by watching others; thus such learning can fairly be called natural and effortless. But most of what we want kids to learn in school is qualitatively different. Kids do not naturally learn to read simply through the opportunity to observe others reading, although this idea has been suggested more than once in the history of education.

So one Romantic notion is that the child has a natural propensity to learn, but that this impulse is crushed by the unnatural, deadening school routine. This idea—of a bad fit between the child's natural propensities and the procedures at school—lends itself to still another Romantic idea. Recall that Romantic thinkers were fascinated by hidden powers, hidden potential in an individual or in nature. In education, this idea is expressed as the possibility of "unleashing" or "unlocking" learning. The child's intellectual ability is, we are told, much greater than what we are seeing. The right instructional methods will unleash this hidden potential, and we'll see great things from the child.

From a cognitive point of view, this idea is almost certainly wrong. Nothing in the mind is locked or leashed. Sure, we learn much faster and with greater pleasure and enthusiasm when the learning experience is pleasant or when things are put to us clearly and in context, rather than some dry recitation. But the idea that powerful forces lie dormant within us and that these forces can be harnessed? That's a fantasy, a pleasant dream. Everyone can improve at any skill he or she works at. But it does take work, not the simple turning of a key in a lock.

Another aspect of Romanticism expressed in educational programs is the emphasis on the individual. If individuality is paramount in your mind, you could easily conclude that a teacher, however skilled, could never honor the interests and abilities of thirty different students. The terms "one size fits all" or "cookie cutter" are often used pejoratively in this context. Marketing a product as one that honors the individual resonates with a parent who feels that his or her child is a square peg trying to fit in the round hole of schooling. Products may boast that they are "tailored to the individual" or that they "respect your child's learning style."

There is a valid point here, and it does contrast sharply with the Enlightenment view and with the scientific view in general. Let me make this point by stating two extreme positions, neither of which many people would embrace.

Enlightenment position: there are no important differences among kids, so the goal ought to be to find the best way to teach reading (for example) and then use that with all kids.

Romantic position: every child is unique, so it is hopeless to try to define educational "best practices."

FIGURE 2.8: In this shampoo advertisement, one need not make a choice between science and nature. We see the standard trappings of science—a test tube and beaker—harmoniously arranged with leaves and flowers from nature.

The truth is bound to be somewhere in the middle. Most kids are similar enough to one another that it's a realistic scientific goal to talk about "how kids learn" just as we can talk about "how kids digest food" and "how kids breathe." It doesn't mean that our conclusions will apply to every child—some have a digestive disorder, for example—but it ought to apply to a lot of kids. That said, there's no doubt that schooling is more complicated than digestion. The raw memory processes may be pretty similar across kids, but there are surely differences in kids' motivation for school and the particulars of what motivates them, just as one example. I'll have more to say about the role of science in education—what it can and can't contribute—in Chapter Four. For now, let me just note that extreme positions—that schools can safely ignore any and all differences among kids *or* that schools must provide qualitatively different instruction for every child—are not in keeping with what's known about the mind.

Although I introduced Romantic thought as a reaction to the Enlightenment, today the two live together in peace, at least in popular culture. For example, one Pantene shampoo advertisement (Figure 2.8) offers imagery from both Romantic and Enlightenment views.

And the voice-over suggests that the shampoo can "unlock the potential of nature" through the use of "Pantene Pro V science."

What's true of beauty products is true of educational programs. Many programs have a Romantic sensibility, but claim to offer Enlightenment-style scientific proof. For example, the Web sites that promise to unleash your child's hidden potential often claim that their methods are brain based and scientifically proven. The purveyor of "natural" dyslexia treatments emphasizes that they're backed by scientific proof.

In this chapter, I've described some peripheral cues frequently used to boost the credibility of educational programs; I've summarized them in Table 2.1. As evidence, most are neutral. In other words, the mere presence of these cues doesn't mean that an educational program or curriculum is bad, or poorly supported. Not everything that trumpets "All Natural!" is a waste of money. All I'm claiming is that the presence of these cues should do nothing to persuade you that it's a good idea. The exception, I'm claiming, is any that promises to unlock or unleash cognitive ability. That promise will go unfulfilled. For the others, we need only to disregard the peripheral cues to ensure that we don't get sucked into thinking that the program resonates with deeper beliefs that we hold, whether Romantic or Enlightenment.

Okay, so we know what to disregard. But what do we look for? How can you recognize an educational program that really does have scientific backing? In the next chapter, we'll discuss what real science looks like.

TABLE 2.1: Pat phrases that tap Enlightenment or Romantic themes.

Enlightenment Idea	Peripheral Cues	Romantic Idea	Peripheral Cues
Science is the best way to understand the world.	"Research-based" "The research shows" "Brain-based" "Neuroscience" Any technical-sounding jargon Endorsement by credentialed scientists Images of the brain	Intuition is a valid way to understand the world.	"That little voice inside" "Moms just know" "What the doctor [teacher] said just didn't make sense to me"
Learning is governed by laws that apply to all children.	Reference to a single method of teaching all students "Best practices"	The experience of the individual is the most valid way of understanding the world.	"Cookie cutter" (negative) "One-size-fits-all" (negative) "Tailored to your child" "Your child's learning style"
		Nature contains vast hidden powers and hidden potential.	"Unleash learning" "Unlock potential"
		Natural is better.	"Learn the natural way" "Without medication"

3

What Scientists Call Good Science

> If it disagrees with experiment, it's wrong. In that simple statement is the key to science. It doesn't make a difference how beautiful your guess is, it doesn't make a difference how smart you are, who made the guess, or what his name is. If it disagrees with experiment, it's wrong.
>
> —*Richard Feynman*[1]

Imagine that an earthquake strikes your town. Your home shakes, exactly as if a giant shook it for his amusement. Windows rattle, books fall from bookshelves. You jump under a table, wondering when it will end, wondering whether your house will crash around you. At last it stops. You survey your house, call your friends and family—everyone is okay. You hear on the radio that the quake's epicenter was actually several hundred miles away. Towns there were leveled, tens of thousands have died, hundreds of thousands have lost their homes.

How would you react? I think I would, of course, feel bad for all those suffering people, but I would also feel grateful. I'd be thanking my lucky stars that things weren't worse where I lived. What I *wouldn't* do, I would imagine, is pass rumors that another earthquake is coming, even worse this time, centered on my town.

Improbable as it seems, such rumors are relatively common after major earthquakes. This phenomenon was first noted after a large earthquake in 1934 centered in the state of Bihar in eastern India. These rumors were especially rampant more distant from the epicenter, in areas that had suffered less damage.[2] Psychologists were puzzled. Why would people pass these rumors, which would serve only to increase anxiety?

This puzzle caught the attention of psychologist Leon Festinger, who turned the problem on its head. Perhaps it's not that people were spreading rumors and thereby causing anxiety. Perhaps they were already anxious, and the rumors gave them some *justification* for their anxiety. And so the theory of cognitive dissonance was born.[3]

The core of cognitive dissonance theory is that people find it uncomfortable to hold two conflicting thoughts in mind at once. This discomfort motivates people to change one of the thoughts. People are, understandably, anxious following an earthquake, even if the damage around them was minimal. It's unnerving to be confronted with one's powerlessness in face of dramatic natural force.* So these people hold two seemingly conflicting thoughts: (1) I am anxious, and (2) everything is fine because I was not injured by the quake. Festinger's theory predicts that when we hold two conflicting thoughts, we are motivated to change one. It's not easy to make yourself less anxious, so you change the other thought—everything is *not* fine, because another, even larger quake is coming. People closer to the center of the quake, in contrast, have no need to justify their anxiety. They *have* lost property or been injured, or their friends or family have, so it's quite clear to them why they are anxious.

Festinger subjected his idea to more careful testing in the laboratory. In one of his better-known demonstrations, he asked subjects

---

*I have experienced this anxiety. There was a 5.8 magnitude earthquake in Mineral, Virginia, on August 23, 2011, about thirty miles from my home.

to perform terribly boring, repetitive tasks—for example, removing and replacing pegs in a pegboard.[4] After an hour of this tedium, the experimenter told the subject that the purpose was to see if people performed tasks better if they have been told that the task is interesting. The experimenter said that the *next* person coming needed to expect that the task would be interesting. Would the subject be willing to tell the new arrival that she was in for a treat? The crucial part of the experiment was that subjects were offered money to tell this lie: some were offered the relatively modest sum of $1, whereas others were offered $20, a tidy sum in the late 1950s when this experiment was conducted. At the end of the experiment, subjects were asked how much they had liked the pegboard task.

We normally think that paying people to do something produces better results. So we might expect that the $20 subjects would end up rating the task more interesting than the $1 subjects would. But the opposite happened. Why? By getting the $1 subjects to lie about the task, the experimenters ensured that subjects held two conflicting thoughts: (1) the task was really boring, and (2) I just told someone the task was interesting. Subjects can't convince themselves that they didn't just say the task was interesting, so they change the other thought: they tell themselves that the pegboard task wasn't all that bad. The $20 subjects, in contrast, don't really feel that mental conflict because they can justify that second thought; "I just told someone that task was interesting *because I was paid twenty dollars to say it.*" So when asked at the end of the experiment, they said the task was dull, dull, dull.

How Science Works

The story of cognitive dissonance theory illustrates how science operates. Figure 3.1 shows that it's a cyclical process. (When I refer to this figure, I'll call it the Science Cycle.) We start on the right, with some observations of the world. These needn't be technical laboratory findings. They can be casual observations you make on a neighborhood walk, or in the case of psychologist Jamuna Prasad, observations he made of earthquake victims spreading rumors. Then we try to synthesize these observations into a simple summary statement—that's the stage labeled "theory" in the Science Cycle—

and, indeed, scientific theories are really just statements that summarize some aspect of the world. For example, "The planets rotate around the sun in elliptical orbits" summarizes many, many observations of the locations of planets in the night sky. Leon Festinger sought to summarize many aspects of human thought and motivation by claiming that conflicting thoughts create discomfort. Finally, we test whether the summary statement is accurate, as in Festinger's experiment with the boring pegboard task. The test produces new observations, and so we're back at the top of the Science Cycle.†

So what happens next? We make another trip around the Science Cycle, pushing the theory to make more refined predictions, and testing it in more varied circumstances. Eventually we'll find a failure, a circumstance in which the theory predicts something other than what we observe. Finding such a failure is actually a good thing. Why? Because that's the way science advances. Failures are the motivators of improved theories. If we develop a theory that is very hard to disprove, even after many tests, then we start to have some confidence that this theory is a good description of the world and will be of some use to us. (How we use scientific theories will be taken up in Chapter Four.)

How do you find a flaw in a theory, so that you can then go on to try to devise a better one? Criticisms might be leveled at any of the three stages in the scientific process depicted in the Science Cycle: observation, theory, or test.

1. Someone might point out that there was a problem with the *observations* in Festinger's pegboard experiment. If you read the article

---

†This is called the hypothetico-deductive model of science because you use a theory to deduce a hypothesis, which is then tested. Philosophers of science were quick to point out that there are logical problems with this model, among them that too many theories can make the same predictions. A more constrained version of this model is called "inference to the best explanation," in which you're not happy with just any model that fits the data but with the simplest model that, if correct, would explain the data. These concerns are beyond our purposes here, and in point of fact most scientists don't often think about the logical implications of the methods they use. But it should at least be acknowledged that there's a logical issue here. For relatively readable introduction to these very complex issues, see Newton-Smith, W. H. (2001). *A companion to the philosophy of science*. Malden, MA: Blackwell.

describing the experiment, you'll see that data from 15 percent of the subjects had to be excluded; these subjects either were suspicious about the real purpose of the experiment or refused to do some of the tasks. That's a pretty high percentage, so I might claim that the observations from this experiment are invalid, and suggest that we need better data.

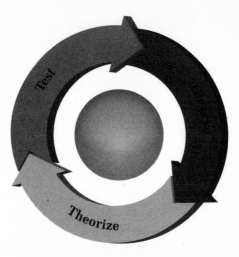

2. Someone might think that the experimental data are okay, but criticize the *theory*. Indeed, cognitive dissonance theory was initially criticized for being rather vague.[5] For

FIGURE 3.1: The scientific method, about as simplified as possible. Observations of the world are abstracted into theories, which are then tested. The results of the test constitute new observations about the world, and the cycle continues.

example, how much inconsistency is required before I'm motivated to change one of my thoughts? Will any type of inconsistency do? Suppose I think my physician is quite competent, but then I see him in a restaurant rudely berating a server. Will I feel dissonance? On the one hand, you can be a good clinician and still be a rude boor. On the other hand, shouldn't a doctor be compassionate and sensitive? I might criticize the cognitive dissonance theory as being insufficiently developed if it cannot make a clear prediction in cases such as this.

3. Someone might propose a new *test* of the theory, drawing a new prediction from the theory that had not yet been considered. The original theory said little about how important the conflicting thoughts were to me; if there was a conflict, there was dissonance. Thus the theory seemed to predict that dissonance would arise even if the thoughts concerned minor matters. Merrill Carlsmith and his colleagues tested that prediction by repeating the boring-task experiment and showing that only *face-to-face* lies caused dissonance.[6] When subjects wrote an essay describing the task as interesting, there was no dissonance, presumably because subjects did not really

take the lie to heart. Carlsmith had no problem with the existing data or with the theory, but he proposed a new test, which then showed the theory to be wanting.

I've gone through this example to emphasize two things about good science. First, science is dynamic, not static. Although Enlightenment thinkers viewed the world as dynamic, their view of science was fixed. Seventeenth-century scientists thought of nature as God's grand book to be decoded, and they expected that scientific knowledge, once gained, would be final. Newton's laws were seen as absolute. The description of heavenly bodies was *done*. Many nonscientists hold this view today, a view all too often reinforced by the presentation of science in school. We learn facts and laws in textbooks as though they are unchangeable. Scientists, in contrast, view theories as provisional. That's why Figure 3.1 depicts the scientific method as a cycle. It never stops, and the best theory we have of any phenomenon is always taken to be just that—the best theory we have now. It is expected that the theory will fail in some way and that a superior theory will eventually be proposed.

The provisional nature of scientific theory is important to keep in mind when we contemplate using scientific knowledge to improve education. We can't change curricula and methods yearly, but we have to acknowledge that the very best scientific information we have today about how children think and learn may be out-of-date in a decade or two. The consequences of this new knowledge for an educational program may be minor, but they may not, and we would do well to bear this fact in mind when considering educational philosophies written fifty or a hundred years ago.[‡] Piaget died thirty years ago; Vygotsky, almost eighty. Great as these

---

[‡]Of course, that doesn't mean that if it's old, it's wrong. My colleague Angeline Lillard has argued that one hundred years ago, Maria Montessori anticipated many findings of modern science in regard to children's cognitive development. Lillard, A. (2005). *Montessori: The science behind the genius*. New York: Oxford Press.

minds were, they created their theories of child development in ignorance of decades of data.

The second thing to note about the cyclical nature of the scientific method is that it's self-correcting. We not only assume that the current theory is provisional and will eventually be proven wrong; we also assume that a better theory can be and will be developed. But essential to this process is that the theory be open to criticism. That's how we find flaws.

The whole system by which scientific theories are generated and evaluated is set up so that other people have ample opportunity to lodge criticism. The consequence of this somewhat combative nature of science is that most scientists get used to being wrong. It's not just that scientists are wrong more often than they are right—that's probably true in other fields too—but we get our noses rubbed in it, in public.§ After a while, most scientists realize that insisting that you're right in the face of valid criticism only makes you look stupider. You might as well admit the error, and if you find the error before someone else does, you might as well admit it before someone else points it out. Astronomer Carl Sagan put it admirably:

> In science it often happens that scientists say, "You know that's a really good argument; my position is mistaken," and then they actually change their minds and you never hear that old view from them again. They really do it. It doesn't happen as often as it should, because scientists are human and change is sometimes painful. But it happens every day. I cannot recall the last time something like that happened in politics or religion.[7]

---

§For example, Felice Bedford, a friend and colleague at the University of Arizona, published an article in 1997, much of which argued that I had committed a logical fallacy in making a particular claim about learning. I think the claim ended up being well supported for other reasons, but she was right about the fallacy. Bedford, F. L. (1997). False categories in cognition: The not-the-liver fallacy. *Cognition, 64,* 231–248.

This is a sense in which science is radically different from other ways of understanding the world. When you're wrong, everyone else can see it. I can modify my inaccurate theory, or I can abandon it and try something completely new. But I can't just put my head down and pretend I don't notice the problem, or bluster and call people names and hope to distract people from my error.

Science moves forward—that is, our understanding of natural phenomena gets deeper—as we make more circuits around the Science Cycle. Very often when people talk about "good science," they get to the nitty-gritty of how experiments are designed, whether people use the right statistics on their data, and so forth. That's important, but as we've now seen, there are two other, equally important stages where things can go right or wrong: the creation of theory and the observation of the world. Let's look at each of the three stages more closely and examine what must be in place for each to be conducted correctly.

Observing the World

Why is there not a scientific field called "ethicology"? Wouldn't it be marvelous (or at least interesting) to apply the scientific method to the study of ethics? We could, over time, zero in on the one set of ethical principles that would be most fitting for humans. Why are there not university departments of ethicology, as there are of biology, chemistry, and psychology?**

The answer gets at one of the limitations of scientific observation: the scientific method is applicable only to the natural world. It is mute on matters of morality, ethics, or aesthetics. You may have strong opinions as to whether *Twilight* or *Swann's Way* is the better novel, but your opinion is not based on science. And because science applies only to the natural world, it does not, by definition, apply to the supernatural. (The word *supernatural* often implies something from the occult, but I'm using the term here to include

---

**Applying the scientific method to questions of ethics has been tried, notably by John Dewey. See, for example, Dewey, J. (1903). Logical conditions of a scientific treatment of morality. *Decennial Publications of the University of Chicago* (First Series), *3*, 115–139.

anything outside nature, including God.) As physicist Steven Hawking noted, "The usual approach of science of constructing a mathematical model cannot answer the questions of why there should be a universe for the model to describe."[8]

If not all problems are amenable to scientific analysis, we had better ask whether the sorts of problems we face in education can be addressed with the scientific method. At least some of these problems would seem to be part of the natural world, so our answer would be a tentative yes. There are no supernatural forces at work when children learn to read or to work math problems, and these cognitive abilities don't have important ethical or aesthetic components. These processes can be studied scientifically, and significant progress has been made in understanding them in the last fifty years.

There are other vital questions in education for which the scientific method is wholly inappropriate. Should we present American history so as to encourage patriotism or so as to ingrain a questioning attitude toward government and toward institutional authority in general? What is the role of the arts in K–12 education? Who is ultimately responsible for children's education: parents, teachers, or children themselves, and does the answer to this question change as kids get older? Educating children raises dozens of questions, and, powerful as the method may be, science is applicable to just a fraction of them. Thus we have to be clear about which questions science might address and how. I'll have much more to say about that in Chapter Four.

So the first principle of good observation in science is to pick a problem that one can observe. The second principle is that when we say "observation" we really mean "measurement." As the great German physicist Max Planck put it, "An experiment is a question which science poses to Nature, and a measurement is the recording of Nature's answer."

Why is measurement so important? Suppose I have a theory about dieting. I propose that there is a consistent relationship between calorie intake and weight loss: if you reduce calories by 25 percent, you will lose 1 percent of your weight each week. So according to my theory, a two-hundred-pound person who reduces his calorie intake by 25 percent will lose two pounds every week he diets.

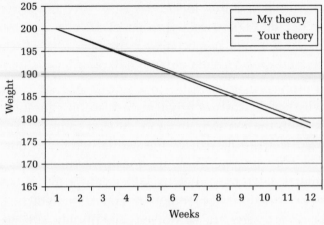

FIGURE 3.2: The predictions of two theories of weight loss.

Now suppose that you have a different theory. You agree that a 25 percent reduction in calories will lead to a 1 percent loss in weight each week, but you think it's 1 percent of how much you weigh *at the start of the week,* not when you started the diet. So the dieter will lose 2.00 pounds the first week, 1.98 pounds the second week (that is, 1 percent of the 198 pounds he weighed at the start of the second week), 1.96 pounds the third week, and so on.

Your theory of weight loss is pretty different from mine; we disagree about the basis of weight loss. But the theories make really similar predictions. At the end of twelve weeks, the predictions differ by one pound (Figure 3.2). So to determine whether your theory or my theory of weight loss is better, we'll need a pretty accurate scale.

Now imagine that we don't have scales at all. Imagine that we can judge weight only by looking at people and saying to ourselves, "Hmm, I think he looks thinner." If that were the case, it would seem almost hopeless to determine whether your theory or my theory of weight loss is better. In fact, if there were not scales, it would be pretty hard to get past the very general, very obvious observation, "When people eat less, they tend to lose weight."

When it comes to many of the qualities that we care about in education research, we are in a comparable position. We don't have scales. We want kids to be creative, to be good collaborators, to be good critical thinkers. But our ability to measure these qualities is quite limited. This means that I might spin an interesting theory about what makes someone creative, but I can't test my theory. And if you have a different theory, we can't design an experiment to tell us which theory is better.

This problem is especially salient in light of current trends emphasizing "twenty-first-century skills" in schooling. The impetus comes from the claim forwarded by some economists that the nature of the job market is changing.[9] Whereas most jobs in the latter part of the twentieth century called for repetitive physical work (for example, assembly line work in a factory) or repetitive cognitive work (for example, telephone sales), high-paying jobs in the twenty-first century are much more likely to call for nonrepetitive cognitive work—that is, jobs where people are frequently confronted with problems that they have not solved in the past. Furthermore, these problems are likely to demand different types of expertise for their solution, so people will need to pool their expertise—that is, to collaborate. Thus the prized worker would be (1) creative, (2) an effective problem solver, and (3) a good team player. So, one might argue, schooling should build those skills, to prepare our students for these jobs.

But if you're hoping that science can help us know how to teach kids these qualities, you'll need to be patient. Researchers are working on ways of measuring creativity[10] and group cooperation,[11] but this measurement problem is not easily solved. Obviously, the fact that we're not yet very good at measuring things like creativity or morality or citizenship does not mean that we shouldn't try to teach kids to be creative, moral, upright citizens. It means that we can't expect science to help much in bolstering our efforts to teach these things. But again, we shouldn't expect science to have all the answers. What's important is clarity in our own minds about what science can and can't do. Measurability is an important factor in how susceptible something is to scientific investigation. Measurability does not speak to importance. Importance is determined by our values.

Speaking Theoretically

I'm sure you have wondered what impact your siblings had on you, especially the impact of birth order (or of being an only child).

If you're the youngest in the family, like me, maybe you felt somewhat overshadowed by your older siblings, who had, and would forever have, the advantage of a few years on you. For their part, my older sisters always felt that my parents went kind of easy on me when it came to discipline—my sisters always said of my parents, "We broke them in for you."

Suppose I tell you that I have a theory about birth order. I claim that the oldest child in a family is typically academically serious and is the highest achiever at school. I explain that the firstborn talks with adults more than her younger siblings do, and is under greater pressure from the parents to act like an adult from a young age. You respond with the example of your spouse's older brother, who flunked out of school and now, at age thirty-two, lives in his parents' basement, drinking beer and playing Xbox. I patiently explain that sometimes the child will sense the expectations of the parents and rebel, casting aside conventional marks of success and marching to his or her own drummer. Sometimes it's even possible that the child will rebel in some parts of his life and try to live up to the parents' expectations in others.

Now in one sense, my theory seems pretty cool. It makes a prediction, but when the prediction turns out to be wrong, my theory does a quick pivot and can *still* account for the data. Actually, a theory that can account for all data is not cool. In fact, able-to-account-for-all-data is not just an undesirable feature; it's a fatal flaw. That sounds strange. Wouldn't a theory that can account for everything be not just acceptable but desirable?

The logic here is a bit convoluted, so let's start with a famous example, suggested by Karl Popper, the philosopher who emphasized this point.[12] I start with observations in the world, so let's suppose that I'm observing swans. I see lots of white swans and none of other colors, so I propose a theory: "All swans are white." According to the Science Cycle, I'm supposed to test my theory. How could I verify that it is true? I don't really get anywhere by taking you to the zoo or to a local lake and pointing out white swans. Finding *some* corroborating evidence for a theory is usually pretty easy. After all, I probably wouldn't have come up with the theory in the first place if I hadn't seen some white swans, so I'm just showing you the ones

I've already seen. And no matter how many white swans I show you, the theory is never really proven. There might be a nonwhite swan in a spot I haven't searched yet. Although proving my theory correct is impossible, proving it incorrect is easy. All it takes is one black swan, and we know that I'm wrong.

The problem with my birth-order theory is that I can't test it. Firstborns are predicted to be high achievers . . . except when they are not high achievers. Show me a firstborn, and I actually can't tell you whether he or she will be high achieving. That means I can't generate a test of the theory and therefore can't move around the Science Cycle. I'm stuck. And if I can't test the theory, I can't falsify it, *and proving theories false is the main way we get to newer, better theories.*

I've made the process sound as though there's a "one strike and you're out" rule. That is, I can keep piling up confirmatory evidence—that is, white swans—and it won't mean much, but when I see one black swan, boom. Back to the drawing board. Indeed, Einstein is often quoted as having said, "No amount of experimentation can ever prove me right; a single experiment can prove me wrong."[13]

It's actually not quite that simple. For example, when asked what sort of evidence would shake his confidence in evolutionary theory, biologist J.B.S. Haldane reportedly said, "A fossil of a rabbit found in Precambrian rock." The Precambrian period ended about 570 million years ago, a time when the only animals looked more like sponges, jellyfish, or worms, from which mammals would evolve much later.

But suppose a Precambrian rabbit fossil *were* found. Would biologists really conclude that evolution had been disproved? The answer is almost certainly no. Evolutionary theory provides such a good fit to so many observations in biology that it would be foolhardy to jettison the theory. Biologists would instead try to figure out how to retain the most important features of evolution that make it such a successful theory, while accounting for the Precambrian rabbit.

So wait a minute—doesn't that make evolution an unfalsifiable theory? I find data I don't like, so I start desperately looking for a back door? Not really. Biologists would recognize that the Precambrian rabbit posed a significant problem, but they would retain evolution as the *best available* theory. Sometimes a difficult-to-explain observation is later shown to fall within the predictions of the theory after all. A classic example is the observation of irregularities in the orbit of Uranus in 1845. The planet simply was not behaving as Newton's theory predicted. One option in the face of these data would have been to abandon Newton's theory. But the theory got so many things right that it seemed rash to discard it. Astronomers instead posited that the irregularities must be caused by another body exerting a gravitational pull on Uranus. That prediction was later confirmed, and led to the discovery of a new planet, Neptune.[14]

How do you know whether to hang on to a theory and hope that the anomalies will be explained later, or whether to ditch the theory? There are no hard-and-fast rules for making that decision. In general, the more data that a theory accounts for, the more willing scientists are to put up with a few things that it gets wrong. If the theory wasn't very successful to start with and then you see observations that conflict with it, you're less likely to continue believing it. Ultimately, it's a judgment call. Reasonable people can differ on whether a theory ought to be abandoned or retained.

When data are mixed, they can become a Rorschach inkblot, revealing the prior beliefs of the viewer. Nowhere is that more apparent in education research today than in the evaluation of charter schools. Charter schools are public schools that have a special agreement with the state; they are subject to fewer regulations than other public schools, so teachers and administrators have more freedom to run the school as they see fit. In return, the school is subject to greater accountability to the state. The school must show that students are learning. (They also receive less money than other public schools, on average.)

Now if you believe that government is more often part of the problem than part of the solution, you probably believe that government regulations can't be good for education. Thus you would deduce that charter schools, being freed from at least some regulation, will outperform other public schools. Some studies show that kids attending charter schools learn more than comparable kids attending other public schools,[15] but other studies don't show that.[16] Such comparisons are complicated to conduct, for technical reasons I won't go into here, but these technicalities give people ammunition with which to criticize studies that draw conclusions they dislike. So people looking at the same dozen or so studies draw polar opposite conclusions. And they think that the *other* guys ought to give up on their theory.

A final property of theories is especially important when we contemplate rejecting an old theory in favor of a new one. Good science is cumulative. That means that for a new theory to replace an old one, it must do what the old one did, and something more. Science is always supposed to move forward. That's been one of the criticisms of pseudosciences like astrology.[17] The failings of astrological theory are well known, and have been for a long time. Yet there is no attempt to use those failed observations to improve the theory. Attempts to advance astrology have been halfhearted, and the theory does not look much different from what it did hundreds of years ago.

A similar problem plagues theories in American education. Historians have pointed out that there is a pattern of education theories being tried, found wanting, and then reappearing under a different name a decade or two later.[18] In the Introduction, I cited the case of whole-word reading, which was introduced in the 1920s and belatedly discredited in the 1960s. When the theory reappeared in the 1980s as "whole-language" reading, there were already ample data to show that this "new" theory was wrong. Scientific theory is supposed to be cumulative, and a new theory—which is what whole-language reading purported to be—should have been expected to account for existing data that were obviously relevant to the theory.

Earlier in this chapter, I mentioned the twenty-first-century skills movement. It provides a more recent example of theoretical retreading. The argument sounds perfectly plausible: our students spend too much time memorizing arcane bits of information. They don't learn how to solve problems, how to be creative, how to *think*. Further, hasn't anyone noticed that schooling hasn't changed over the course of a hundred years? Kids sit at desks, lined up in rows that face the teacher standing before them. Kids today need education that is relevant in a world of Google and smartphones.

These very same concerns—that schooling must be made relevant to life and to work—have been voiced for more than a hundred years.[19] In the 1920s, the idea was called progressive education. In the 1950s, it was called the Life Adjustment Movement. In the 1990s, it was the Secretary's Commission on Achieving Necessary Skills (SCANS). As a consequence of each movement, school curricula were filled with projects that appeared to have real-world applicability, kids went on more field trips, and so forth. After about a decade, people started to notice that students lacked factual knowledge. They'd visited a sewage treatment plant and they'd created a school garden, but they couldn't come within fifty years of the dates that the Civil War was fought. A "back to basics" movement followed, which emphasized factual knowledge and denigrated thinking skills as so much fluff. After about a decade of that, people would claim that the curriculum focused exclusively on facts and that kids didn't know how to apply them to real-world problems. And the cycle would begin again.

Both factual knowledge and thinking skills are essential for students to be able to solve meaningful problems. Imparting both to students is difficult, there is no doubt. Unfortunately, we keep taking on this problem in the same ineffectual way. We address half of it, later despair of the other half, and then ignore what we were getting right in our rush to correct what was undone. Put this baldly, it seems incredible. Yet that has been the pattern.

Testing, Testing

The third and final aspect of the scientific process is testing a theory. We start with observations of the world, then we abstract summary statements from those observations, and then derive new predictions, things we believe that, under certain conditions, we will observe in the world. In the epigraph for this chapter, physicist Richard Feynman suggests that this step is the one that separates science from other ways of understanding the world. So what qualities do we look for in a scientific test?

Recognizing a good study versus a bad one boils down to keeping in mind a list of things that can go wrong, and successfully spotting if any of these traps or pitfalls is present. Table 3.1 is a list of the sorts

TABLE 3.1: Some problems to watch for in education research studies.

Problem	Example
Differential attrition (drop-out) rates between groups	I might compare two tutoring methods for math. After six weeks, I find that kids receiving method A are doing better in math than kids receiving method B, so it looks as though A wins. But a closer look at the data shows that lots of kids getting method A quit the experiment during the six weeks, and very few getting method B quit. So it may be that those few kids who finished method A were an especially determined bunch, and were not really comparable to the kids getting method B.
Simpson's paradox	Suppose a large city has been using a reading program for ten years. I examine the reading achievement scores and see that they have dropped significantly during that time. I might conclude that the program was a failure. But then I look at the scores of wealthy, middle-class, and poor children separately, and I find that reading scores have gone up for each of the three groups! How could overall scores drop if each group is gaining? Poor kids don't score as well as rich kids, so if the percentage of poor kids in the city increased during that decade, the average score might drop, even though each separate group is gaining.
Experimenter expectancy effects	When an experimenter has an expectation as to what a subject is likely to do, the experimenter can, through body language or subtle intonations in instructions, communicate that expectation without meaning to. Many subjects will perceive this expectation and will try to live up to it, either in an effort to be helpful or in an effort to appear "normal."

(continued)

TABLE 3.1: (*continued*)

Problem	Example
Nonrepresentative volunteers	If you are testing children in a laboratory, you must ask yourself, "Who has the time and inclination to bring their child to my lab during working hours on a weekday? Is this family different from other families in some way?"
Correlation versus causation	The fact that you observe that two factors are related doesn't mean you can draw a causal link. For example, ice cream consumption and crime are correlated, but not because ice cream makes people criminals. Hot weather makes people want ice cream, and it also makes people more short tempered, which increases violent crime. Surprisingly often, people conclude cause-and-effect relationships from correlations—for example, the relationship of race and academic performance.
The end of the experiment	If subjects are aware that an experiment is about to end, they will typically try a little harder, so as to "go out with a bang." These data will not be representative of the rest of the subject's performance.
Types of sampling (how you pick the subjects for an experiment)	*Random sampling:* from a large group, a smaller group is selected, at random, for testing. *Stratified:* I first divide my overall group into subgroups (for example, men and women) and then sample randomly from each subgroup. This is done to ensure proportionate representation of subgroups when that's deemed important. *Haphazard (or convenience) sampling:* you select people for your experiment based on whom you can recruit. This method is very likely to bias your results. *Other types of sampling:* cluster, purposive, quota.

TABLE 3.1: *(continued)*

Problem	Example
Carryover effects in repeated testing	If the experimenter tries more than one intervention, the influence of intervention 1 can easily "carry over" to intervention 2. For example, a teacher might try one method of classroom management and then four weeks later try another. He must recognize that the class might respond to the second method differently than they would have if they had never experienced the first classroom management method.
Regression toward the mean	Suppose someone scores very poorly on the SAT. She then takes a test preparation course, and her score improves. We're likely to think that the score went up because of the course. Perhaps not. If I take the SAT, my score will vary depending on which particular set of questions appears on the test I take, whether I'm feeling especially alert that day, and so on. If I get a really low score, that probably means I'm generally not going to score that well on the SAT, but also that *I had an unlucky day too*. So if I took it again, it's likely that I would have a luckier day, and my score would be at least somewhat higher. (The same logic applies to people who get a very high score; their score is likely to go down if they retake the test.)

of concerns one might have about a study in education research. You can skip the list if you want to. It's really meant only to impress upon you that there are a heck of a lot of ways that you can screw up an experiment, and this list barely scratches the surface of the sort of methodological and statistical knowledge that one needs in order to conduct education research well.

Spotting strengths and weaknesses in research is a narrow skill. Someone who is quite good at sizing up one type of experiment will not be nearly as good at sizing up others. For example, I've been reviewing articles in cognitive psychology for about twenty years. Mostly those were studies of particular aspects of learning and movement control. When I became associate editor of a cognitive psychology journal, I covered a broader array of topics, but I was still one of six associate editors, each with his or her own specialty— and the journal didn't even cover all of cognitive psychology!

This problem—the many ways that scientific studies can go wrong— puts me in mind of a moment from the movie *Body Heat*. An arsonist (played by Mickey Rourke) is visited by an attorney (played by William Hurt) who has helped him out of tough spots before. Now the tables have turned, and the attorney is planning a crime. He seeks the arsonist's advice, and the arsonist says, "Anytime you try a decent crime, you got fifty ways you can [mess] up. You think of twenty-five of them, and you're a genius. And you ain't no genius." Science, like crime, is complicated, and there are many ways it can go wrong.

The advantage that scientists have over criminals is that they don't need to keep their work secret. In fact, they are forbidden from doing so. It's so well understood that scientists can miss things that they are *required* to make their work open to scrutiny, so that others can criticize it and improve on it. To appreciate the nature and importance of this feature, let's examine one of its more celebrated failures: the story of cold fusion.

It would be great if nuclear power plants could use fusion rather than fission, as they currently do. The energy produced by fusion is enormous; the required fuel—isotopes of hydrogen—can be found in water; and the radioactivity produced by the reaction is short-lived and harmless. Unfortunately, fusion occurs under conditions of enormous heat and pressure, meaning that it requires more energy to create the reaction than is released by it. Thus it has not been a practical source of energy.

Imagine the excitement, then, when two scientists—each a professor at a respected university—reported that they had produced a fusion reaction at room temperature. Stanley Pons and Martin Fleischmann did just that at a press conference on March 23, 1989.

The odd thing about the announcement, however, was that they held the press conference before the experiments were published in a scientific journal. Publication in a scientific journal is the first sense in which science must be done "publicly." Before your work is published, it will be sent to between two and five scientists familiar with the research topic. You will have described exactly how you did the work; they will make sure that the logic of the experiment and the conclusions are sound, and they will judge the importance of your findings. That's the process commonly called "peer review."

Pons and Fleischmann held the press conference before others had a chance to look carefully at what they did. And the details of the methods provided at the press conference were so sketchy that other scientists were frustrated because they couldn't fully understand the nature of the experiment.[20] Ultimately, the details of the experimental method *were* published, and many scientists attempted to reproduce the cold fusion results and failed.[21] So you could say that the truth eventually won out.

The truth won out, but a lot of time and energy was wasted in the interim. Look at these headlines from the days following the press conference:

Nuclear fusion in a test tube developed by Utah professors—*Financial Times*

Scientists claim technique to control nuclear fusion—*Dow Jones News Service*

Scientists pursue endless power source—*The Times of London*

Taming H-bombs? Two scientists claim breakthrough—*Wall Street Journal*

Test-tube nuclear fusion uses hydrogen bomb's energy—*Toronto Star*

Nuclear fusion breakthrough reported—*Boston Globe*

Researchers around the world stopped what they were doing and scurried to study and reproduce Pons and Fleischmann's experiments. It turned out that the most important part of the finding—the observations that indicated a fusion reaction—were due to errors they had made in their experiments.[22]

So the most basic sense in which science is "public" is the peer review process. Other people must evaluate your work before it's published. Another sense in which science is public concerns the manner in which it's published. You can't provide just a thumbnail sketch of what the experiment was like. You have to describe everything: characteristics of the subjects, model numbers of lab equipment, *exactly* what happened in the experiment, how the data were analyzed, and so on. The goal is to write a description of the procedure that is so complete that another researcher could do the experiment herself.

Being public about the methods of science is important not only because it's hard to think of every possible objection to your work but also because scientists are subject to the confirmation bias too.[23] When we conduct a study, we know what we expect to find, and we are likely to (unconsciously) skew our impression of the results to confirm our expectation. Again, the ever-quotable Richard Feynman: "The first principle is you must not fool yourself, and you are the easiest person to fool."[24]

Safeguarding Science

So what makes good science? I've named seven principles (Table 3.2). Table 3.2 could have been twice as long. And recall that just one of these principles—"scientific tests are empirical"—was the basis for *another* list of potential problems to watch for (Table 3.1), which itself could have been ten times longer. The implication is obvious. Judging whether or not a scientific claim is well founded requires a lot of thought and a lot of expertise. That creates problems for individuals and problems for practitioners.

For the individual, the obvious problem is in knowing what the scientific evidence *really* says on complex matters. In a few instances—

TABLE 3.2: Seven principles of good science

Stage of Scientific Method That Is Affected	Principle	Implication for Education
Entire cycle	Science is dynamic and self-correcting.	If we use the scientific method, we can reasonably expect to develop a deeper understanding of learning in school.
Observation	Scientific method applies only to the natural world.	Some important questions in education do not concern the natural world; rather, they concern values.
Observation	Scientific method works only if the phenomenon under study can be measured.	Some important aspects of education do concern the natural world, but the phenomena are difficult to measure.
Theory	Theories cannot be proven true. They can only be falsified, but when to abandon a theory as false is a judgment call.	The fact that it's a judgment call must not prevent us from rejecting poorly supported education theories so that we can seek out better ones.
Theory	Good theories are cumulative.	Education has a history of reintroducing theories under a different name, even though the theory has been tested and found wanting.
Test	Scientific tests are empirical.	Interpreting empirical tests is always difficult, and doing so is much more difficult in education, where there are so many factors that might be causal. Evaluating these tests requires considerable expertise.

(*continued*)

TABLE 3.2: (continued)

Stage of Scientific Method That Is Affected	Principle	Implication for Education
Test	Scientific tests are public.	Because science is so difficult to evaluate, it's crucial that science be conducted in a way that allows everyone to evaluate it. Some of education research is peer reviewed, but not all of it.

notably, the safety of medications—we are protected by laws. A new medication must pass a rigorous scientific screening process (in the United States, overseen by the Food and Drug Administration) before it can be sold. There are loopholes through which charlatans enter the marketplace with snake-oil remedies, but if a nonscientist wants to know what scientists think about an issue, it's not hard to learn. Scientific consensus views are regularly published by institutions that scientists have created. If you want to know what the medical community thinks about the link between vaccines and autism, there are Web sites (for example, www.healthfinder.gov, maintained by the U.S. Department of Health and Human Services) that publish consensus statements. If you want to know whether a particular type of psychotherapy has scientific support, you can visit the Web site of the Society of Clinical Psychology.[25] If you want to know what physicists think about climate change, you'll find a statement on the Web site of the American Physical Society (and comparable groups in other nations). I know that some people don't really trust the scientific community. That's a different issue. I'm talking about access to the collective view of that community, and in most cases, you can get that view pretty easily.

Practitioners face a different problem. Suppose you're a doctor. You go through medical school and residency, learning the most up-to-date techniques and treatments. Then you go into family practice, and you're an awesome doctor. But science doesn't stand still once you've finished your training. You were up-to-date the year you graduated, but researchers keep discovering new things. How can you possibly keep up with the latest developments when, according to PubMed.gov, more than nine hundred thousand articles are published in medical journals each year?[26] Medicine has solved this problem for practitioners by publishing annual summaries of research that boil down the findings to recommendations for changes in practice. Physicians can buy summary volumes that let them know whether there is substantial scientific evidence indicating that they ought to change their treatment of a particular condition. In other words, the profession does not expect that practitioners will keep up with the research literature themselves. That job goes to a small set of people who can devote the time needed to it.

In education, there are no federal or state laws protecting consumers from bad educational practices. And education researchers have never united as a field to agree on methods or curricula or practices that have sound scientific backing. That makes it very difficult for the nonexpert simply to look to a panel of experts for the state of the art in education research. There are no universally acknowledged experts, a topic I'll discuss in some detail in Chapter Six.

Every parent, administrator, and teacher is on his or her own. That's why I wrote this book. But before we can talk about spotting good science amid fraud, we must cover one more topic. We've talked about what properties scientists look for when considering whether science is well done, but we haven't yet talked about what to do with good scientific findings. The lab, after all, is not the classroom, and how to move from one to the other is not obvious. That is the subject of Chapter Four.

4

How to Use Science

> "A plowed field is no more part of nature than an asphalted street—and no less."
>
> —*Herb Simon*[1]

When President Obama extols science, saying, "Science is more essential for our prosperity, our health, our environment and our quality of life than it has ever been before,"[2] he does not seek to persuade Americans of the importance of science. They already believe it. Surveys show that very high percentages of Americans (usually close to 90 percent) say that they are "very interested" in new scientific discoveries, and think that such discoveries have a positive impact on our quality of life. Furthermore, relatively few Americans see a downside to science. When prompted with possible negative effects—for example, that science "doesn't pay enough attention to the moral values of society" or that science "makes our way of life change too fast"—a substantial minority of Americans agree, but the percentage is much lower than that observed in similar surveys in other countries. Americans see more advantages and fewer disadvantages to scientific advances than people from any other country for which comparable data are available (Brazil, China, European Union, India, Japan, Malaysia. Russia, South Korea).[3]

Americans also see it as natural and right that the federal government should pay for scientists to do their work. More than 80 percent agree with the simple statement "The government should fund basic research." Indeed, 35 percent of Americans think that the federal government spends too little on science, and only 10 percent think that it spends too much (Figure 4.1).[4] (The remainder think that the level of spending is about right, or have no opinion.)

The seeds of that public attitude and of enormous federal expenditures on scientific research may be found in World War II. The average citizen may not have been aware of the massive scientific efforts, organized by the U.S. Office of Scientific Research and Development, that went into developing radar, sonar, and advances in fuses, missile guidance systems, ordnance, aviation, and so on. But Americans were certainly aware of the role of science in the development of the atomic bomb. And they certainly were aware of the availability of penicillin. Although penicillin was identified as effective in treating bacterial infections in 1928, there was no way to produce it on a large scale. As late as June 1942, there was virtually no penicillin available to treat infections. Yet two years later, some two billion units of penicillin went with Allied soldiers to France on D-Day, the product of a new method of growing a new strain of penicillin (originally discovered on a moldy cantaloupe) in a liquid by-product of corn. Whether or not the atomic bomb

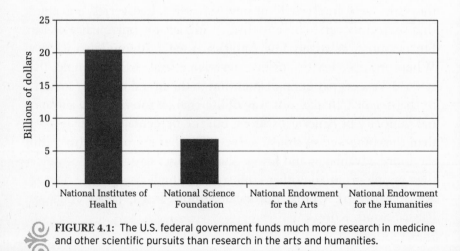

FIGURE 4.1: The U.S. federal government funds much more research in medicine and other scientific pursuits than research in the arts and humanities.

ultimately saved Allied soldiers' lives by averting the need to invade Japan is a matter of debate. That penicillin saved lives is not.

President Roosevelt knew exactly how important science had been to the war effort. In the autumn of 1944, when it began to look probable that the Allies would win the war in the next year or two, President Roosevelt asked Vannevar Bush, the head of the U.S. Office of Scientific Research and Development, to write a report outlining his vision of postwar scientific research. Many federal scientific projects responded to particular wartime needs that private sources simply could not address. Leaving the development of battleworthy radar to private firms was not an option. But after the war, these needs would disappear. Should federal expenditures on science continue, or should they drop to near zero, the level before the war?

Bush argued that funding for science should continue, but with a different focus. The great majority of wartime monies had gone to "applied" research—that is, research meant to solve a specific problem. Bush's report made a strong case for the importance of what he called "basic" research during peacetime.[5]

Bush described basic research as that "performed without thought of practical ends. It results in general knowledge and an understanding of nature and its laws." Bush argued that basic research is actually the driving force behind successful applied research. Understanding the laws of nature could have far-ranging and unanticipated benefits. Bush went so far as to call scientific progress the "one essential key to our security as a nation, to our better health, to more jobs, to a higher standard of living, and to our cultural progress"—a formulation not far from that used by President Obama sixty-five years later.

Bush also reminded the president of the essential role that the federal government played in these scientific success stories, and he argued that the government ought to stay involved. Applied and basic research would inevitably compete for limited funding that private firms could allocate to research, and applied research would usually win. After all, applied research solves short-term problems and thus is likely to earn money. Bush argued (without much data to back him up) that basic research would ultimately pay for itself in improved productivity. (This argument would be supported by economic research in the 1950s.[6])

Bush's vision was that basic research tells us the secrets of nature. Applied research exploits that knowledge in the creation of new technologies. What, then, is education research, basic or applied? Education research is clearly applied—it is directed not at fundamental questions of nature but at solving a problem: How do we best educate children? We would imagine that the outcome of basic research, especially knowledge of how children think and learn, would be informative to education research. Great strides have been made in our knowledge of neuroscience—surely newfound knowledge of the mind and brain can help us improve schooling, right?

Clarifying the Relationship Between Applied and Basic Research

Surely newfound knowledge of the mind and brain can help us improve schooling. I've heard this phrase (or ones like it) countless times, and it increasingly reminds me of the Underpants Gnomes. In one episode of the animated television series *South Park*, a little boy swears that his underpants are stolen at night by gnomes. He and his friends stay up late and find that the Underpants Gnomes are real, and they follow them to their underpants processing facility. When pressed, the Gnomes explain their business plan, shown as a chart (Figure 4.2).

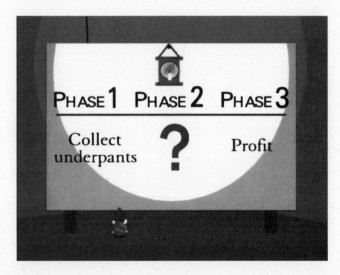

 FIGURE 4.2: The business plan of the Underpants Gnomes.

Since the episode's original broadcast in 1998, references to Underpants Gnomes have been used as a metaphor for poorly thought out business or political plans. In the case of education research, I think a similar plan is at work (Figure 4.3).

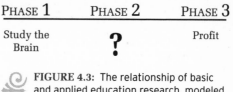

PHASE 1	PHASE 2	PHASE 3
Study the Brain	**?**	Profit

FIGURE 4.3: The relationship of basic and applied education research, modeled after the business plan of the Underpants Gnomes.

I realize that the Underpants Gnomes analogy may be a bit strained, but it highlights an important point. The need to flesh out phase 2 is obvious in the Underpants Gnomes' business strategy. It is no less important in thinking about using basic research to improve education, although the need is less plain because it seems so *obvious* that learning more about how the mind and brain operate should improve education. In the remainder of this chapter, I will argue that such knowledge can help, but that the process is far from obvious.

To get a more detailed view of what phase 2 in Figure 4.3 might look like, we need to better understand the relationship between basic and applied research. We need to get beyond saying that "applied researchers can draw on basic research" to establishing a more systematic and general description of how that actually happens.

A useful starting point comes from the work of Herb Simon.[7] Simon was a polymath, making profound and lasting contributions to several fields, including economics, organizational behavior, computer science, psychology, management theory, and political science.* Perhaps it was his position at the center of diverse fields that gave him such clarity about basic and applied research.

---

*He was awarded the Turing Award by the Association for Computing Machinery (often called the "Nobel Prize for computer science") for his contributions to artificial intelligence. He was awarded the American Psychological Association's Award for Outstanding Lifetime Achievement Contributions to Psychology for his work in human decision making and problem solving. And he won the Nobel Prize in economics for his contributions to microeconomic theory.

Simon's description of the difference between them begins as Bush's does, more or less. In basic research, the goal is the discovery of laws that describe natural phenomena. You take the world as it comes to you, and try to summarize it with general principles. Applied research, in contrast, is goal driven. You don't want to describe the world as it is; you want to change the world to make it better. That's the meaning behind the epigraph of this chapter: a plowed field is no more or less "natural" than an asphalted street because in each case, humans have altered the world to fulfill a purpose. Examples of applied sciences might include all the branches of engineering, architecture, urban planning, and education research.

Applied sciences typically call for the construction of an artifact—an object that serves the purpose of changing the world so that it's more like what we want it to be. A civil engineer builds a bridge. An urban planner designs a park. And an educator writes a lesson plan.

Basic sciences can contribute to applied sciences by helping one understand how an artifact might work. For example, knowledge of physics and of materials science is useful to a civil engineer designing a bridge. She will use knowledge gleaned from these fields to predict whether the construction plan and materials she has in mind will yield a bridge that will stand or fall. Similarly, cognitive science might help an educator predict how the mind of a third-grader will respond to a lesson plan: will she find it comprehensible, will she remember it later, and so on. So far, so good, and kind of obvious.

But here's a less obvious point to consider. I can use principles of physics to help me design a pendulum clock that will keep marvelous time in my living room, but that clock won't work at all on board a ship. The ship's rolling movements will render the pendulum movement useless. Similarly, a sundial won't work in my living room. In determining whether an artifact is meeting the intended goal, we can't attend only to the artifact. We must consider how the artifact interacts with the *environment* in which it is situated. Basic sciences may be useful here as well. We could use knowledge of physics to determine how much the movement of a ship affects the mechanism of the clock: Will a pendulum clock work despite the gentle rocking of a houseboat moored to a slip?

Method One: Draw on Basic Scientific Knowledge

Now we're in a better position to specify what happens during phase 2 of the Underpants Gnomes' plan for education. Basic science can aid applied science by providing useful descriptions of the components of the artifact and the environment in which it's situated. Simon called these the inner and outer environments. In the case of education, we expect that the inner environment would be the mind of the child, and information from cognitive psychology would be relevant—that is, as educators design lesson plans, they could draw inspiration from our knowledge of how the mind works. If the inner environment is the mind of the child, then the outer environment is the classroom; we ought to be concerned that, just as a clock works well or poorly depending on the environment, a particular lesson plan (or curriculum, or whatever) that might work for a child in one environment will not work at all in another environment. So basic science should be used to describe the environment—that is, the classroom.

This all sounds fairly straightforward, but we'll spend most of this chapter elaborating on the difficulties that arise when one applies this method to education. Most of the time, these difficulties are ignored, and people try to get the benefit of the cloak of science on the cheap. Toward the end of the chapter I'll describe a second, altogether different way that basic science can lend a hand to education. This method is subject to fewer problems, but it's expensive. Likely for that reason, it's rarely used.

Problem 1: Goals

What would you say about a mother who forbade television, video games, participation in school plays, sleepovers—even play dates? She does allow her child to participate in some activities—namely, homework and at least two hours of practice each day on a musical instrument. The goal? To ensure admission to Harvard University and to produce a math whiz or music prodigy. You may recognize this recipe for success as that of Amy Chua, also called the Tiger Mother. She published a piece in the *Wall Street Journal* describing her parenting style, under a title that seemed self-consciously provocative: "Why Chinese Mothers Are Superior."[8]

And provoke it did. Chua took it for granted that the stereotypical academic success of Chinese students was true, and averred that the success was due to the tough-love parenting practices of Chinese mothers, who, she claimed, bully, criticize, spy on, and prod their children to great academic achievement.

Much outrage was directed at Chua, and virtually none of it questioned whether or not her methods "worked." Few, if any, criticized her by saying "Bah, that's no way to get your kid into Harvard!" Rather, they criticized her child-rearing goal: academic success, seemingly at any price. Chua claimed that she wants her kids to be happy too; she said kids become happy when they are good at something, but being good at something requires practice, and kids don't want to practice, at first. But American readers—accurately, I think—felt that, when push came to shove, Chua was ready to choose that her child be good at something rather than be happy. Readers were not shocked by her methods because they thought they were ineffectual. They were shocked by her methods because they disapproved of her goals.

The French biologist Jean Rostand said, "Theories pass. The frog remains." In other words, the frog—or, more generally, the natural world—is always present, available to let us know whether our theory (of frog physiology, or whatever it is) is any good. In basic sciences like biology, it's clear to everyone whether or not the theory is any good, because we all agree on the yardstick by which it's measured: agreement with nature.

That's not so for applied sciences. The goal of an applied science is up for grabs. It is completely up to the individual as to what would make the world "better" and thus would be an appropriate target for applied scientific research. Does Amy Chua's method of parenting "work"? If you share her goals, that's an open question, and you could use methods of science to answer it. If you don't share her goals for parenting, the question makes no sense.

In education research, the problem is still worse. It would be bad enough if we had a few different goals for educators to choose from, and there were an acrimonious debate about which was correct. Instead, the goal is underspecified or completely unstated. Thus we guarantee confusion and stagnation in research.

We invite confusion because how to use or respond to facts from basic science depends on one's goal. Consider, for example, data from psychologists showing that people have many different mental abilities—that is, that there is not a single type of intelligence. This idea is best known to educators through Howard Gardner's theory of multiple intelligences, although the idea has been strong in psychological theory since the 1930s; what has been controversial is the number of mental abilities and how to characterize them.[9] Suppose that debate were settled, and there were reasonable agreement that there are, say, five types of intelligence: verbal, mathematical, spatial, musical, and emotional. (The last of these being the ability to understand the emotions of others and to understand and regulate one's own emotions.). Let's pretend that the evidence for this five-factor theory is very strong indeed, and insofar as we can *know* something scientifically, we know this fact. Some people are good with words, others with numbers; others are skilled musically; and so on. What would that mean for schooling?

What it means for schooling depends on your goals for schooling. Suppose I think that children attend school for *self-actualization*, a term from psychological theory that means to become all that you can become, to fulfill your potential. In this vision of education, schools should help children identify their strengths and develop them. With this goal in mind, the theory from psychology outlining the five types of intelligence is a godsend. My goal is to help each child discover his or her abilities—well, here's a taxonomy of ability! When I see a child struggling verbally but excelling musically, I'll have a way of thinking about why that's so, and I'll know that I should be sure to offer every musical opportunity to this child, while not pressing so hard on reading and writing.

But now suppose my goal for schooling is not self-actualization but preparation for the world of work. When today's children someday seek a job and career, they will not compete only with the child down the street or across town; they will compete with children in Berlin, São Paulo, and Nanjing. We owe it to our kids and to their future prosperity to prepare them for this eventuality. With this goal in mind, the theory of intelligences is not just useless to me but possibly destructive. Most kids aren't going to make a living by playing music, so I'm going to see music as an add-on, a fun extra that kids really ought to do on their own time. I don't want a psychologist telling them

Insert name of your school or district

Choose one
- will strive for
- will promote
- will provide

Choose two
- high standards
- a caring environment
- a learning community
- a child-centered sensibility

so that each student

Choose one
- acquires
- develops

the skills and knowledge to

Choose two
- be a responsible and productive citizen.
- be a life-long learner.
- be college- or career-ready.
- achieve his or her full potential.

FIGURE 4.4: Do-it-yourself school mission statement. Just move downward, choosing one or two phrases as directed.

that music is, in some sense, the equivalent of a practical ability like mathematics. *The implications for education of a scientific fact depend on the goals of schooling.*

Those goals, however, are usually undefined. Yes, schools have mission statements. So too do school districts and state departments of education. But let's face it—they are typically not crisp, certain statements of purpose. Rather, they are dewy-eyed platitudes. If you find yourself in need of such a statement, I've got you covered (Figure 4.4).

Such statements may serve other purposes, but they cannot help us when we're trying to understand the implications of basic science for education. Science can affect education only if there is a clear statement of education goals.

Now, this problem shouldn't be blown out of proportion. Even if the goals of schooling are not explicit, aren't they kind of obvious? We want kids to know some science, some history, some math, and so on. That's true enough, especially at the younger grades. But as kids get older, our long-term goals seem to loom larger. Do we want kids to learn American history so that they will be proud of their heritage or so that they will learn to thoughtfully question those in authority? If a kid doesn't like math, is it okay for him to stop studying it once he knows enough to balance a checkbook and do his taxes? Or should every kid at least try to get through precalculus, so that we're not shutting him off from future technical careers? How much emphasis should English classes place on aesthetic appreciation of literature versus more practical pursuits, such as expository writing? These are the kinds of questions that make school boards squirm because any answer will make *someone* angry. So people pretend that schools can be all things to all students, and the questions go unanswered. But the hidden cost to not answering the question "What are the goals of schooling?" is that education researchers can't do their job.

Problem 2: Feedback

A mayor can expect that constituents will feel justified in bringing the problems of the city to the mayor's attention, even when the mayor is trying to enjoy a meal in a restaurant or shopping for groceries. New Yorkers are not known as the bashful sort, so we might expect that they would not be shy about approaching their mayor with unsolicited complaints or comments. That may be the reason that Ed Koch, New York's mayor during the 1980s, would often beat them to the punch by asking for their opinions: a buoyant "How'm I doing?" became something of a catchphrase for Koch.

Some of this was political show, of course, but some part of it may have been a real desire for feedback. Sure, the mayor had access to opinion polls, but those might be written in a biased way, or the data might be "groomed" before Koch ever saw it. As General George Patton said, "No good decision was ever made in a swivel chair." A good leader is hungry for reliable, on-the-ground feedback.

We often take feedback for granted, but it is essential for systems of all types: political, corporate, biological, and so on. In education, we can describe two functions of feedback. One is to provide information for ongoing correction. Even highly reliable systems have some error, and you need feedback about the error to correct it. For example, consider your ability to control your body. You probably have the general sense that you are highly accurate in making simple movements—reaching for a cup of coffee, stepping up on a curb, and so forth.

Try this. Pick a spot on your desk (or wherever you're reading this book), close your eyes, and try to hit the spot with your finger. You'll probably be pretty close, but you are unlikely to hit it directly. Now do the same thing again with your eyes open. If you are mindful of what you're doing, you'll notice that you make a pretty rapid movement that puts your fingertip in the ballpark of the target; then your hand slows down, and you move it the rest of the way to the target. During that moment that you slow down, you're actually gathering feedback—you're using vision to determine where your fingertip is relative to the target—so that you can compute the rest of the movement to put your finger exactly where you want it.[10] Before you start the movement, your brain calculates what your muscles should do to move your hand to the target. That calculation is imperfect, however, even for a highly practiced skill like moving your hand. You need feedback along the way if you are to finish the movement exactly on target.

Analogous processes happen in the classroom. Just as your brain plans a sequence of muscle movements to get your hand to a target, a teacher plans a sequence of activities that will move the student's mind toward a particular goal. The goal might be "knowledge of grammatical rules" or "a positive attitude about reading" or "an understanding of the consequences of bullying." When you move your finger to a target, the corrective procedures you make mid-movement are essential to reaching the target. The same is true of teaching and learning.

You need feedback in the middle of a complex action (a movement, or teaching) so that you can make corrections. You also need feedback at the end so that you can evaluate whether you've met your goal. If you have no feedback, how can you evaluate whether or not whatever you're doing works? For example, many businesses have diversity awareness programs meant to teach their workers to respect variations in employee personality, age, ethnicity, and other dimensions. Yet only 36 percent of companies using such programs make any effort to evaluate whether the training has any impact![11]

These points are fairly obvious for educational practice, but what do they have to do with education research? Feedback is necessary in education research in order for us to know whether or not the artifact is doing the intended job. If my goal for education is to improve creativity in kids or to make them more moral citizens, I need a way of measuring morality or creativity in order to know that my efforts are getting somewhere. As I write this, we have reasonably good tests in hand to measure content knowledge in most of the major subject matter areas. We don't have good tests to measure students' analytic abilities, creativity, enthusiasm, wisdom, or attitudes toward learning.

This caution is not to say, "If we can't measure it, we shouldn't try to teach it." Our goals for schooling should be set by our values. The feedback problem is not about what should be taught—it's about one limitation on science's ability to help us reach our goals. This point is easily summarized: if someone approaches you with a curriculum that he claims will boost kids' creativity, you might ask yourself how he knows whether or not it works.

Problem 3: The Outer Environment

A teacher recently told me a story about switching schools. He had long been a physical education instructor at a fairly traditional boys' school, but when his wife's firm transferred her, he ended up teaching at a somewhat larger, coed school with a very progressive sensibility. Students had much more latitude in selecting their work, and there was a lot of emphasis on collaboration and cooperation in all aspects of the school day. Given my description, you can imagine how things went on this teacher's first day, when he tried to organize a soccer game of third-graders by naming captains and encouraging them to alternate picking teammates from among the remaining students. Some told him that they didn't feel like playing soccer and wanted to do something else. Some protested his method of organizing teams. One little boy calmly told the teacher that he didn't know what he was doing. "You're new. You should ask *us* how we do things. That's what we're here for."

This example illustrates the importance of the outer environment. A teaching method that had worked well in numerous classes for better than a decade imploded. Why? Because the sensibility of the class was different from any the teacher had encountered before. Students expected choice and collaboration in every lesson, features that had not been expected at his old school. His lesson plan was a pendulum clock placed on a ship. (He is a resourceful teacher, and it didn't take him long to find his groove at the school.)

We need some description of the outer environment. We need to use basic science to characterize classrooms. For example, maybe the critical features of a classroom are the emotional warmth, the degree of organization, and the academic support offered.[12] The problem, though, is that scientists know much more about children's minds than they do about classrooms. There are serious, ongoing research programs addressing this issue, but the going has been slower.[†]

Problem 4: Levels of Analysis

Let's go back to the question raised by the Underpants Gnomes and the answer we've been working with. The question is "How can we use basic scientific knowledge to improve education?" and the answer is "Basic science provides a description of the inner environment and the outer environment." I just finished saying that we shouldn't expect too much by way of a description of the outer environment—the science just isn't as far along on that problem. What about the inner environment? Do we know a lot about children's minds? We do, but applying that knowledge is not as straightforward as you might imagine. Understanding why calls for some heavy lifting, but it's probably the most important point in this chapter.

Let's start this way. Take someone who knows a lot about children's minds. She has considerable experience in tutoring individual kids, and she is terrific at it. Would we predict that this person will also be a great classroom teacher with, say, twenty-eight children? Our intuition says "not necessarily." But why not? A classroom, after all, is composed of individual children, and if we propose that this teacher knows a great deal about individual children, why shouldn't she be terrific in the classroom? Because kids interact, and those interactions pose challenges that the teacher never encountered when she taught individuals. Certainly, her prior experience and her skill will be of some benefit, but we can pretty much bet that there are aspects to handling a class that will be new to her.

[†]The logistics of doing research on classrooms is more difficult. Why? (1) To study a child, you need parental permission. To study a classroom, you need permission from school officials, who are understandably reluctant to grant it. After all, the mission of the school is to educate, not to conduct research, and what if the study interferes with education? (2) If I gain access to a school, I might be able to observe, say, twenty classrooms. But that school also contains, say, 450 kids. It's easier to complete a study of kids because there are more of them.

The term *levels of analysis* describes this phenomenon: when you've analyzed something and understand it, your understanding applies only to what you've studied, not necessarily to a *group* of the things you've studied. We can generalize this principle. Just as knowing a lot about teaching an individual child does not mean that one will be equally successful in running a classroom, being a successful classroom teacher does not mean that one will necessarily be skilled in running a school, and a good school principal will not necessarily make a good district leader (Figure 4.5).

You can see in Figure 4.5 that I've defined the "child" level of analysis as an evaluation of whether or not the child has met some goal we set for schooling. "There's DeAndre. Can he multiply two-digit numbers consistently?" Or "There's John. Does he know his colors?" When we evaluate "the child," we're saying, "I want kids to be able to do X . . . can this child do it?"

District

School

Classroom

Child

(for example, motivation, math, reading)

FIGURE 4.5: Some levels of analysis in education.

Well, what about levels below—that is, more fine grained than that of "the child"? That's the province of educational psychologists and cognitive psychologists. We want to know the mental processes that underlie abilities like "reading success" or "proficiency in mathematics" (Figure 4.6).

Okay, what mental abilities does a child need to be proficient in mathematics? I may propose that three abilities must be in place: the child must have memorized a small number of math facts (like $2 + 2 = 4$); the

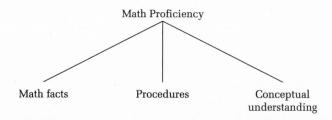

Math Proficiency

Math facts   Procedures   Conceptual
                                        understanding

FIGURE 4.6: Hypothetical mental contributors to proficiency in mathematics.

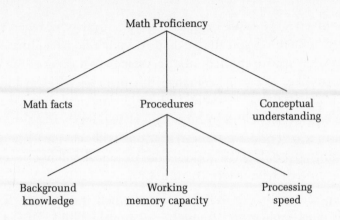

FIGURE 4.7: Hypothetical mental contributors to the use of mathematical procedures.

child must know relevant math procedures (that is, algorithms, ways of solving standard problems); and the child must have a conceptual understanding of why and how those algorithms work. Each is a hypothetical entity I use to build a theory of a child's overall math competence.

But then someone might ask me, "What about these *procedures*? What does it take for a child to know how to use procedures?" In response to that question, I might try to come up with a theory of the mental processes underlying mathematical procedures. "Well, the child needs some background knowledge—that is, she has to memorize the procedures; and she needs working memory capacity—that's the mental space in which she's going to manipulate numbers with these procedures; and then she needs processing speed, which is sort of like the mental fuel to get this work done." (Figure 4.7).

As you'd guess, people ask, "How does working memory work?" and we get even more detailed. If this deconstruction of mathematical proficiency isn't very clear to you, don't worry about it. Here's the main point. As we pick these mental processes apart, we're creating new levels of analysis—I'll call them educational processes and cognitive processes (Figure 4.8).

It is clear that what we know at one level of analysis doesn't necessarily translate up perfectly—my knowledge of how to tutor kids individually might *help* me as a classroom teacher of twenty-eight, but it sure doesn't guarantee that I know all I need to know. The same thing applies at these other levels of analysis. Knowing something about how kids acquire math facts might help me improve students' overall math proficiency, but we actually have the same problem we had in going from one kid to a classroom. Kids interact, so

District

School

Classroom

Child
    (for example, motivation, math, reading)

Educational processes
    (for example, math facts, reading strategy)

Cognitive processes
    (for example, working memory, attention)

FIGURE 4.8: More levels of analysis in education research.

a classroom has features that individual kids don't have. In the same way, I might understand something about math facts, but math facts *interact* with other mental processes to produce math proficiency. So what I know about math facts may not apply perfectly well once it's in the context of all those other contributing processes.[‡]

The semi-independence of these levels is wonderful for researchers because it reassures them that it makes sense to study just one level. For example, suppose a researcher said, "I study reading." I might reply, "That's dumb. You know that reading must be composed of other, more basic processes like attention, vision, and memory. Why don't you study attention, vision, and memory? Once you've got those figured out, you'll understand reading!" Then another researcher might say, "No, Willingham, *you're* dumb. We know that the mind is a product of the brain. What we ought to do is study the brain!"

The semi-independence of these levels means that each ought to be studied on its own. Knowing a lot about cognitive processes is not

---

[‡]This distance problem is also a significant challenge for people trying to apply neuroscientific knowledge to education. There is a lot of excitement about "brain-based education" right now, but getting from the basic scientific data to something usable in the classroom is not easy. You need to translate not only the cognitive scientific data into educational practice but also the neuroscientific data into cognitive data. For more on this problem and how to solve it, see Willingham, D. T., & Lloyd, J. W. (2007). How educational theories can use neuroscientific data. *Mind, Brain, and Education, 1,* 140–149.

a guarantee that I'm going to understand reading, for just the same reason that knowing how to teach one child is not a guarantee that I'll be able to run a classroom. If you want to understand reading, you have to study reading.

As I said, that's wonderful for researchers, but there's a less-wonderful implication for the application of basic scientific knowledge to classrooms. Information from lower levels is not guaranteed to apply to higher levels in a straightforward way, and *all the information from basic sciences that we hoped to apply to education is at the lower levels.* The lowest level in Figure 4.8 that educators might care about is the child—educators want children to learn. Changing things at lower levels is not enough. For example, suppose you and I had this conversation:

ME: I figured out how to increase a child's working memory capacity!

YOU: Cool! Can she read with better understanding? Is her understanding of fractions richer? Does she like learning more?

ME: Uh. . . I don't know.

YOU: (*pause*) Oh.

Here's an example of how the application of cognitive principles can sound good, but fail. The spiral curriculum was introduced in the early 1960s by cognitive psychologist Jerome Bruner.[13] The idea is that students revisit the same fundamental concepts across several years, each time with greater depth. To a cognitive psychologist, this sounds great. It means that a lot of time elapses between when kids study the same basic idea, which is very good for memory. It means that students will hear the same important ideas from different teachers, so if a student doesn't quite understand the way one teacher explains it, there will be another opportunity the following year. So again, in terms of two processes at a cognitive level of analysis—memory and comprehension—the spiral curriculum sounds like a win.

But once it was implemented in classrooms, it became clear that a spiral curriculum was subject to at least two serious drawbacks. First, students don't stick with any topic long enough to develop a deep conceptual understanding of it. Countries that seem to do a better job teaching math, for example, have curricula in which a small number of topics are studied intensively during the year and then are not revisited.[14] Another drawback of the spiral curriculum was pointed out to me (indirectly) by my oldest daughter. When she revisited a topic in the fifth grade that she had studied in the fourth grade, her reaction was "Not this again!" Never mind that she had not understood it all that well the previous year. As far as she was concerned, "We did this already." Lots of time between practice is great for memory, but it turns out to have unexpected implications for motivation.

Does the levels-of-analysis problem mean that educational psychology is useless? Not at all. There are three ways that basic scientific information from lower levels of analysis can benefit education. First, if we have a detailed theory of how the levels relate to one another, then we can successfully predict what happens when we go from one level to another and so avoid the problem I've described. I'll know how the different pieces interact, so I can predict, "Yup, practicing math facts will help long division, and here's why . . ."

Second, we can use data from educational (or cognitive) psychology when we think that the effect we're looking at is so large and so robust that we are pretty confident that it *will* translate to higher levels in nearly all situations, even if we don't have a detailed theory of how that translation happens. For example, practice is so important to learning that I might predict that it's always going to be important; it doesn't matter whether you are learning to improvise in jazz or learning to garden or learning to integrate in calculus— practice is necessary to improve, and there aren't going to be strange interactions at other levels that make that need go away. This of course doesn't mean that the principle can be applied mindlessly. Another universal fact about cognition is that enforced, repetitive practice is detrimental to motivation.

The third and final way that you can use data from basic science is to evaluate a claim made by the purveyor of an education product. If someone promotes a curriculum or teaching method by claiming that it capitalizes on a feature of the mind, cognitive or educational psychology might have information as to whether the feature of the mind is accurately described. For example, the Core Knowledge Foundation offers a curricular sequence that emphasizes content knowledge[15] and argues that this emphasis is useful because reading comprehension depends on content knowledge. That's a claim about how reading works, independent of any claim about whether or not the core knowledge sequence helps kids learn to read better. In this case, the claim about the mind is correct.[16]

In other cases, the claim is clearly false. For example, type "left brain right brain education" into an Internet search engine, and you will find a great many education products that claim to be based on the scientifically established differences between the right and left hemispheres of the brain. In virtually every case, the characterization of the differences is wildly exaggerated. There are differences in what the two hemispheres of the brain do, but for most tasks, most of the brain is involved, and it doesn't make sense to talk about the left brain as "linguistic and logical" and the right brain as "emotional and artistic."[17]

We've reviewed four challenges to applying data from natural science to education when using the first method of applying basic science to problems. Let's review them:

1. Goals are often unstated or implicit. Because education is a goal-driven enterprise, this vagueness makes it hard to know which findings from basic science are relevant, and to draw implications from those that are relevant.

2. Feedback is essential to knowing whether we're moving toward or away from our education goal, and feedback is lacking for many of the outcomes we might care about (for example, creativity or analytic problem solving).

3. We know much more about children (the inner environment) than we do about classrooms (the outer environment), and we need knowledge of both if we are to apply basic scientific knowledge to education with confidence.

4. Even if you can manipulate a cognitive process and be confident of the cognitive consequence, you can't guarantee the same outcome in education because (a) you may unintentionally change other cognitive processes too, and (b) the changed process may interact with other cognitive processes in ways you didn't predict.

These four problems must always be solved when we seek to apply basic scientific knowledge in education research. For some topics—for example, learning to read—the problems are largely solved, and there are real opportunities to use basic science in education. For others—for example, teaching students to think critically—the answers are less clear. Feedback is a particular problem in critical thinking research, because critical thinking is so difficult to measure. As we'll see in future chapters, clarity about whether these problems are solved can help you evaluate claims that an educational program is "research based."

This first method—drawing on principles of basic science—is, unfortunately, very easy to do sloppily. You can take a finding that sounds somewhat peripherally related to whatever educational panacea you're peddling, wave it around, and say "Look: research!" It's cheap, because the research already exists. But as you've seen in this section, it's pretty difficult to do it well.

Method Two: Two Problems, Not Four

Thus far we've discussed one way of applying basic scientific knowledge to education: characterizing the inner and the outer environment. But there is a second method. This method is easier to do well, because there are fewer problems to be solved. But it's very expensive because there will not be existing research waiting for you to use. The researcher will be starting from scratch.

Recall the Science Cycle from Chapter Three (illustrated again here as Figure 4.9).

The stage in the cycle marked "Test" refers to the testing of a prediction. When we create an artifact in an applied science, we want to test whether the artifact is doing what we

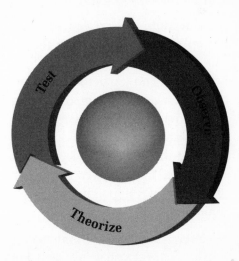

FIGURE 4.9: The Science Cycle.

expect—that is, whether it is meeting the goal that we've set. Even when the knowledge that we're applying from the basic sciences is very sound, we can't necessarily be certain that the artifacts we create will behave as expected.

For example, consider the problems architects face when they plan a large building, such as the Epic tower in Miami, a forty-eight-story residential building. In the case of the Epic, architects needed to be sure that the building could withstand wind forces that one would expect at its location on Biscayne Bay. Basic science can provide wonderfully accurate information about the outer environment: the wind forces and other weather elements to which the Epic would be exposed, and the way that those forces differ at ground level compared to an altitude of five hundred feet, the height of the building. Basic science could also provide excellent information about the inner environment: the tensile, compressive, and shear strength of the materials used, for example. You might think, therefore, that the architects could calculate with great confidence how their design would stand up to wind forces. But they (like all builders of skyscrapers) were not satisfied with the predictions derived from this basic scientific information, accurate though it might be. They constructed a highly detailed scale model of the building and put it in a wind tunnel, to be sure that it reacted as predicted (Figure 4.10).

In education, we create a series of lesson plans for algebra, for example, in the expectation that kids who experience those lesson plans will meet some criterion for knowledge that we have set. But how do we know whether this new set of lesson plans is more effective than whatever we were doing to teach algebra before? Don't we need to compare the new method to the old method? Making such comparisons is the bread-and-butter of basic science. It's the Test phase of the Science Cycle. So the second way that basic science can be used in an applied pursuit like education is to take advantage of methods developed in the basic sciences to evaluate whether our applied methods are effective.

An interesting feature of this second method is that the inspiration for the method you're testing could come from anywhere. In the first method, we were talking about using basic science to derive a method of teaching, say, chemistry. But now we're talking about

FIGURE 4.10: At top, a wind tunnel containing a scale model of the Epic skyscraper, surrounded by models of neighboring buildings. At bottom, the model of the Epic skyscraper showing sensors that would detect movement of the model in the wind tunnel.

using techniques from science to *compare* two methods of teaching chemistry, and those two teaching methods could come from anywhere: my experience, another teacher's experience, or thin air.

In applied sciences, you can often create the artifact without basic scientific knowledge. For example, people have been building bridges for thousands of years, and for most of that time, builders were not guided by scientific knowledge of physics. The Ponte Fabricio was built around 62 BC, centuries before classical physics was well formulated—yet it still stands and is still in use (Figure 4.11).

Even when we do not have basic scientific knowledge guiding the building of the artifact, we can still use the scientific method to *evaluate* the artifact. Bridge builders of old would have done so implicitly: keep using the designs that lead to strong, enduring bridges; discard the designs of the bridges that collapse. Craft knowledge comes from this sort of experience. The scientific method just makes such comparisons more reliable by making them more systematic, as we discussed in Chapter Three.

Thus, even though basic scientific knowledge may provide very little solid information for how to design a curriculum that will improve civic engagement, we can still use the scientific method to compare

FIGURE 4.11: The Ponte Fabricio in Rome. This bridge is functional, beautiful, and enduring, and it was built long before classical physical principles were worked out.

two existing curricula to see which one does a better job of promoting civic engagement. Compared with the first method, this method poses fewer challenges. We still need to define the goal, and we still need some reliable feedback measure. That is, we need to decide what we mean by "civic engagement" and how to measure it. But we needn't worry about the other two problems—characterizing the inner and outer environments, and that complex interactions lead to surprising outcomes.

Happily, the two problems that stick with us using this method can be solved provisionally. In other words, I could say, "All right, I know this definition isn't perfect, but let's say that 'civic engagement' means participating in civic institutions. And I'll measure it by asking high school seniors whether they do volunteer work at such an institution, whether they follow news stories about these institutions in local media, and whether they say that they have an interest in these matters." I can then use scientific methods to compare two curricula for their success in promoting civic engagement.

The danger in this strategy—and it is significant—is that if my definition or measure of civic engagement is dopey, I can easily kid myself into thinking that I have successfully compared the two curricula when in fact my comparison was flawed from the start because I used a dopey definition or a dopey measure. But you've got to start somewhere, and it seems to make sense to measure things as best you can and to try to improve the measures as you go, rather than to throw up your hands in despair.

In sum, the second method is more straightforward than the first. If I scientifically compare two curricula or two teaching strategies, or parochial schools versus public schools, I do need to worry about what's being measured and how. But if the measurement seems pretty straightforward—for example, a reading test for third-graders, of which there are several good ones—we can conduct a good study. Sure, there are lots of ways to mess up a research project, but we're at least playing to the strengths of the scientific method, meaning that the ways to mess up the study are understood, and there are strategies for dealing with them.

In the first method I described, the payoff can be much greater, but the likelihood that you'll actually see some payoff is much lower.

The second method simply compares two bridges and tells you which does a better job. At the end of the day, you're likely to know which of those two bridges is better, but you're left without any information as to how to build an even better bridge. The promise of the first method is that you'll be able to use scientific principles to inspire a better bridge than anyone has yet imagined, because you understand in the abstract what makes a bridge long lasting and strong. But as we described in this chapter, deriving practical artifacts from those abstract principles is not straightforward.

So for all the talk about brain science leading to a revolution in education, that road seems much more difficult than the process of comparing existing curricula and teaching methods. Perhaps the old adage has it right: one good thief is worth ten scholars. In other words, the smart thing to do is to find the best existing curriculum and copy it. Then perhaps tweak it here and there, and use the scientific method to see whether your tweaked version has made it still better. Perhaps. But I think that this vision is too pessimistic about the contribution that basic science might make to education research. I do think that progress in our understanding of learning, reading, and mathematics—the three topics most heavily studied—have already paid dividends. Just how much help basic science has provided to education is, of course, a matter of opinion, and justifying my opinion would take us too far afield.

We've examined in some detail what scientists call "good science" (Chapter Three) and the challenges and opportunities in using good science to improve education (Chapter Four). Armed with this knowledge, we can begin to examine ways of evaluating scientific claims about education that you encounter.

Part Two

The Shortcut Solution

5

Step One: Strip It and Flip It

> He who would do good to another must do it in Minute Particulars
> General good is the plea of the scoundrel, hypocrite, and flatterer
> For Art and Science cannot exist but in minutely organized Particulars.
>
> —*William Blake*[1]

So far, this book has described evidence that we believe things for poor reasons (Chapter One) and that we are especially susceptible to reasons that sound consistent with sensibilities from the Enlightenment or the Romantic era (Chapter Two). I've described what constitutes good science (Chapter Three) and how to use it (Chapter Four). It's time to get specific about how we can differentiate good science from bad.

This chapter and the three following outline a four-step process to help you evaluate the likely scientific soundness of a proposed curriculum, teaching strategy, textbook—anything that is purported to help children learn. Note that I said the *likely* scientific soundness. I freely admit—no, I emphasize—that what I'm recommending is not a substitute for a thoughtful evaluation by a knowledgeable scientist. Rather, it's a workaround, a cheat. As such, it's imperfect. The great advantage is that it doesn't require a knowledgeable scientist.

When someone approaches you with an education product—whether you're a parent, a teacher, an administrator, or a policymaker—he is asking you to change something. He wants you to change what you do in your home, classroom, or school in a way that is going to affect the children in your charge. As a shorthand, I'm going to use the term *Change* to refer to a new curriculum or teaching strategy or software package or school restructuring plan—generically, anything that someone is urging you to try as a way to better educate kids. I will use the term *Persuader* to refer to any person who is urging you to try the Change, whether it's a teacher, administrator, salesperson, or the president of the United States.

To get started in your evaluation, you need to be very clear on three points: (1) precisely what Change is being suggested; (2) precisely what outcome is promised as a consequence of that Change; and (3) the probability that the promised outcome will actually happen if you undertake the Change. All other considerations are secondary at this point and should be considered distractions. "Strip it" is a method to get to these minute particulars that Blake refers to in this chapter's epigraph. (We'll get to "Flip it" in due course.)

Strip It

To strip a claim to its essentials, I suggest that you construct a sentence with the form "If I do X, then there is a Y percent chance that Z will happen." For example, "If my child uses this reading software an hour each day for five weeks, there is a 50 percent chance that she will double her reading speed." Of course, the agents might vary: the person doing X might be a student, a parent, a teacher, or an administrator, and the person affected by the outcome (Z) might be any of those. Note too that the value of Y (the chance that the desired outcome will actually happen) is often not specified. That's fine. Right now all you're trying to do is be clear about the claim made by the Persuader, and if she has left Y out, she's left Y out.

For example, have a look at the front page of the Web site shown in Figure 5.1.

FIGURE 5.1: The front page of a Web site that makes a clear claim for its product.

This Web site—unlike many—is quite clear in its claim. X is the use of colored overlays when reading. The promised outcome (Z) is improved reading, and the term "correct the processing problem" is used, so the claim seems to be not simply that things get better but that the problem will be corrected. The chances that the colored overlays will work (Y) are less clear from this page, but on another page of the Web site, one sees the claim that 46 percent of people with "reading problems, dyslexia, and learning difficulties" can be helped by the method. So the stripped claim offered on this Web site is "If your dyslexic child uses colored overlays when reading, there is a 46 percent chance that your child's reading problem will be corrected." At this point you should suspend judgment as to whether that sounds likely true or false. All you're trying to do now is to gain a clear idea of exactly what is being claimed.

Exhibit 5.1 is another example. It's abstracted from a blog, but I could easily imagine its being part of a professional development session on student motivation. It's titled "Five Ways to Get Students Excited About Learning."

EXHIBIT 5.1: Summary of Advice for Teachers on the Teaching of Writing, Drawn from a Blog Entry

Five Ways to Get Students Excited About Learning

1. **Learn everywhere!** When you enter a classroom, the door usually closes behind you. Why? You probably carry the world in your pocket, via your cellular phone. Why should learning be insulated? Classroom walls not only keep out distractions, they keep out opportunities.

2. **Write for everyone!** As a teacher you no doubt read your students' papers carefully. But you are just one person. Your students can reach an audience of millions, in an instant, and each of those potential readers can provide feedback on your students' writing.

3. **Write with everyone!** Why must learning be a solitary enterprise? Increasingly, our work is collaborative, the product not of an individual's labor but of a group's best efforts and compromises. Working in isolation is no longer an option. The 21st century is about connection.

4. **Make mistakes!** Mistakes are not failures. The only people who don't make mistakes are people who never do anything, and if you never made mistakes you'd never learn anything. The problem is that people don't embrace mistakes as opportunities to learn.

5. **Have fun!** Who decreed that learning must be drudgery? We learn most when our minds are open, when we feel playful.

The Change recommended in Exhibit 5.1 is much harder to strip using the "If I do X, then there's a Y percent chance that Z will happen" formula, and that's informative. X is hard to pin down, and Y is unspecified. To be fair, this advice was drawn from a blog entry, so perhaps I shouldn't take it all that seriously. At the same time, though, you see a lot of advice to teachers that is similarly frothy. Such advice is difficult to disagree with, but it doesn't help because it is so indefinite.

Stripping Emotion

In Chapter Two, we discussed pat phrases and images meant to call to mind themes from Enlightenment thought (technical jargon, the terms "research-based" and "brain-based") as well as phrases from Romantic thought ("unleash," "natural," "tailored to your child," and so on). The "If X, then Y percent chance of Z" format ought to rid you of those peripheral cues to belief. What else will it do?

It will also trim emotional appeals, which can be very powerful indeed. Suppose that you're a speechwriter for the president. He has emphasized the importance of mental health services for returning veterans in his most recent budget proposal, and he asks you and another speechwriter to work something about the topic into his next speech. Each of you spends a few minutes jotting down ideas and then you compare notes. Which of these two options seems more effective for the president's speech?

1. Point out that 15 to 20 percent of soldiers returning from Iraq show signs of depression or posttraumatic stress disorder. (Note: he'll need to signal that this disorder is serious.) The figure rises to about 30 percent for soldiers on their third or fourth tour. Rates of suicide among soldiers have not been this high in a quarter of a century.[2] Funding has increased, but it is still inadequate, and many soldiers are left untreated.

2. The president had a great uncle who served in World War II and was among the soldiers who liberated a Nazi concentration camp. When he came home, he went up into the attic and was unable to leave the house for six months. At that time, there simply was no mental health support for those who had seen the horrors of

war. Have the president tell that story, then segue to this idea: today we have that support, but we must be sure it is available to every one of the soldiers who selflessly put his life on the line to protect our freedom.*

Politicians don't persuade with statistics. They persuade with emotions. In recent presidential elections, the policy wonk with facts at his fingertips—Al Gore, Michael Dukakis, Bob Dole—has lost to the candidate who can connect with the electorate on an emotional level. This was nicely captured in a political cartoon I recall from the 1984 campaign. There had been a brutal recession in the early 1980s, and the cartoon depicted the average American as a patient in a hospital bed, connected to a monitor labeled "Economy," which showed a precipitously dropping indicator. Presidential candidates Walter Mondale and Ronald Reagan, dressed as doctors, stand by the bedside. The patient says to a shocked Mondale, "I know you're a better doctor, but he"—pointing to a smiling, grandfatherly Reagan—"makes me feel better."

Emotional stories may add personal texture to a problem that we understood only abstractly, or make a problem seem more urgent, but they don't provide compelling reasons to do any particular thing. Why? Because emotional appeals don't provide evidence that a particular solution will work. That's equally true in education.

Persuaders in education seek to rouse different emotions, depending on their audience. For administrators and policymakers, it's most often fear. For example, consider these quotations from a column written by *New York Times* columnist Thomas L. Friedman in 2009.[3] (I've seen similar arguments dozens of times.)

> "Just a quick review: In the 1950s and 1960s, the U.S. dominated the world in K–12 education. We also dominated economically. In the 1970s and 1980s,

---

*The president actually used this story as part of a Memorial Day speech when on the campaign trail in 2008; he was taken to task for erring in some details when he first told the story. A video of the speech can be seen here: http://www.youtube.com /watch?v=SV1sxq8mqvA.

we still had a lead, albeit smaller, in educating our population through secondary school, and America continued to lead the world economically, albeit with other big economies, like China, closing in."

"There are millions of kids who are in modern suburban schools 'who don't realize how far behind they are,' said Matt Miller, one of the authors [of a recent study]. 'They are being prepared for $12-an-hour jobs—not $40 to $50 an hour.'"

What are we to do?

"President Obama recognizes that we urgently need to invest the money and energy to take those schools and best practices that are working from islands of excellence to a new national norm."

The Persuader refers to broad economic trends and extrapolates a dark picture to the near future. Foreign, better-educated kids are in America's rearview mirror, gaining fast, and economic ruin will follow when they pass us. Fear makes us more open to suggestion: "That sounds terrible! Quick—tell me how to fix it!" But in fact, the message mentions a solution only briefly—invest money to take best practices from one school and put them in another—and provides no supporting evidence that this measure will work. In fact, this self-evident solution—take what works one place and implement it elsewhere—is a notorious flop among those who know the history of education policy. Successes depend on many factors that are hard to identify, let alone replicate.

When Persuaders target teachers, they more often use emotional appeals centering on hope, not fear. Most teachers you meet are optimists. They believe that all children can learn and that all children have something to offer the classroom. Teachers are also optimistic about the possibility that they can help children fulfill their potential.

An unpublished survey I conducted of several hundred teachers showed that the most frequent response to the question "Why did you become a teacher?" was "I wanted to make a difference in the world." But teachers are not optimists to the point that they are out of touch with reality. A teacher knows when there is a child with whom she is not connecting. She knows if some aspect of her teaching has become grooved, familiar, and a little stale. When they talk to teachers, Persuaders offer a Change as a way finally to reach that unreachable child or to put the passion back into the teaching.

Administrators often try to sell teachers on an idea by dangling hope before them. Administrators know that "buy-in" is vital—if teachers don't believe that a Change is a good idea, they won't implement it in their classroom. Thus administrators see a need not merely to persuade teachers but also to inculcate zeal for the Change. Fear does not encourage zeal. It encourages grudging compliance. Hope breeds zeal. That is why professional development sessions sometimes feel like evangelical revival meetings. But hope, like fear, is not a reason to believe that a Change will work.

Stripping Claims That the Persuader Is "Like You"

When you change a Persuader's claim to "If I do X, then there's a Y percent chance that Z will happen," the emotional language ought to vanish. So too should another set of peripheral cues to persuasion: those primed to make you think that the Persuader is *like you*. Many Web sites and professional development marketers will claim quite directly, "I know what it's like . . ." The developer of the product will go to some pains to make clear that he's a teacher or a parent. Consider this example, from a Web site touting an ADHD treatment: "Your friends think he just needs consistency. Your doctor wants to medicate him. Your husband doesn't see why you can't control him. Your mom thinks he just needs a good spanking." By predicting the reactions of friends and family—reactions that would make a mom feel guilty or inadequate—the author signals, "I know what it's like to be you."

But being "like me" doesn't really increase the chances that you've got a solution to the problem I face. Lots of people "know what it's like" and haven't found a shortcut to reading comprehension or a way to motivate frustrated kids or a method to help children with autism connect with other kids. And let's face it: being similar to your audience is an easy credential to inflate. I once attended a professional development seminar in which the speaker told story after story of his experiences in the classroom, all of which were, in turn, funny or poignant, and all of which showed that he "got" teachers. I later learned that he had been a classroom teacher for one year, twenty years earlier. He'd been doing professional development ever since, telling, I suppose, the same set of classroom stories.

Stripping Analogies

Stripping claims also removes the potentially powerful and often misleading role of analogies. When we reason by analogy, we use what we know about a familiar situation to make predictions about an unfamiliar situation. For example, suppose I said to you, "Did you know that robins love onions? It's true. They don't often get access to them, but when they do, they just go crazy for them! Now that you know this, let me ask you this question: Do you think that blue jays like shallots?" Admittedly, this would be a strange conversation, but you see the point.

I'm inviting you to draw an analogy. You know that blue jays, like robins, are common American birds that lay eggs, build nests, and share many other features. Shallots, like onions, are pungent, edible roots. So given that robins like onions, it's at least *plausible* that blue jays like shallots, even if it's not guaranteed (Figure 5.2).

It's not guaranteed because the properties between analogous things never overlap *completely*. Or as Coleridge more eloquently put it, "No simile runs on all four legs."[4]

Nevertheless, when analogies are suggested to us, we tend to use them. That's why politicians so frequently offer analogies to defend their policies. For example, analogies were rampant in the United States during the buildup to the Persian Gulf War. Those who favored intervention drew an analogy between Saddam Hussein and

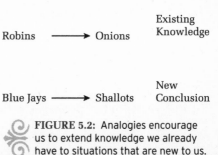

FIGURE 5.2: Analogies encourage us to extend knowledge we already have to situations that are new to us.

Adolph Hitler: both were dictators of militaristic countries with regional aspirations who invaded weaker neighbors. Most Americans think that earlier action against Hitler could have saved many lives, so if Saddam is like Hitler, military action seems to make sense. But other politicians countered with a different analogy. Iraq is like Vietnam. Both were distant lands that did not directly threaten the United States. Most Americans regret the Vietnam war, so this analogy suggests *not* undertaking military action.

You would think that people would not be taken in. Surely we make judgments based on the merits of the case, not based on a rather shallow analogy suggested by a politician. But experimental data show otherwise. In one study, subjects read a fictional description of a foreign conflict and were asked how the United States should respond, using a scale from 1 (stay out of it) to 7 (intervene militarily).[5] The description they read did not explicitly offer an analogy, but instead dropped hints that were to make subjects associate the scenario with either World War II or Vietnam: for example, the president was said to be "from New York, the same state as Franklin Delano Roosevelt," or "from Texas, the same state as Lyndon Johnson." Later, they were asked to judge how similar the fictional scenario was to each of these conflicts.

There were two fascinating results in this study. First, people *were* influenced by the hints. Those who read the story with the World War II hints favored intervention more than people who read the same story with the Vietnam hints. Second, people *thought* that they weren't taken in by the analogy. Both groups said that the story they read was not very similar to World War II and not very similar to Vietnam. In short, people thought, "I see how you're trying to influence me, but I'm too smart for you. The analogy you're suggesting doesn't really apply." But their judgments of how to respond showed that they were influenced nevertheless.

Analogies are sometimes offered in discussions of education, and that's another reason to strip claims. Consider this snippet adapted from a talk to a school board, similar to many that I've heard in the last five years.[†] The speaker was there to talk about the role of new

---

[†]This example, like many I'll use, was inspired by a real talk, but I've changed it enough that it's not clearly attributable to the original speaker.

technologies in education. Students today carry phones with more computing power than the desktop machines of ten years ago. Many students are in contact with friends via social networking sites and text messages literally during every waking hour. What do those facts imply for education? Here's the nub of the speaker's argument:

> Let's consider what these new technologies have meant for various industries. Magazine publishing is almost defunct, and newspapers are desperately playing catch-up, trying to figure out a way to adapt. Remember those drive-up places to get your film developed? Remember stores that rented movies? Those are gone. People no longer use travel agents. They no longer use maps.
>
> All of these industries are obsolete, unnecessary. And they all have something in common; each was based on the delivery of information. These industries no longer exist because the Internet offers personalized, immediate access to almost limitless information.
>
> So what does that mean for schools? *Education is in the business of delivering information.* The pattern in other businesses has been for information delivery to become more mobile, real-time, and collaborative, and also to be more personalized. The question for teachers and administrators is, "How are you going to adapt?"

The speaker's message was clearly emotional—he was quite literally suggesting that everyone in the audience was going to be as obsolete as a VHS video player, and soon. But this suggestion was by analogy. Obviously he's right when he says that various industries have been rendered irrelevant by new technology. But it's not obvious that every industry that delivers information is doomed. Education differs from these other industries in that a personal relationship (between teacher and student) is known to be central.[6] I don't need or want a personal relationship with the person who makes my airline reservation.

Other peripheral cues discussed in Chapter Two will also disappear when you strip a claim. Persuaders naturally want to appear authoritative. They will brag about academic degrees (if they have them). They will claim associations, however tenuous, with universities, especially prestigious ones, or they will claim to have consulted with Fortune 500 companies. They will boast about the authorship of books and articles; they will boast about speaking engagements. These are all indirect ways of saying, "Other people think I'm smart." They are not claims about the efficacy of the Change, but rather are claims about the Persuader. I'll have much more to say about how to evaluate the Persuader in Chapter Six, but here's a preview: characteristics of the Persuader are a very weak indicator of scientific credibility. Stripping the claim will help you ignore them.

Flip It

Psychologists have long been interested in how people make decisions. We might bet that decision making is a complex cognitive process, but we'd also bet that certain things about that process can be taken for granted—for example, that the particular way you describe the decision I have to make shouldn't influence what I decide to do, provided that both descriptions are clear. That perfectly reasonable assumption turns out to be incorrect. People *are* affected by the description of the choice they are to make. That's why, when you are choosing whether or not to implement a Change, I suggest you Flip it.

Flip Outcomes

To understand the meaning and purpose of the advice to Flip it, have a look at Figure 5.3.

One package advertises the ground beef within to be 85 percent lean, and the other as 15 percent fat. The meaning of the two labels is, of course, the same. If beef is 85 percent lean, then the remainder

FIGURE 5.3: The two labels shown describe the same information, but they sure don't sound the same.

is fat, and if it's 15 percent fat, then . . . you get the idea. The labels may be interchangeable in their *literal* meanings, but they sure don't sound the same, do they? Indeed, in one study, subjects were asked to sample cooked ground beef and were told either that it was "75 percent fat free" or that it was "25 percent fat." Subjects in the former group rated the beef as better tasting and less greasy.[7]

This is one example of a large family of phenomena psychologists call *framing effects*. In framing effects, the way a problem or question is described influences the solution or answer we provide. This is why I suggest that you Flip it. When you hear about an outcome (that's Z in our Strip it formula) it's worth thinking about flipping it.

How might this be relevant to education? Just as a grocer would prefer to tell you how lean beef is rather than how fat it is, a Persuader would rather tell you how many children will be reading on grade level if you adopt her Change, and would rather not talk about the converse—how many will not. Although such framing seems like an obvious ruse, experiments show that providing information about success rates rather than failure rates actually makes people rate programs as more successful.[8] So when you hear that a curriculum promises that "85 percent of children will be reading on grade level," flip it. Recognize that 15 percent won't. This failure rate may still seem acceptable, but it's worth having it clear in your mind.

Flip What You're to Do

Another somewhat obvious framing effect doesn't concern the outcome (Z in our Strip it formula) but rather concerns what you're asked to do (X in the Strip it formula). Sometimes a problem is presented as though it is inevitable that we must take action. After all, there's a problem! Something must be done! But inaction is not always the worst possible choice. Years ago, a dentist told my father that his teeth were in terrible shape. He took about five minutes frightening my dad with all the details, and then another five describing an elaborate set of measures he might take to delay the inevitable, ending with, "Now if I do all that, I think you can keep your teeth for another ten years." So Dad asked, "Okay, what if I don't do any of that stuff. How long would my teeth last?" The dentist was taken aback that anyone would consider such a plan, but

Dad persevered, and finally squeezed an answer out of him: "I don't know. Ten years, maybe?"

There are many problems in education with a similar profile: they are real problems, but there is no proven method of dealing with them. Thumping the table and insisting "Something must be done!" misses the point. Yes, lots of kids don't know as much civics as they ought to.[9] That doesn't mean we should plunge ahead with any civics program that we happen to lay hands on. Do we have some reason to believe that the new program will not make things worse? Is there reason to think that things might get better if we were to take no action? Or perhaps the "cure" being offered will avoid some problems but make others still worse. For example, some critics argue that children with attention deficit hyperactivity disorder (ADHD) should not be given medication. I understand the drawbacks: medications can have side effects, and the child may feel labeled by the diagnosis. Stopping the medication may solve those problems, but it incurs other costs; kids with untreated ADHD are at greater risk for dropping out of school, teen pregnancy, drug abuse, clinical depression, and personality disorders.[10] So here's another way to flip the Persuader's claim: you should also ask yourself, "What happens if I *don't* do X?"

Flip Both

A final framing effect is somewhat less obvious; you need to combine the two we've discussed. This won't seem as complex once we make it concrete, so let's start with an adapted version of the problem used in the classic experiment on this phenomenon.[11]

Imagine that an island nation of six hundred people is preparing for the outbreak of a deadly disease. There are two alternative medicines that can be used to fight the disease, but the constraints of time and money mean that the islanders can select only one. The scientific estimates of the medicines are as follows:

Medicine A: Two hundred people will be saved.
Medicine B: There is a one-third probability that six hundred people will be saved, and a two-thirds probability that no people will be saved.

Which of the two programs would you favor?

Before you answer, you should know that other subjects saw the same problem, but with a different description of the medicines:

> Medicine A: Four hundred people will die.
> Medicine B: There is a one-third probability that no people will die, and a two-thirds probability that six hundred people will die.

Notice that Medicines A and B have the same consequences in the two versions of the problem. "Two hundred people will be saved" is the same outcome as "Four hundred people will die." So in this experiment, as in the hamburger situation (lean versus fat), we vary the description of the outcome (people saved versus deaths); but unlike the hamburger situation, this one requires that a choice be made (rather than just rating the appeal of the burger).

The findings were striking. When offered the first description— which emphasizes the people saved—72 percent chose Medicine A. But when offered the second description, which emphasizes deaths, just 28 percent chose Medicine A, even though the choices in each pair are comparable. Why? Most psychologists interpret this as part of a very general bias in how we think about risk and outcomes. We are *risk averse* for gains, and *risk seeking* for losses. That means that when we must make a choice between two good outcomes (where we stand to gain something), we like a sure thing. Hence, when the medicines are described in terms of lives saved, we go for the sure thing—the 100 percent chance that two hundred people will be saved. But when losses are salient, suddenly we're ready to take risks to reduce the loss. Hence, in the second problem description, people are apt to choose Medicine B, hoping for the outcome where no one dies.

Now let's put this into the Strip it formula. In the first flip, I asked you to think about whether there is another way to describe the outcome (Z)—that's the lean versus fat hamburger business. In the second flip, I asked you to compare the outcome of adopting the Change (X) to the outcome when you do nothing (not X), as in my dad's dentistry experience. In the island disease problem, we've combined them. Everyone was asked to consider a choice of what to do (X), but the outcome was described positively or negatively (Z).

Let's put this into an education context. Suppose that you're a school principal, and the central office in your district closely monitors the percentage of kids who read at grade level, as defined by a state-mandated test. With your current reading program, 34 percent of kids in your school are reading at grade level, and 66 percent are not. If you adopt a new reading program, there is some chance that it will work well, and things will improve. But there is also some chance that things will get worse—teachers will be unfamiliar with the new program and so won't implement if effectively, or the program just may not be as good as what you're doing now. We can frame this choice in terms of losses:

> Choice A (keep doing what you've been doing): 66 percent of kids read below grade level.
> Choice B (adopt new program): there's a two-thirds chance that 90 percent of kids read below grade level, and a one-third chance that 10 percent of kids read below grade level.

Or we can frame the choice in terms of gains:

> Choice A (keep doing what you've been doing): 34 percent of kids read at or above grade level.
> Choice B (adopt new program): there's a two-thirds chance that 10 percent of kids read at or above grade level, and a one-third chance that 90 percent of kids read at or above grade level.

Naturally, I've fabricated the figures in these choices, but I'm sure you get the point. When we think about adopting a Change, we understand that there's some chance that it will help, but there is also some chance that it will not work or even make things worse. We can frame these possible outcomes either as gains or losses. *When things are described as losses, we are more likely to take a risk.* So when a Persuader emphasizes again and again that things are really bad, what is she really saying? She's saying that the current situation means a certain loss! The Persuader is egging you on to take a risk. When the island problem was described in terms of losses (deaths), people were more ready to go for a risky solution to try to minimize the losses. If the Persuader instead emphasized *gains,* you would be more likely to stick with what you're doing—where your gains are certain—rather than taking a risk to try to increase your gains.

Whether or not the risk is worth it is, of course, a matter of the odds of the gains and losses, as well as how good the gains seem to you and how bad the losses seem. What I'm emphasizing here is that you should look at these outcomes from all possible angles, because your willingness to try something risky is influenced by whether you think of yourself as trying to get something good or trying to avoid something bad.

So to summarize, Flip it means that you

1. Consider whether the promised outcome can be described another way. If it's described positively, is there a negative side to it? (For example, a "pass rate" can also be described as a "failure rate.") The new description may sound fine to you, but it may not. Try it.
2. Consider not just the consequences of undertaking the Change, but the consequences of doing nothing.
3. Combine the two flips. When comparing the consequence of undertaking the Change (versus doing nothing), also be sure to make that comparison with the outcome flipped. That is, compare the Change to doing nothing when you think of the outcome as good, and compare the Change to doing nothing when you think of the outcome as bad.

Claims Not Worth Your Time

I've emphasized that this first step—Strip it and Flip it—is meant to be devoid of evaluation. You are simply to gain clarity on the claim. We're not going to go deeply into the process of assessing evidence until Chapter Seven, but some claims are, on their face, unworthy of attention: some are boring, some are unacceptably vague, and some are unlikely to affect students. Let's look at each of these.

Old Stuff
One possibility is that the claim, once stripped of fluff, is revealed as something humdrum because it is already familiar. This phenomenon is especially prevalent in so-called brain-based education. As described in Chapter Two, neuroscientific terms seem so impressive, so unimpeachably *scientific* that it may not occur to you that the findings, though perfectly true, don't really change anything. Table 5.1 shows some neuroscientific findings that I have seen emphasized in books and blogs.

Vague Stuff
Once stripped, some claims are revealed as, well, pretty mundane. But others, though far from mundane, are very hard to size up because they don't yield to your best efforts to put the claims into the format "If I do X, then there is a Y percent chance that Z will happen." In other words, you can't quite figure out either what you're supposed to do (X) or what is supposed to happen after you do it (Z). That problem ought to strike you as quite serious. You are embarking on this educational Change because you think it's going to do some good. If you don't have it clear in your mind what Z is supposed to be, then you can't know whether or not the Change is working. And if you don't have X clear in your mind, that means you're not sure whether you're doing the right thing to make Z happen.

When I say that X must be clear, I really mean more than that. I don't just mean that the Persuader should be specific about what you (or the student) is supposed to do; I mean that you should feel confident that you can predict the impact of the Change on the *student's mind*. Think about it this way. What prompts students to learn new information, or a new method of analysis, or critical thought? It's the student's mental activity that makes these things happen. Listening to a teacher or reading a book or creating an artifact—students learn from these activities only insofar as the listening,

TABLE 5.1: Some common neuroscientific claims, stripped.

Neuroscientific Finding	Stripped
Dopamine, a neurotransmitter associated both with learning and with pleasure, is also released during video gaming. Video games may be an ideal vehicle through which to deliver educational content.	Kids like games, so if we could make learning more like games, kids would like learning.
Although the brain weighs just three pounds, it commandeers about 20 percent of the body's glucose—the sugar in the bloodstream that provides energy. When glucose in the brain is depleted, neural firing is compromised, especially in the hippocampus, a structure vital to the formation of new memories.	A hungry child won't learn very well.
The prefrontal cortex of the brain is associated with the highest levels of decision making and rational thought. It is also the last part of the brain to be myelinated—that is, to be coated in the insulation essential to effective neural functioning. The prefrontal cortex may not be fully myelinated until twenty years of age.	Sometimes teenagers do impulsive things.
There is massive brain plasticity during the early years of life. Brain plasticity is the process by which the physical structure of the brain changes, based on experience. New networks are formed, and unused networks are "pruned" away—that is, are lost.	Little kids learn a lot.

reading, or creating gives rise to the right mental activity. I might provide what I think is a brilliantly clear explanation of the relationship of medieval vassals and lords, but if you're not really paying attention, it won't do any good. Or consider that sometimes you are paying attention, but the ideas being communicated to you just don't click. When we say "it's not clicking," we mean that the

Student thought ◄———— Teacher ◄———— Principal ◄———— District ◄———— State

FIGURE 5.4: The chain of influence in education. This description is not meant to be comprehensive. Many factors are omitted, and there are more mutual influences.

ideas are bumping around in our thoughts (because we are paying attention), but they are not coming together into a coherent whole. Understanding is a mental event. The act of teaching is an effort to precipitate such mental events by shaping the thoughts of students. Students' mental events can be thought of as the last link in a chain (Figure 5.4).

At the far left of Figure 5.4 are the thought processes that will drive learning, understanding, enthusiasm, and so forth. The teacher tries to create an environment that will move the student's thoughts in particular directions. The school administration tries to support the teacher's efforts, or the administration tries to get the teacher to teach in ways the administration thinks is most effective. The district does the same, influencing school administrators. The state legislature writes laws in an effort to influence how districts and schools are administered.

The point here is to emphasize that (1) Changes in the educational system are irrelevant if they don't ultimately lead to changes in student thought; and (2) the further the Change from the student's mind, the lower the likelihood that it will ultimately change student learning in the way people hope. For example, suppose a state legislature writes a law dictating that contracts between teachers' unions and school districts cannot forbid the use of student test scores in the evaluation of teachers.‡ The law doesn't say that districts *must* use test score data—it just says that such use can't be forbidden. The hope, of course, is that some districts will use test score data. An additional hope is that principals, who at most schools have a prominent voice in the evaluation of teachers, will emphasize those test scores rather than ignore them. Further, the hope is that teachers,

---

‡In fact, the Race to the Top initiative of 2009 was a federal law, which said, among other things, that states interested in applying for a pot of federal education grant money could not have a law on the books forbidding the use of student test data in teacher evaluations.

aware that their principals will base teacher evaluations on test scores, will try to ensure that their students will perform better on state-mandated tests. Finally, the hope is that the Changes teachers make will, in fact, change student mental processes so that they will learn more and score better on the tests.[§] If anyone in this process does not or cannot act as expected, the law will not have the intended effect. As the chain of influence necessary for the Change gets longer and longer, there is a greater and greater chance that it won't work.

Take, for example, the Change of placing an interactive whiteboard in a classroom.[**] It would seem that this tool could be quite useful in a classroom. For starters, the teacher can capitalize on all of the software on the Web. The United Kingdom invested heavily in interactive whiteboards, and today virtually every UK school has at least one. But the impact on student achievement has been minimal. It turns out that the presence of an interactive whiteboard in the classroom does not necessarily change teaching for the better, or even change teaching at all.[12] Teachers need not only the whiteboard but also substantive training in its use, expert advice about how to exploit it in lesson plans, and time to gain expertise and confidence.

It's not just technological Changes that are underspecified. Many Changes that urge project learning or group learning have this characteristic. Just as dropping an interactive whiteboard into a classroom is not enough to ensure that students will learn, assigning group work is not enough to ensure that students will learn how to work well in groups. These pedagogical approaches call for much more independence on the part of students, and therefore they depend on the teacher's having strong relationships with the students and a good understanding of the existing relationships between students. The teacher uses this knowledge in hundreds of moment-to-moment decisions that guide the groups in the work

---

[§]Of course, the motivation for the law was probably not to get teachers to teach better but to fire teachers who were already not teaching well. The chain of action required in this case is different.

[**]An interactive whiteboard is used as a screen on which one can project an image from a computer. The screen is touch sensitive, so the teacher (or student) can interact with the computer by touching the screen.

without micromanaging them. Thus Changes that suggest lots of group work in the classroom are almost always underspecified. The methods are terrific when they work well—in fact, I think that for some types of learning they are probably the ideal—but they are very difficult to implement well, and I seldom see a Persuader acknowledge this difficulty.

There is an inevitable tension here. On the one hand, teachers and administrators are understandably leery of Changes that amount to classroom micromanagement. Classrooms are dynamic places, and teachers need flexibility to change what they are doing based on moment-to-moment evaluations of students' understanding and motivation. On the other hand, the greater the flexibility, the less one can say with any confidence exactly what the Change amounts to. There is a happy medium. A Change might include considerable detail as to how it is to be implemented without prescribing what must be done moment to moment.

The clarity of the outcome is just as important as the clarity of what you are supposed to change. Readers of this book are interested in evidence and will surely want to know whether or not a Change is actually working. For example, suppose that my first-grader's teacher has told me that my son is struggling with reading, and I notice that he shows no interest in reading at home. I hear about a technique called Language Experience[13] that is supposed to help struggling readers, and I decide to give it a try. Language Experience is quite specific about what you're supposed to do:

1. You have the student dictate something to you (a story, a description, anything that the student would like to relate).
2. You write down what the student says, periodically stopping and reading aloud to the child what you have written so far.
3. When the child is finished, you read the whole piece aloud to him or her.
4. You save the piece so that the child can reread it himself or herself.

The method is clear enough. The outcome, less so. The technique is supposed to help make reluctant readers more interested in reading. Okay, but how are you to know that's happening?

At some point you need to evaluate whether or not the Change is working so that you can either continue it or give up and try something else. To know whether it's working, you'll need three pieces of information: (1) how to recognize the positive change when it happens; (2) how large the change is supposed to be; and (3) when to expect it.

Knowing what a Change is supposed to do is not quite the same as being able to evaluate whether or not it's actually happening. When we discussed good science (Chapter Three), we emphasized the need for things to be measurable. The same principle applies here. If a Persuader promises that a Change will make kids like reading more, how will I know that they do? I could just ask them: "Do you like reading more than you did six weeks ago?" But then again, maybe children's memory for that sort of thing is not that accurate. Then too, if the child says, "Yes, I like reading more," but then seems just as miserable during reading time at school, should I be persuaded by what she says, or by how she seems to act? If I am to evaluate whether a Change is working, I need something concrete, and something that is well matched to what I was hoping the Change would do. For example, perhaps I was prompted to look for a reading program because my child complained about reading in school and because he seldom read books at home. So I could see whether the Change prompts less complaining and more reading.

I also need some idea of what constitutes "success." Suppose that in the week before he starts this new reading program, my son doesn't pick up a book once. If, three weeks into the program, he is looking at books once each week, am I satisfied? Or does that Change seem too small? In addition, I need to know when to expect that the good outcome will have happened. For example, you'd think it pretty odd if I told you that I had been using a reading program for two years with no sign of its helping, but that I was still hopeful that eventually it would do some good. Okay, so two years without results is too long. What's more reasonable? Two weeks? Two months?

It's important to define the signs of success *before* you embark on the Change. Once you're committed, your judgment of how it's working is all too likely to be affected by cognitive dissonance. You'll recall that cognitive dissonance refers to discomfort that is a consequence of holding two conflicting beliefs simultaneously. Dissonance motivates us to change one of the beliefs. (Remember the boring pegboard task that subjects ended up rating as interesting?)

Cognitive dissonance may make it hard to evaluate how an educational Change is working. Once you have been embarked on a Change for a while, you've invested your time and that of the students or your child, and you may have a financial investment. Thus, if the Change isn't really working that well, you will hold two incompatible thoughts in mind: (1) I invested heavily in this program, and (2) this program brings no benefits. It's hard to rewrite history and pretend that you *haven't* invested in the program, so you are likely to seek out reasons to persuade yourself that the program *is* working, even if you're grasping at straws.

The best way to protect yourself from this profitless self-delusion is to write down your expectations before you start the program: how big a change you're expecting, when you expect to see it, and how you'll know the change is happening. Writing down these expectations makes it difficult for you to persuade yourself that something is working when it's not, because you have already defined for yourself what it means for the Change to be "working."

All Things to All People

In the Broadway musical (and later, Hollywood movie) *The Music Man,* con man Harold Hill comes to a small town in Iowa and persuades the townspeople that he is organizing a boy's marching band. When pressed to describe how he plans to teach the boys to play, Hill describes his "think system." If a boy thinks the melody and hums the melody, he will, when presented with an instrument (even for the first time), be able to play the melody!

Some claims about Changes are equally extravagant, but are not quite as transparently false. From a cognitive perspective, if a Persuader makes either of two promises, they are very unlikely to be kept: (1) that a Change will help with all school subjects, or (2) that a change will help all kids with a disability. Let's consider each in turn.

Suppose that instead of being tutored in academic subjects, students performed a set of exercises tapping basic mental processes that underlie *all* cognition. You don't just tutor the student in history; instead, you make memory work better, or you improve critical thinking. Many of the "brain games" software packages and cognitive training centers make such claims.

Unsurprisingly, a notion this plausible has been around for a while. In the nineteenth century (and before), it was the rationale for students to study Latin. The thinking was that, although useless for communication, Latin is a logical language requiring logical thought and that this logical habit of mind will transfer to other mental work. In addition, learning Latin is difficult. Kids will learn mental discipline, which will also translate to other intellectual pursuits. As more than one wag has put it, "It doesn't really matter what kids study, as long as they don't like it."

These ideas were tested by Edward Thorndike, an important learning theorist at the turn of the twentieth century, and often considered a founder of educational psychology. Thorndike reported that training in one task led to improvement in that task, but the skill seldom showed much transfer to other tasks. It seemed *not* to be the case that studying Latin makes you all-around smarter or more mentally disciplined or better at learning new things.[14] This finding has more or less held up over the last century.[††]

A more modern take on this old idea is not to use Latin or some other subject matter to improve a basic mental process but rather to train the basic mental process itself with content-free exercises. Working memory has been the favorite target for this strategy. Working memory is the mental "space" in which you manipulate and combine ideas. You can test the capacity of working memory by asking someone to keep something briefly in mind—a list of letters, say—and then to recount what you asked her to keep in mind. People with larger working memory—those who can keep more stuff in mind simultaneously—tend to do better on standard

---

[††]Thorndike, E. L., & Woodworth, R. S. (1901). The influence of improvement in one mental function upon the efficiency of other functions. *Psychological Review, 8,* 247–261. Note that there must be some process by which learning makes you better at solving unfamiliar problems—after all, adults are better at this than kids are, so their experience must be transferring to the new problem in this situation. But it's far from obvious how that works.

tests of reasoning.[15] It's long been reported, however, that training working memory, like studying Latin, doesn't lead to good transfer. Someone who practices keeping letters in mind will get better at keeping letters in mind, but if then asked to remember numbers, shows little or no transfer.[16]

There has been a new ray of hope in this area of research in just the last few years. Some laboratories are reporting that people trained in certain working memory tasks not only improve on that task but also *do* show transfer to other working memory tasks; however, they don't show any advantage on reasoning tasks.[17] So at this point, there's reason to be suspicious of any Change that, once stripped, promises an across-the-board improvement in cognition.

The problem is not just that you can't train basic cognitive processes like working memory. The problem is that when you practice a cognitive skill—critical thinking, say, or problem solving—the newly acquired skill tends to cling to the domain in which you practiced it. That is, learning how to think critically about science doesn't give you much of an edge in thinking critically about mathematics.

There are two reasons that critical thinking sticks to subject matter: sometimes you need subject knowledge to recognize what the problem is in the first place, and sometimes you need subject knowledge to know how to *use* a critical thinking skill.[18] Consider this problem:

I am taking a trip on Route 66, all the way from Chicago to Los Angeles. It's a total of 2,451 miles, and I want to document the trip. I have enough memory in my digital camera to take 150 pictures. If I want them evenly spaced, I should take one picture every how many miles?

Although this problem seems straightforward, many people get it wrong, and they typically make the same mistake. They divide 2,451 by 150 and come up with 16.34 miles. But if I take my first picture in Chicago (mile 0), I'll snap my 150th picture 16.34 miles *short* of the end of Route 66 at the Santa Monica Pier. Think of it this way. Suppose I said I wanted to take only two pictures. Now how many miles should separate my shots? If I divide 2,451 by 2, I get 1,225.5. I take my first picture in Chicago, and my second only halfway along the trip. Thus the formula to solve the problem is not (number of miles) ÷ (number of pictures). It's (number of miles) ÷ (number of pictures −1).

You can see why many people get this wrong. Someone who is very likely to get it *right* is a person who builds fences or is familiar with iterative loops in computer programming. Buying the right number of fence posts is analogous to my picture-snapping problem, and computer programmers learn about this off-by-one error because many data structures have indices that start at zero rather than one. The fact that these folks are likely to get the problem right shows that sometimes solving a problem is not a matter of critical thinking. It's a matter of recognizing, "Oh, this is *that* sort of problem." This recognition process (and its importance) is familiar to teachers of mathematics. Students may encounter a formula for solving a particular type of problem and can apply the formula with ease. But when later confronted with a word problem, they have a hard time figuring out which of the many formulas they have learned is appropriate. This is not a matter of critical thinking. It's a matter of having worked enough of these (and other) problems so that the deep structure of the problem is apparent to you, just as a builder of fences would recognize that her knowledge applies to the Route 66 problem.

At other times, you might know exactly which critical thinking strategy you are supposed to use, but lack the knowledge required to apply it. For example, students who have been exposed to the scientific method know that experiments typically have an experimental group and a control group. These two groups are supposed to differ in some important way (for example, the experimental group gets a new math curriculum, and the control group gets the old one); otherwise they are supposed to be comparable. But ensuring that the groups are comparable frequently requires knowing something about the thing you're testing. For example, if I'm testing the efficacy of a math curriculum, shouldn't I check to be sure that kids in the experimental and control groups have roughly the same knowledge of math before the experiment begins? Yes, that sounds like a good idea. Are there other things I ought to check because they might affect kids' learning of math? Here's a list of some factors. Which ought to be measured before the experiment begins, to ensure that the two groups are equivalent?

Factors That Might (or Might Not) Be Important to Equate When Comparing Math Curricula

Gender	Attitude toward math
IQ	Attitude toward school
Learning style	Liking for the teacher
Working memory capacity	Relationship warmth with the mother and with the father
Handedness	Family income
Spatial ability	Highest educational degree of mother

Here's the point. If we plan to test whether the new curriculum is better than the old, we need to make sure that the kids in the two groups are the same. But kids have an endless number of attributes. We could easily add to the list of factors. It's impractical to test each kid on every attribute. What we really need to do is test kids on the attributes that matter to learning math. Okay, which attributes matter to learning math? Well, knowing the answer to that question is a matter of background knowledge. So here's a critical thinking skill (evaluating whether or not a study was well done) for which we know what to do (make sure that there is a control group), yet we can't do it in the absence of the relevant background knowledge. So when I see a Change promise to improve a skill (such as "critical thinking") and it makes no mention of the need for knowledge to go with it, I'm suspicious.

There's a second type of across-the-board claim that ought to make you leery. This one does not cut across the cognitive abilities of one child, but rather concerns a single ability in many children. I am suspicious of Changes that promise to remediate a problem in *any* child. Why? Because each of the outcomes we care about for schooling is complex. Lots of cognitive and noncognitive processes contribute. Put another way, if a child is having problems with reading, there are many possible reasons for that. Thus a Change might help with reading difficulties that are due to a problem in processing sounds, but that's not going to work for a child who has a problem with visual processing. Hence, when a Persuader claims that a Change will help *any* reading difficulty, the needle on my nonsense detector flutters close to the red zone.

In this chapter, we've covered the first of three steps in evaluating claims about educational Changes. Table 5.2 summarizes all of the subcomponents of Step One: Strip it and Flip it.

TABLE 5.2: Summary of the steps suggested in this chapter.

Suggested Action	Why You're Doing This
Strip to the form "If I do X, then there is a Y percent chance that Z will happen."	To get rid of emotional appeals, peripheral cues, and proffered analogies that may influence your belief. The scientific method is supposed to be evidence based and uninfluenced by these factors.
Consider whether the outcome (Z) has an inverse; if so, restate the stripped version of the claim using the inverse.	To be sure that you appreciate all the consequences of the action—for example, that a "85 percent pass rate" implies a "15 percent failure rate." We are subject to framing effects; we think something is better if the positive aspects are emphasized rather than the negative.
Consider the outcome if you fail to take action X.	To ensure that the promised outcome if you do X seems much better than if you don't do X. When there is a problem, it's tempting to lunge toward any action because it makes you feel that you are taking some action rather than standing idle.
Consider the outcome if you fail to take action, this time using the inverse of Z as the outcome.	To ensure that doing something versus doing nothing looks just as appealing when you think about good outcomes as when you think about bad outcomes. People are generally less willing to take risks to increase their gains— they would rather have a sure thing. But they don't want a sure thing for losses—they will take a risk to try to minimize them.

(continued)

Suggested Action	Why You're Doing This
Evaluate whether the stripped promise is something you already know.	To be sure that what's being sold to you is something you can't do yourself. Technical talk—especially neuroscientific talk—can make old ideas seem cutting-edge.
Evaluate whether the Change is clear; "clear" means that you feel confident that you know how the Change will affect students' minds.	To ensure that the Change is implemented as intended. Changes that sound good can go awry if they are not implemented in the classroom as intended or if students don't do what you're hoping they will do.
Evaluate whether the outcome (Z) is clear; "clear" means that there is some reasonably objective measure of whatever outcome you expect, how big the change in the outcome will be, and when it will happen.	To be sure you will be able to tell whether or not the promised outcome is happening.
Check the outcome against this list of frequently claimed but unlikely-to-work promises.	To be sure that claims are not made that are unfeasible, from a cognitive perspective—for example: An improvement in all cognitive processes An improvement in a specific cognitive process (for example, critical thinking) irrespective of material An improvement for all students who struggle with a complex skill such as reading

I urge you not simply to think about the actions in Table 5.2 but to write down your thoughts about them when you are considering a Change. Forcing yourself to write things down will make you take more time with each action, and articulating your thoughts will increase their precision. It's well worth the time now, given that a

Change usually represents a significant investment of time, money, and energy, not to mention the time and energy of your kids.

Suppose you've run through all the evaluations suggested in Table 5.2, and you think the Change is worth pursuing. Now suppose that the Change is promoted by a well-known figure in education; a prominent professor; or a former secretary of education who, in your opinion, has always seemed to have a lot of horse sense. You've decided that the Change sounds pretty good; if an authority figure says so too, how persuasive should you find that? That's the subject of Chapter Six.

6

Step Two: Trace It

> I was bold in the pursuit of knowledge, never fearing to follow truth and reason to whatever results they led, and bearding every authority which stood in their way.
>
> —*Thomas Jefferson*
>
> *Nullius in verba* (translation: "Take nobody's word for it")
>
> —*Motto of the Royal Society of London*

Bernhard Dohrmann is a businessman and entrepreneur of wide-ranging interests. Unfortunately, he has also had his share of legal problems. In 1975, he was convicted of securities fraud for selling railroad cars that did not exist. In 1982, he was charged by the Federal Trade Commission with misrepresenting the prices of investment diamonds. The case was settled out of court, with Dohrmann's company returning $6.7 million to investors. In 1991, Dohrmann was charged by the U.S. attorney's office with sixteen counts of criminal contempt; it seems he lied about his company's sales figures when selling bonds to investors. He was sentenced to prison for this crime in November 1995.[1]

With such a history of legal problems, what's a troubled businessman to do? Why, go into the educational software business, of course!

Dohrmann started a company called Life Success Academy that marketed (and continues to market) Super Teaching. Super Teaching consists of a system that projects images to three screens; the central screen shows whatever images a teacher typically uses in a lesson plan. The flanking screens show "seemingly random" images of nature, or real-time footage of the teacher or the audience. This practice is said to be consistent with "whole brain learning."[2] Systems initially were to sell for $160,000 *per classroom;*[3] the current price is down to $29,500.[4]

Although Super Teaching had been around since at least 2002, things started to look really promising for the Life Success Academy in December 2007, when the company signed an agreement with the University of Alabama in Huntsville. The university would help test and refine the Super Teaching method and would in return share in profits from future sales. In early October 2008, the university unveiled Super Teaching with a ribbon-cutting ceremony. The president of the university attended, but the honor of cutting the ribbon went—not inappropriately—to Tony Robbins, motivational speaker and late-night infomercial pitchman.[5]

A year-and-a-half later, the University of Alabama in Huntsville dissolved its relationship with Bernhard Dohrmann and the Life Success Academy.[6] Things had heated up six months earlier. A blog that covers Alabama politics had posted a lengthy summary of Dohrmann's criminal past, provocatively headlined "Why Is UAH Involved with 'a Very Dangerous Con Man'?"[7] A month later, the university's student newspaper published an article titled "Learning at the Speed of Con."[8]

It's hardly news that an educational Change attracted serious attention despite the fact that there was no evidence supporting it. If that were uncommon, I would have had no reason to write this book. The question that ought to interest us here was nicely put in a *USA Today* article: "Some observers are wondering why it took the university six months to terminate the relationship after unsavory details of the entrepreneur's past came to light—and why due diligence did not stop the university from signing the contract in the first place."[9]

This point initially seems self-evident: What in the world were officials at the University of Alabama in Huntsville thinking? Dohrmann's sketchy past would seem to raise plenty of red flags, and fancy detective work was hardly required to find out about it.

Googling Dohrmann's name produces enough relevant information. Furthermore, in 2002, the local Huntsville paper had published *on its front page* a highly unflattering story about Dohrmann, detailing his criminal record.[10] Yet key officials at the university were unapologetic about the partnership. The chief information officer had this to say about Dohrmann's history: "That's totally immaterial. People are not vetted for their past. That's not our normal process here."[11] This argument may strike you as far-fetched: A criminal past of fraud is immaterial when you're thinking about a business relationship?

But then again, maybe there's something to this argument. It is not unreasonable to say, "I judge each case on its merits. It's foolish to base a decision on some *guess* as to someone's character; I'm interested in *evidence* about the program. Super Teaching looked promising, and the university was well protected in the signed contract."

In fact, you could argue that such an attitude would be consistent with much of what I've urged in this book. Let's not forget our discussion in Chapter Two, in which I pointed out that medieval thinkers venerated authority so much that Oxford University declared that undergraduates were to read only Aristotle and those who defended him. I approvingly recounted the change in how people weighed evidence, in which they ultimately rejected belief based solely on authority and embraced the scientific method. Well? Why is it stupid to *believe* Aristotle solely because he's been right in the past, but smart to *disbelieve* Dohrmann solely because he's been wrong in the past? In each case, am I not simply assuming that people who have been right in the past will continue to be right, and people who are wrong will continue to be wrong? Should the experience of the Persuader—for better or worse— influence whether or not you believe that the Change will work?

When Authority Fails

Should you believe what someone says about a subject simply by virtue of his or her authority?* In this book, we're interested in

---

* Note that we're using the term authority to mean "knowledge" or "expertise" ("She's an authority on the subject") rather than to mean "power" ("His subversive activities got him in trouble with the authorities").

EXHIBIT 6.1: An Explicit Breakdown of What Happens When We Believe Someone Because of His or Her Authority

Proposition A: Simon the Scientist has good scientific reasons for believing X.

Proposition B: Billy the Believer has good reasons for believing that Proposition A is true.

Therefore, Billy believes that X is supported by scientific evidence.

Source: Lund, M. On arguments from authority in scientific inquiry. Unpublished manuscript.

whether or not a claim is scientifically supported, so the structure of the argument based on scientific authority would look like that shown in Exhibit 6.1.

This looks a little more complicated than it is. We're really interested in Billy here. Billy doesn't understand the science behind X. But Billy believes that Simon does. Billy knows that Simon says, "The scientific evidence supports X." So Billy, without understanding the science, trusts that the scientific evidence supports X. This is belief by authority. Simon is an authority on science, so when he says something about science, Billy is more likely to believe it.

Our goal is to develop some rules as to when the logic outlined in Exhibit 6.1 is sound and when it's not. That's why I broke up this relatively simple situation into the three statements. That way we can see cases where the logic fails in each of the statements. We'll examine four such cases.

Simon Is Not a Good Scientist

First, Billy's conclusion might be incorrect if Simon actually is not a good scientist. The whole point of believing an authority is that he or she is, in fact, an authority! Small wonder, then, that in education research, Persuaders are often eager to present their credentials. Exhibit 6.2 lists some of the more common earmarks of authority among Persuaders in education.

EXHIBIT 6.2: Examples of Ways That Persuaders Seek to Establish That They Are Authorities on Education

- Academic degrees: PhD, MA, MSW, EdD, and so forth.
- Affiliations with academic institutions, whether as a graduate or an instructor ("Dan Willingham has served as an adjunct instructor at the Sebastian Weisdorf University.")
- Publications and public speaking ("Dan Willingham is the author of dozens of articles and four books. He has lectured throughout the world on education theory.")
- Affiliation with prominent companies ("Dan Willingham has been a consultant to several Fortune 500 companies.")
- Affiliation with government agencies ("Dan Willingham's software uses a federally protected technology, and he is collaborating with the Ministry of Higher Education in Malaysia to bring this technology to classrooms there.")
- Quoted or featured in popular media ("Dan Willingham has been quoted in the *San Francisco Chronicle* and other leading publications. His opinion is regularly sought by reporters on education issues.")

Note: All the examples about the author are fictitious, although he is quite the authority, believe you me.

Marginally Useful Guides

What should you make of these sources of authority? Some are at least potentially relevant. If you have a degree in a scientific field, that increases the chances that you have some expertise in that field.

The depth and breadth of your knowledge are hardly guaranteed, it's true. Some degrees are simple shams, purchased from online diploma mills; one such "school" granted a master's degree to a pug dog.[12] And it's no secret that even bona fide universities vary considerably in the rigor of their programs. Still, an advanced degree from a real university is a start. It means that the Persuader committed at the very least one year, and possibly six or more, to serious study of the topic.

I think that having the status of a full-time researcher—at a university, a think tank, or a business—is also a meaningful credential. If someone makes her living as a scientific researcher, you have reason to think that she's knowledgeable on the subject. Now, researchers at schools of education come in for a lot of criticism. As historian Ellen Condliffe Lagemann put it, "Since the earliest days of university sponsorship, education research has been demeaned by scholars in other fields, ignored by practitioners, and alternatively spoofed and criticized by politicians, policy makers, and members of the public at large."[13] Indeed, some data indicate that even researchers at education schools are not so sure about the quality of research there.[14]

Two factors have, I think, contributed to the terrible reputation of researchers at education schools. First, many people think that they can judge education research, just as they think that they can judge what makes for a good teacher. Thus, when we hear conclusions drawn by an education researcher that conflict with our own impressions, it rankles in a way that findings from other scientists do not. A biologist could come up with any theory concerning reproduction in the mud dauber wasp, and it wouldn't run counter to my intuitions. But I have intuitions aplenty when it comes to education, and as we saw in Chapter Two, I have a mental bias to dismiss theories and data that run counter to my beliefs.

A second reason that education research is belittled turns out to be useful to our purposes here. You should remember that not every professor at a school of education is a scientist. Many academic disciplines can be related to education: history, sociology, psychology, critical theory, gender studies, linguistics, economics, political science, and so on. You'll find representatives of all these disciplines at schools of education. This situation does not lead to an interdisciplinary synergy, resulting in fertile cross-pollination of ideas and perspectives. People more often ignore one another because it's hard to understand the work of someone from a different discipline: he or she makes different assumptions, uses different tools, and has different goals. Thus education research can look chaotic. Education researchers seem to agree on very little, and that doesn't give the public the feeling that much progress is being made. For the narrow purposes of this book, you should bear in mind that someone's status as a professor at a school of education is a reasonably reliable sign that this person's work has scholarly integrity, but it does not necessarily signify that the person applied scientific methods in evaluating the Change. There are other scholarly methods of understanding the world, and many methods are represented at schools of education.

Useless Guides

If the first two items on the list (Exhibit 6.2)—an advanced degree and a research job—are only marginally trustworthy, the remainder are even less so. These "credentials" amount to having been hired to give a speech, to advise people in business or the government, or to answer a reporter's questions. Each is a vote of confidence, yes, but it's a vote of confidence given just once, with no opportunity to retract it. For all you know, the Persuader did his consulting at the Fortune 500 company, and the officials there ended up thinking he was a nitwit. Then too, you don't know the basis on which the Persuader was selected to be a consultant in the first place. To some extent, these earmarks of expertise are self-perpetuating. If you were responsible for selecting a speaker for your school district, wouldn't you be reassured to see that the person you were thinking about had given many such talks before? "This guy can't be all bad—look at all the other districts who thought he was an expert." This is social proof, which we discussed in Chapter One, and it's self-reinforcing. The more you're in the public eye, the easier it is to stay in the public eye.

Occasionally you'll see a ploy akin to reverse psychology: someone will try to gain credibility by saying that experts ridicule him! The Persuader says, "Everyone thinks my theory is wrong. They laugh at me; they don't take me seriously. Well, they laughed at Galileo! They laughed at the Wright brothers!" This strategy has been dubbed the "Galileo Gambit," and it's obviously wrong. A few scientists who were ridiculed turned out to be correct, but not everyone who garners scorn will be vindicated. They laughed at Galileo, but they also laughed at the Three Stooges. I have a sneaking suspicion (but can in no way prove) that when you see the Galileo Gambit used, the Persuader probably does not expect to convince people that ridicule means he's right; rather he hopes to convince people that even if he is scorned, at least he is not ignored. It's a backhanded attempt at authority: important people take me seriously enough to grapple with my ideas, although they don't fully appreciate them. When you see the Galileo Gambit, you are looking at a Persuader whom experts ignore.

Remember, we're trying to figure out when you should trust an authority, and we're doing that by examining when authority can go wrong. The first case we've seen is one in which Simon is actually *not* a good scientist. Billy is mistaken about Simon's credentials. The trustworthiness of a Persuader's credentials is pretty hard to verify without a considerable investment of your time and, in many cases, without a certain amount of expertise yourself.

Claims Are Misunderstood

There are other ways that you can go wrong when you trust an authority. Simon may be a good scientist, but Billy the Believer may misunderstand Simon's claim about X. That may happen because Simon's belief is misrepresented by a third party. It also may happen when someone reads Simon's work and draws what he sees as a natural conclusion, even though Simon never made the claim at all.

One of the most common of such misunderstandings concerns Howard Gardner's theory of multiple intelligences. Gardner's theory claims that the human mind has eight basic intellectual capacities: verbal, spatial, bodily-kinesthetic, musical, interpersonal, intrapersonal, naturalistic, and mathematical. People often believe that strength in one intelligence can be leveraged to amend a deficit in another intelligence; for example, the student who struggles in math but is talented in music might be helped by putting mathematical concepts to song. Gardner never said that, and, in fact, the idea runs counter to the theory. Gardner sought to prove that these intelligences really are different—for example, that interpersonal (understanding others) and intrapersonal (understanding oneself) intelligences are not different manifestations of the same ability but are fundamentally different types of mental processes. One of the ways that Gardner supported these distinctions was to suggest that the different intelligences use different "mental codes." By analogy, Microsoft Word and Adobe Photoshop use different types of files—they are not compatible or interchangeable. In the same way, the different intelligences use different mental representations to get their work done.[15]

So it's not just that the multiple intelligences theory is silent regarding the fungibility of intelligences; it actually predicts that they are *not* interchangeable. Why do so many people believe that the theory makes the opposite claim? I have no way of knowing, but I've always suspected that it's raw hope. It would be so wonderful if it were true: the student who has long struggled with math or with reading can suddenly be helped to succeed when his other strengths are recognized. It would be like finding a forgotten key that opens the treasure chest.

Scientific Expertise Is Misapplied

Another possibility is that Simon is a good scientist with excellent credentials, but he doesn't really know anything about X. Nevertheless, he offers an opinion on X, and Billy believes him because Billy doesn't notice that Simon's expertise is specific to other matters. Advertisers have long counted on our insensitivity to the specificity of expertise. For example, tennis great Roger Federer endorses products manufactured by Nike and by Wilson. That makes sense; we'd certainly expect an athlete of his caliber to be knowledgeable and discerning about athletic equipment. Federer also endorses Mercedes Benz cars and Rolex watches. Now this is a bit more of a stretch, but we could say, "Well, he's a rich guy, so he probably knows more about the finer things in life than the rest of us. He's not a watchmaker, sure, but maybe he understands what makes a Rolex glamorous." But it's really hard to make a case for Federer's endorsement of Gillette shaving gel; in what sense is he an authority on shaving gel?

Or consider radio talk show host Laura Schlessinger, whose show is called the *Dr. Laura Program*. Schlessinger's show consists mostly of people calling in and asking for advice about romantic relationships,

parenting, and other interpersonal issues. One would assume, therefore, that she is a psychiatrist (that is, an MD) or that she has a PhD
in clinical psychology or counseling. She doesn't. She has a PhD from
Columbia in physiology. Her dissertation concerned the effects of
insulin on lab rats.[16] She did further her training in counseling at the
University of Southern California,[17] but she's "Doctor" Laura because
of her training in physiology. If being called "doctor" is supposed to
give her authority as a counselor, there's a mismatch between the
credential and the authority we're according her. We are in error.

This error in judging whether someone's background is relevant
explains our feeling that something was amiss when a university
official asserted that Bernhard Dohrmann's criminal past was "totally
immaterial." Dohrmann's past might well be considered immaterial
if, for example, I were thinking about buying the house across the
street from him. Does his record of shady business deals predict that
he'll be a bad neighbor? Probably not. But if his criminal record
were one of harassing neighbors, obviously that would be relevant.
It's little wonder that people thought Dohrmann's track record in
business should have been considered as the university contemplated
entering a business agreement with him.

Authorities Conflict

What do we do when two people who seem to be equally good
authorities on a subject disagree (Exhibit 6.3)?

EXHIBIT 6.3: When Two Equally Authoritative Sources Disagree, Which Should You Believe?

Proposition A: Simon the Scientist has good scientific reasons for believing X.

Proposition B: Simone the Scientist has good scientific reasons for believing that X is false.

Proposition C: Billy the Believer has equally good reasons for believing that Proposition A is true and for believing that Proposition B is true.

Of the four problems I'll describe, this is probably the most prevalent in education research, and it's understandable why that's the case. There will be disagreement among authorities when there is not a reasonably successful scientific model of a phenomenon. If you ask one hundred cognitive psychologists, "What makes people creative?" you're going to get a lot of different answers. Even if the hundred psychologists you ask are really top-flight scientists, they won't agree, because creativity is poorly understood. If, in contrast, you asked the same hundred psychologists, "When you look at an object, how do you know how far away it is?" you'll get much higher agreement. It's a well-studied problem, and we know a lot about how that process works. The questions that educators care about are more often similar to the creativity question than to the distance question. That's why education researchers, even authoritative experts, often disagree.

Small wonder that many teachers are suspicious of education research, and that it seldom influences their teaching.[18] Part of this suspicion comes from a sense that researchers reduce everything to things that are easy to measure and, in so doing, miss most of the rich texture of the classroom.[19] My own experience in talking to teachers indicates that there is another factor: a sense that different people make different claims about what "the research shows." Just as statistical legerdemain can make data appear to support any conclusion, so too can "the research" be shape-shifted as one sees fit. One can hardly blame teachers, who are in the classroom every day, observing firsthand what works and what doesn't, for not changing their practice on the basis of what looks like foolery.

Our purpose thus far has been to list the ways that an argument from authority—trusting that a conclusion is scientifically supported because a knowledgeable person said that it is scientifically supported—can go wrong. We've examined four ways (Exhibit 6.4).

It sounds as though we're working up a good head of steam toward the conclusion that "you can't believe something just because an authority tells you it's so!" The Royal Society of London—one

> **EXHIBIT 6.4: Situations in Which an Argument from Authority Can Go Wrong**
>
> 1. What we take to be signs of authority turn out not to be very reliable, and the person is not, in fact, scientifically knowledgeable.
> 2. We might arrive at a false belief because we misunderstand the position taken by the scientist.
> 3. The person might be a good scientist, but be in error because he or she takes a position on a topic outside his or her area of expertise.
> 4. Two people with equally good claims to authority might disagree on an issue, leaving it unclear which authority to believe.

of the world's oldest scientific societies, dating to 1660—seems to have gotten it right in its motto, offered as an epigraph to this chapter: "Take nobody's word for it." That seems to be in the spirit of this book, the point of which is to allow you to judge the merits of scientific research yourself. But dismissing authority can't be done quite so quickly.

Can Authority Work in Education Research?

Each of us trusts authorities all the time. On what basis do I evaluate the advice dispensed by my doctor? Or my electrician, or my accountant? I trust them exactly because they have relevant training; they are credentialed. Believing them because they are authorities is not just a matter of convenience for me. I can't do otherwise but trust them.[20] Naturally, this trust doesn't *always* benefit us. We've all had that uneasy feeling of wondering whether our doctor really knows what he's doing. But for the most part, the trust seems to work out. If so, it must be that the four problems listed in Exhibit 6.4 are generally absent when we trust the authority of our doctor or electrician. Why?

There seem to be three crucial differences between my doctor and an education researcher. First, when it comes to doctors, plumbers, and the other professionals whom I trust, *I don't have to do the vetting.* I believe, with some justification, that a license to practice the profession is meaningful. Hence, the first problem noted in Exhibit 6.4 is solved: someone credentialed to be knowledgeable probably is.

Further, the professionals in these fields decide whether a particular subfield requires further training or a separate license. Auto mechanics may become certified to work on particular makes of cars. Any physician is somewhat knowledgeable about heart problems, but if there is a serious issue, the patient is sent to a cardiac specialist. Hence, problem 3 (Exhibit 6.4) is largely solved: experts are reluctant to take positions beyond their expertise because there are acknowledged specialists.

Another important difference between education research and fields with trustworthy experts is that we believe there is a settled truth in these other fields. For example, last week I called an electrician to diagnose and repair a problem: the lights in my living room kept flickering. It didn't even occur to me that there might be two or three opposing schools of thought on how to solve this problem. As I consider it now, I recognize that there might be more than one way to fix it, but I expect that different electricians would acknowledge that even though they have their own favorite method, the other methods are at least *okay.* Hence, the fourth problem (Exhibit 6.4) doesn't come up. In education, experts think that other experts' methods are *terrible,* are likely to damage children, and so on.

The third difference between education researchers and doctors or accountants concerns the role of the consumer in fixing the problem. In fields with acknowledged experts, practitioners try mightily to minimize our contribution to solving the problem. My auto mechanic doesn't invite me to turn a few screws as he's fixing my car, or to chip in my opinions about what to do next. He (accurately) figures I'll be more of a nuisance than anything else. So too, my physician tolerantly answers my questions, but doesn't volunteer more detail than I request. In both cases, their main message to me is, "To keep things running smoothly, you do exactly as I say." My job is to execute their instructions, whether it's changing the oil more frequently or getting more exercise. We have an unspoken understanding that my ability to understand *why* I'm to do these things is limited. Sure, I may ask questions and try to understand things better, and on occasion my questions even prompt my doctor to make some small changes. But I always yield to his authority. I would never think of using his diagnosis as a springboard for a homegrown plan of care.

This arrangement does not hold in education. Teachers and parents are not willing simply to do what education researchers tell them. Researchers don't have that kind of credibility, and they don't deserve it. In consequence, parents and teachers *interpret* what education researchers suggest, and sometimes their interpretation is not in keeping with what the researcher believes the science supports, as we described in the case of Gardner's theory of multiple intelligences. That's the source of the second problem we discussed (Exhibit 6.4).

In sum, we trust authorities when (1) a reliable licensing body certifies their expertise; (2) there is a settled truth in the field on which experts agree; (3) the settled truth allows experts to diagnose problems accurately and to prescribe remedies that work in most situations and that do not require creativity or skill from the nonexpert. So where do we stand in education? None of the three conditions have been met.

As noted, there is not a licensing body that testifies to the skill of education researchers. The closest you can come is to look for academic degrees or full-time employment as a researcher. I've argued that these credentials are not meaningless, but neither are they terribly reliable.

As for education research yielding a "settled truth," it is fairly obvious that we're not there; researchers don't have a corpus of knowledge that is universally agreed on even for limited education goals, such as "How much emphasis should be devoted to phonics in the teaching of reading?"

In fact, the problem is still worse. Education researchers often don't even agree on first principles of how research ought to be done. For example, the National Mathematics Advisory Panel was created at the request of President George W. Bush, and set the task of summarizing what is known about how kids learn mathematics. The panel was composed of nineteen eminent researchers, who wrote a report, published in 2008.[21] Before the year was out, there was a special issue of the flagship journal of the American Educational Research Association devoted to critiques of the report.[22] The thirteen articles in this issue centered on two themes: claims that the members of the panel adopted too narrow a view of what math education should contain, and claims that the panelists adopted too narrow a view of what was acceptable research. Education researchers do not agree on the fundamentals of research, so it's difficult to find anyone who all education researchers would agree is an authority.

There is a high-profile attempt to solve the problem of authority in education. Called the What Works Clearinghouse (WWC), it was created in 2002 through the Department of Education, with the goal of sifting through the research dross and providing polished summaries of the research gems.[†] The WWC focuses on interventions (for example, curricula) rather than education theory. The idea is to summarize studies that have evaluated a particular reading program, dropout prevention program, and so on. Researchers employed by the WWC set high standards for what research is considered worthy of inclusion, so that consumers will know that the summaries they read are based on high-quality science.

As I write almost a decade into the project, it's hard to find people who think it has been a smashing success. Complaints have often focused on the standards set by the WWC.[23] In an effort to be rigorous, the WWC considers only certain types of experiments, which arguably limits the perspective of reviewers, and the WWC sets stringent quality criteria so that few studies end up making the grade.

So what's the final word on authority? We began by making explicit the logic behind an argument from authority (Exhibit 6.1, repeated here as Exhibit 6.5).

[†]Another, smaller-scale effort is the Best Evidence Encyclopedia (www.bestevidence.org), run by the Johns Hopkins University School of Education. Researchers there do not write research summaries themselves, but rather seek out high-quality research summaries that have been published elsewhere, and put them into more reader-friendly language.

EXHIBIT 6.5: Our Original Breakdown of an Argument from Authority

Proposition A: Simon the Scientist has good scientific reasons for believing X.

Proposition B: Billy the Believer has good reasons for believing that Proposition A is true.

Therefore, Billy believes that X is supported by scientific evidence.

Source: Lund, M. On arguments from authority in scientific inquiry. Unpublished manuscript.

In the course of this chapter, we've seen that there are multiple reasons to doubt proposition A and proposition B. We are thus encouraged, in Jefferson's lively epigraph to this chapter, to beard every authority who stands in our way. How are we to be bold in our pursuit of knowledge? If we can't take an authority's word for it, how do we evaluate the strength of evidence ourselves? That's the topic of Chapter Seven.

7

Step Three: Analyze It

Most institutions demand unqualified faith; but the institution of science makes skepticism a virtue.

—*Robert K. Merton*[1]

Let's pretend that it's 2005 and that you hear about Brain Gym, a program of physical movements that the Web site claims "enhance[s] learning and performance in ALL areas."[2] The front page of the Web site from 2005 claims that the program is used in more than eighty countries and that the company has been in business for more than thirty years, so there seem to be plenty of people who find it valuable. The Web site headline tugs at both Enlightenment and Romantic heartstrings: "Brain Gym develops the brain's neural pathways the way nature does . . ."

Even though it's 2005, long before *When Can You Trust the Experts?* was published, let's suppose that you strip the claims here. The core idea is that students who perform twenty-six relatively simple exercises will observe dramatic academic improvements. The promises on the Web home page are that the exercises enable one to

- Learn anything faster and more easily
- Perform better at sports
- Be more organized and focused
- Start and finish projects with ease
- Overcome learning challenges
- Reach new levels of excellence

These promises may seem a bit grand, and you'll note that Chapter Five warned that you ought to be suspicious of any Change that claims to help cognitive processes across the board. But when you click on the "research" link, you find a twenty-one-page document with dozens of technical-sounding studies. Admittedly, many were published in *Brain Gym Journal*, which certainly sounds as though it must have close ties to the company, so perhaps those should be discounted. But there are also publications from the journals *Perceptual and Motor Skills* and *Journal of Adult Development*.

Staying in the year 2005, suppose you leave the Brain Gym site and do a general Web search of the term "Brain Gym." You find lots of Google hits on the United Kingdom's government Web site. You have a hard time working out whether there is an official relationship between Brain Gym and UK schools, but the references to the program certainly seem positive. Your search also yields an article in the *Wall Street Journal*[3] and two somewhat older articles from British newspapers, all of which mention Brain Gym in a positive light.[4] The citation of some scientific studies, the implicit approval of the UK government, and recognition in mainstream newspapers might well make you think that Brain Gym is legitimate.

Now suppose that you're doing these Web searches in 2011 instead of 2005. You probably would soon discover a 2006 column by Ben Goldacre, who writes a regular feature titled "Bad Science" for the *Guardian*, a British newspaper. Goldacre excoriated Brain Gym as "nonsense" and a "vast empire of pseudoscience."[5] A year later, two leading British scientific societies (the British Neuroscience Association and the Physiological Society) wrote a joint letter to every local education authority in the United Kingdom to warn them that Brain Gym had no scientific basis.[6] Days later, the creators of Brain Gym agreed to withdraw unsubstantiated scientific claims from their teaching materials. According to one newspaper report, the author of the Brain Gym teacher's guide admitted that many of the claims there were based on his "hunches," rather than on scientific data.[7] Oddly enough, it was not until December 2009— some twenty months later—that a spokesperson for the British government would admit that it had been promoting a program that was without scientific basis.[8] This is especially curious because Brain Gym had changed the claims featured on its Web home page

nearly a year earlier, in February 2009.[9] The previous list of promises had been changed to this notably less grand set:

- Promote play and the joy of learning
- Draw out and honor innate intelligence
- Build awareness regarding the value of movement in daily life
- Emphasize the ability to notice and respond to movement-
  based needs
- Encourage self-responsibility
- Leave each participant appreciated and valued
- Empower each participant to better take charge of his own
  learning
- Encourage creativity and self-expression
- Inspire an appreciation of music, physical education, and the
  fine arts

In one sense, this story is cheering. The purveyors of an educational
intervention overstate what it can do, scientists draw attention to
this fact, and the claims are withdrawn. But that doesn't mean that
there is a system that effectively guards against nonscientific claims
in education. Brain Gym was adopted in thousands of schools, and
it drew the critical attention of journalists and the two British scientific societies only because it was so commonly used and because
it was endorsed by the UK government. If "the system" really
worked, scientific claims would be evaluated *before* the programs
became popular. So here's the challenge. *If you had been looking at
Brain Gym in 2005, what clues were present that would tell you that its
scientific basis was weak?* How should you think about evidence? In
this chapter, we'll examine three relevant topics: how to use your
experience to evaluate new claims, what looks like evidence but
isn't, and how to use the technical scientific literature.

How to Use Your Experience

We've said that educational Changes have, at their heart, the claim
"If you do X, there is a Y percent chance that Z will happen." It's
natural that when you hear this claim, your mind will automatically
play out the hypothesis: you'll imagine doing X, and you'll imagine
the outcome, judging whether or not Z really is likely to happen.

Suppose you heard, "Check out this software. If your child uses it for just fifteen minutes each day, her reading will improve two grade levels in six months." You will judge how easy or difficult it will be to get your child to use the software, and you'll make some prediction about whether she'll learn. Obviously, this prediction is heavily influenced by your experience with your child, your impressions about learning to read, and probably your impressions about computer-assisted learning.

On the one hand, the heading of this section may surprise you—in fact, we might say it ought to surprise you. The message of this book has been "You can't trust your own experience. You need scientific proof!" The point of the scientific method is to put human experience into an experimental context. On the other hand, it seems foolish to jettison all of our prior nonexperimental experiences; surely having observed my daughter at close hand for ten years gives me some useful information when trying to judge whether or not she's going to learn from the software. Is there not a way to use this less formal knowledge wisely? When do our experiences offer a reliable guide, and when are they likely to fool us?

When Our Experience Misleads Us

Two common problems are associated with the use of our informal knowledge. First, we are wrong when we think with certainty, "I know what happens in this sort of situation." I think to myself, "My daughter loves playing on the computer. She'll think this reading program is great!" I might be right about my experience—my daughter loves the computer—but that experience happened to have been unusual; perhaps she loved the two programs that she's used, but further experience will reveal that she doesn't love to fool around on the computer with other programs. Another reason my experience might lead me astray is that I misremember or misinterpret my past experience, possibly due to the confirmation bias. Perhaps it's not that my daughter loves playing on the computer; actually, *I'm* the one who loves playing on the computer. So I interpret her occasional, reluctant forays on the Internet as enthusiasm. We all know parents (not us, naturally) who project their own dreams and opinions on their children.

Misremembering your experiences can happen even when you've had ample opportunities for observation. For example, when I was in graduate school, I knew a professor who had lived as an adviser in an undergraduate dorm for about twenty years, so he was quite familiar with undergraduate life. His experience led him to conclude that the raising of the drinking age (which happened in the mid-1980s) had only made students drink alcohol secretively; in fact, he thought they drank more. He was not and is not alone in this belief. More than one hundred college and university presidents have signed a public statement declaring that raising the drinking age has failed to encourage responsible drinking among young people, and that new ideas are needed.[10] But empirical data show that they are wrong. For example, nighttime traffic fatalities for eighteen- to twenty-year-olds dropped when the drinking age was raised to twenty-one. Alcohol-related health problems also decreased in this age group.[11]

Why would so many college presidents think that raising the drinking age has backfired? I expect most were not looking at data; they were, like my professor friend, thinking back on their experiences with students, and these are the types of experiences that are especially prone to the confirmation bias. The confirmation bias is more likely to arise with events (1) that you are remembering, rather than experiencing right now; (2) that are ambiguous in their meaning, rather than clear; and (3) that may be hidden or unremarkable, rather than quite obvious. Trying to compare incidents of problem drinking ten years ago to the present day obviously requires memory. "Drinking to excess" is also somewhat ambiguous; if a student is acting belligerent, it's hard to know whether the two beers he drank contributed to his mood, or whether he just had a bad day. And student drinking is nonobvious in that students drink on the sly—the professor was guessing at how much secretive drinking was going on.

So it's risky to use your experience to generalize about that sort of event. A teacher may think that her students have trouble staying on task when they work in groups, but like student drinking, that may be hard to assess. Whether or not students are working well in groups is at least sometimes a judgment call. And if I have several groups in my class working simultaneously, might not the one or two that are having a hard time stand out among the others? Might I not be more likely to remember those groups?

Double-Checking on Your Experience

There are ways of evaluating your experience to give you more confidence that you're right. First, you should recognize that sometimes your experience does not have the problems I've mentioned, and therefore merits full confidence. Some experiences are, by their nature, unambiguous: for example, if my daughter has failed math, I don't have to wonder whether the confirmation bias is making me believe that she failed math. It's an unambiguous event, and one that is not likely to be subject to the tricks of memory. Other experiences might in principle be ambiguous, but in your view the conclusion is unmistakable. "Students are fascinated by demonstrations in science; they are *always* drawn in." Or "My son will work on any problem, no matter how difficult, if he feels that I'm working with him."

Now it appears that I'm offering conflicting advice. I'm saying, "Don't trust your memory if the situation is ambiguous. Unless you're really, really sure." Just how clear is a case supposed to be before you have confidence in your conclusion? There are steps you can take to double-check. For example, you can compare your "common sense" with that of other people. Does your spouse agree that your son will work on any problem so long as you are there? Ask a few fellow teachers, "Are your students as enthusiastic about science demonstrations as mine are?"

Note that when you use your experience to evaluate a proposed Change, you're not just remembering what has happened; you're also predicting what will happen. You're thinking "students like science demonstrations," not just as an idle observation, but as a means of judging the likelihood that a Change will work as you expect. For example, you might think that the Change will be more likely to succeed because it uses lots of science demonstrations. You can put your commonsense intuitions to the test by *forcing* yourself to generate reasoned support for outcomes that you *don't* think will happen.

For example, suppose you're a teacher and you attend a professional development session at which a Persuader recommends that homework be eliminated. Your initial reaction is, "That's crazy! Kids have to practice certain skills, and if they don't practice them at home, they'll have to practice them at school. We'll lose valuable time that ought to be spent on critical thinking." Okay, so there's your experience predicting what will happen. Now imagine that you've implemented the Change as the Persuader recommended, and, as you predicted, the outcome was bad. Write a list of the bad outcomes that occurred and the reasons for the bad outcomes. Now, imagine that you implement the change, and the outcome is *good*. List the good things that happened and the reasons these outcomes occurred. Give this your best shot, even though you initially think the idea is dumb. If you're stuck, ask a friend to help you.

You may be surprised to find that the outcome you don't expect is not as outlandish as you imagined. Sometimes the exercise of making the best case we can for something we don't believe helps us avoid the confirmation bias. It helps us see that there is more than one way of looking at things. And if, try as you might, you can't see a way that the Change will turn out differently from what you expect, your confidence should be a little higher that you're right.

So far we've talked about how you can avoid drawing the wrong conclusion about what you have actually experienced in the past. A different problem arises when we use our experience to draw conclusions not just about what has happened (my daughter likes using the computer), but about what *caused* events to happen. That is, we use our everyday experience to draw conclusions about a broader theory. For example, let's suppose that I'm right—my daughter really does enjoy using the computer, and she has a real knack for learning to navigate programs. It would be a mistake for me to conclude that observation shows that the left brain–right brain theory of thinking must be correct, because my daughter is so obviously a left-brained thinker. Why would this be a mistake? Two reasons.

The first is our old friend the confirmation bias. If I believe a theory, I'm likely to notice instances in which my daughter's behavior seems to fit the theory (she's a deft computer user, as a left-brain person should be), and to ignore or discount behavior that doesn't fit: according to the theory, she should show other left-brain behaviors (logical thinking) and *not* show purportedly right-brain behaviors (such as daydreaming). It's asking a lot for me to keep a running tally of each, but to avoid the confirmation bias, that's what I'd need to do.

Another reason that you shouldn't use your casual observations as evidence for or against a theory is that many theories might make the same prediction. The left brain–right brain theory might predict that someone who likes math will also like computers, but so would a theory based on the common observation that both are technical subjects.

Most of the observations we make are casual and therefore imprecise. Because they are imprecise, lots of theories are consistent with them. For example, I mentioned the lack of evidence for learning styles in Chapter One, and I've touched on this topic when I've spoken with teachers. More than once I've fielded angry questions from teachers who think I'm saying that a teacher whose instruction is informed by learning styles must be a poor teacher. They are thinking, *the theory of learning styles informs my teaching, and my students learn a lot. So there has to be something to the idea of learning styles.*

But there is much more to these teachers' practice than learning styles theory. An effective teacher is warm; he knows his subject matter cold and knows compelling ways to explain difficult concepts; he is sensitive to his students' emotions; and so on. Some or all of these features may be what makes him effective, and the use of learning styles actually contributes nothing. The only way to know for sure would be to have the same teacher compare his effectiveness when he uses learning styles and when he doesn't, and to measure with care the results for students. In other words, you'd need to do an experiment.

In sum, your knowledge can help you predict *what* will happen, at least under some circumstances, but it's hazardous to use your experience to draw conclusions about *why* something happens.

Would a Little Breakthrough Be So Bad?

But there is still another way that your knowledge can help you. You can use it to judge how revolutionary a Change is. If a Change sounds like a breakthrough, a radical advance in addressing a difficult problem, it's probably a sham. Why? Unheralded breakthroughs in science are exceedingly rare. A popular image of scientific progress has the lone scientist working in his lab, struggling vainly to solve a problem, and then, in a Eureka! moment, he has a breakthrough idea, which he reveals to an astonished world. This image of scientific progress fits some cases, notably Newton; his achievements in optics and gravitation all came as he worked in isolation at his family's country home, Woolsthorpe, where he had gone to escape the bubonic plague then threatening Cambridge University.

But that image doesn't fit many cases, especially today. Progress is almost always the product of multiple scientific laboratories working on the same problem, sometimes engaging in petty sniping, but one way or another improving each other's work through collaboration and criticism. History is a ruthless editor, however, and the credit for a landmark of science usually goes to one person or at best a pair. James Watson and Francis Crick saw themselves as racing other laboratories to uncover the structure of DNA,[12] but how many of us today are aware of those other researchers? Indeed, how many are aware that Watson and Crick shared the Nobel prize for the discovery with Maurice Wilkins? Beware of breakthroughs developed by the lone genius, especially one who first publicizes his findings on a Web site with a money-back guarantee.

Further, science typically proceeds in a series of steps, some forward, some backward, that creep toward an advance. Scientific breakthroughs nearly always have some foreshadowing. Before a successful therapy for Alzheimer's disease is developed, you will see news of important steps taken at the molecular level, then successful treatment of Alzheimer's in animal models, and so on.

I've suggested that common sense can be an ally, but it should not be your only weapon. A Persuader will often suggest that there is research evidence supporting the proffered change. How can you evaluate it? Let's start by getting clear about what is evidence, and what looks like evidence but isn't.

Stuff That Masquerades as Evidence

When you're evaluating evidence, the first thing to do is to be sure that you understand the evidence that's being offered. After all, why would you adopt a Change if you don't understand the evidence supporting it? By far the best way to gain this understanding is through a conversation with the Persuader, as opposed to, for example, reading something about it. It's generally easier to listen to an explanation because you can stop the speaker when something doesn't make sense, and ask for a different explanation.

The dirty little secret is that when you press a Persuader to explain a Change, you're not only seeking to understand it but also convincing yourself that the Persuader understands it. Einstein's theories are both mathematically dense and conceptually counterintuitive, so it is noteworthy that he said, "If you can't explain it simply, you don't understand it well enough." All too often it happens that the Persuader has a pat set of phrases regarding the "latest brain research" supporting the Change. But if you ask a few questions, the Persuader's confidence noticeably drops, the same phrases are repeated, and the explanation doesn't seem to hang together very well. You don't need scientific expertise to detect this phenomenon. It doesn't mean that the Change won't work, but it's a good sign that the person who is trying to persuade you to use it doesn't understand the purported evidence behind it.

If the arguments marshaled are clear to you, there are a couple of tests you should apply to them. One is to be sure that the Persuader is not confusing a label with proof. A classic illustration comes from *The Imaginary Invalid*, a 1673 play in which Molière lampooned physicians. In one scene, the lead character is examined for his admission to the medical profession by a chorus of pompous doctors. When asked why opium makes people sleepy, the student replies that it does so because it has "a dormitive quality." The doctors nod their heads sagely and say, "Well argued. Well argued. He's worthy of joining our learned body."*

But of course saying that opium makes people sleep because of its "dormitive quality" is no explanation at all. It's giving the thing to be explained a fancy label and then pretending that you've accounted for how it works. Unfortunately, one sees this sort of "explanation" all too often applied to educational products. Students who have trouble reading are said to have "phonic blocks," or a Persuader will dub learning "repatterning" to make it sound technical and

---

*This bit of the play is actually written in a burlesque of Latin, to further ridicule the learned society of seventeenth-century physicians, so any translation can only be approximate.

therefore mysterious. Whether it's fabricated jargon or a bona fide term, if it's invoked merely to label something that you know under another name, it's not doing any intellectual work. It should be discarded, and it should make you suspicious. Technical-sounding terms for ordinary concepts are invoked only to impress.

You should also keep in the forefront of your mind a bait-and-switch technique that's common in the sale of education products. A Persuader will cite research papers that are perfectly sound, but that relate to the Change only peripherally, if at all. Consider, for example, the Dore Program (http://www.dore.co.uk/), a course of treatment meant to address autism. (The claim is that it's applicable to other problems as well, but to keep things simple, I'll discuss only autism.) The logic behind the program is this:

> ### The Logic Behind the Dore Program for Autism
> 1. The cerebellum (a large structure at the base of the brain) is implicated in autism.
> 2. Therefore, autism can be remedied by improving cerebellar function.
> 3. The cerebellum is known to support balance and skill acquisition.
> 4. Therefore, physical exercises will improve cerebellar functioning.
> 5. Therefore, physical exercises will help children with autism.

If you strip the Dore claim, you'll focus on point 5: if your child performs physical exercises, his or her symptoms will improve. There are not scientific studies on the Dore Web site that address this claim. There *are*, however, lots of links to articles in scientific journals that verify a link between the cerebellum and autism (point 1), the link between the cerebellum and skill (point 3), and the link between the cerebellum and exercise (point 4). All of these articles represent good basic science, but they don't directly support (or falsify) the Dore

Program.[13] For example, suppose exercise and autism implicate *different parts* of the cerebellum? The cerebellum is, in fact, enormous, and is involved in many functions.

Another source of "evidence" that should not persuade you is testimonials—that is, first-person accounts from people who have used the product and swear that it helped. Testimonials are, in their way, much more compelling than dry statistics. Compare these two statements for their persuasive value:

1. In 28 percent of cases, parents and teachers report improved behavior and concentration after three weeks of Jamboree ADHD behavioral therapy.

2. I was in tears nearly every day. My son was just about uncontrollable. But after just three weeks of Jamboree therapy, it was like he was a new child! Now he's polite to everyone, and he does his homework without my nagging, *on his own*. For the first time, he'll be on the honor roll!

Poet Muriel Rukeyser wrote, "The universe is made of stories, not of atoms."[14] Perhaps she meant that we experience events as connected, as leading to a conclusion. Certainly, stories are more interesting and memorable than statistics—so much more so that cognitive psychologists sometimes refer to stories as "psychologically privileged."[15] It's no surprise that Persuaders make use of them. But you should ignore them. There is usually someone who is ready to testify to the efficacy of almost anything. To take an extreme example, the members of the Heaven's Gate religious cult happily offered testimony in 1997 that the world was about to come to an end and that they would be rescued by aliens in a spaceship following the Hale-Bopp comet.[16]

Two mechanisms can lead you to think that a futile Change has worked a miracle, and make you a good candidate to offer a testimonial. First, there's the placebo effect, wherein being told that you are under some sort of treatment can provide a quite real psychological boost. Supermodel Elle Macpherson was criticized when she admitted that she used powdered horn from endangered rhinoceroses for "medicinal" purposes, despite the lack of evidence that it brings any benefits. Macpherson's response: "Works for me."[17] The benefit comes not from the treatment, but from the belief.

You've probably heard about placebos relieving pain,[18] but they have also been shown to improve symptoms in kids with ADHD[19] or autism.[†20]

It's also possible that whatever's being treated gets better, but the improvement has nothing to do with the treatment. For example, take one hundred kids in the autumn of second grade who are struggling with reading. Now look again at those kids in the spring. Of those hundred, there will probably be a few—five, maybe ten—for whom something clicks, and their reading dramatically improves. Perhaps they really connected with their teacher and worked extra hard to please her. Perhaps they encountered a book that they wanted to be able to read independently. Perhaps they simply accumulated enough practice that they got the hang of it. If you're the parent of one of those kids, you'll think, "I'm so happy that Robert's reading has improved!" But if you've been giving Robert an herbal supplement guaranteed to improve reading, you are very likely to attribute the improvement to your intervention. And if you were asked to provide a testimonial, you just might comply. And the parents whose kids took the herbal supplement to no avail? Their testimonies will not appear on the Web site.

Testimonials invite you to conclude, "This is what's in store for me if I buy in." But to make a principled prediction as to what outcome you can fairly expect, you need more information than a testimonial can offer. In Chapter Three I noted that positive evidence is not conclusive for a theory. For example, I theorize that all swans are white, and to prove it, I take you to some parks and zoos and show you some white swans. Well, you probably figured that there were *some* white swans around, or I wouldn't have proposed the theory in the first place.

Testimonials show you white swans: "Look, there's one!" You need not just stories of success from people who adopted the change but also stories of failure. You also need stories of success and failure from people who *didn't* adopt the change. The heart of the problem with testimonials is captured in Figure 7.1.

---

†If placebos work, why don't we just give everyone placebos? They don't work for everyone. In fact, they work for a minority of people. But of course, you need only a few testimonials to make a Change look good!

	Things improved	Things didn't improve
Adopted Change		
Didn't adopt Change (or adopted placebo)		

FIGURE 7.1: You need four types of information to fairly evaluate a Change. A testimonial offers just one of the four.

Testimonials offer information only from the upper-left quadrant, and to evaluate whether or not the Change has an impact, you need information from all four quadrants.

Finding and Interpreting Research Studies

What you've done to this point is simply to listen to the arguments of the Persuader and try to evaluate them critically. But a logical argument in support of a Change is not the same thing as scientific data indicating that it works. You want to know whether such data exist. Where are you going to find them?

Your first request ought to go to the Persuader. If someone tells me that a Change is "research based," I brightly say "Great! Can you send me the research? I'd really like to see the original papers *that report data.*" The Persuader almost always says "Sure!" Sometimes I get something. Often I don't. I figure that either way, I've learned something: either I get some research papers, or I learn that the Persuader either doesn't know about the research or can't be bothered to follow through and send it to me.

But of course I don't really expect that the Persuader is going to send me *all* available research papers, especially the ones critical of the Change. What he or she sends is a start, but I need to do a little digging on my own. This process calls for some work. That's why I've saved it for last. I don't advise moving ahead unless what you've heard about the Change to this point sounds good, and you are contemplating it fairly seriously.

Where to Find Research

There are two varieties of research that you might seek. One is a direct test of the Change. For example, the Persuader is urging you to use Accelerated Reader (http://www.renlearn.com/ar/), a specific program for elementary reading. So you could look for research studies that compare how kids read when that program is in use versus how they read when it is not. The other type of evidence you might seek doesn't test the specific Change, but rather bears on a more general claim about how kids learn. For example, suppose that the Persuader urges you to use Accelerated Reader because it emphasizes reading practice. You might seek evidence on the importance of reading practice more generally, not just as it's implemented in Accelerated Reader. Let's start with finding research that tests a specific Change.

The goal here is to find original research, not what someone else has said about original research. Thus much of what you find in a regular Web search will not do: Web sites (even of reputable organizations), blogs, newspaper articles, and Wikipedia are all secondary sources. They might, however, prove useful if they cite original research articles.

Fortunately, there is another, direct way to locate material. There are several search engines available on the Internet that will help you locate relevant research articles. One of the best is Education Resources Information Center (ERIC; www.eric.ed.gov), which is maintained by the U.S. Department of Education. It provides a fairly comprehensive search of articles related to education. PubMed (http://www.ncbi.nlm.nih.gov/pubmed/) is maintained by the U.S. National Library of Medicine and by the National Institutes of Health. This database is very useful for more medically oriented articles (for example, on autism or attention deficit hyperactivity disorder).

Using either will be fairly intuitive to people accustomed to such search engines as Google or Yahoo. There is a search bar into which you type a few keywords. You're looking for research testing the effectiveness of a Change, so the search term should just be the name of the program. If you want to know whether the Dore Program helps kids with ADHD, search on *"Dore Program."* If you want to know whether Singapore Math boosts achievement for math, search for *"Singapore Math."* You *do* want to include quotation marks—that will limit the search to articles that have the exact phrase "Singapore Math." If you enter *Singapore Math*, the search will return articles that have the word *Singapore* and the word *Math*, and you'll end up with articles that, for example, compare math achievement of kids in different nations, but nothing about that particular math program. For some searches, the difference won't matter much, but it's a good habit to adopt.

If you're having trouble finding articles, try to think of whether there is more than one term for what you're interested in. For example, *"whole word"* reading could also appear under the terms *"whole language," "sight word,"* or *"look-say."* Google may be useful in finding such synonyms, and ERIC has a thesaurus that you can consult, so that you'll have greater confidence that you're using the right search term.

You will also want to limit your search to papers that have undergone peer review. You'll recall that I mentioned peer review in Chapter Three; remember the discussion of the "cold fusion" scientists who held a press conference to announce their results, rather than submitting their findings to the criticism of their peers? I expect that by this point in the book, you have an even better understanding of why peer review is so important. The repeated theme in our discussions has been that our judgment is subject to a broad variety of biases, especially those that confirm our preconceptions and flatter our egos. Much of what we call scientific method consists of safeguards meant to increase the objectivity of those judgments. Planning and executing an experiment, analyzing the data, and writing a report—this process can easily take a year. Little wonder that, once it's complete, a researcher is quite convinced that it's *really* good. Needless to say, the study may contain mistakes, no matter how careful the researcher. What's needed is a dispassionate expert to give it a careful read and to determine whether it is scientifically sound. That's the point of peer review.

When you conduct a search on PubMed, almost all the articles that turn up are peer reviewed. Few medical journals will publish an article that has not undergone peer review,[‡] and PubMed doesn't

---

[‡]Whether or not an article undergoes peer review varies by journal. Either the journal editor always sends articles out for peer review, or never does. It's not decided on a case-by-case basis.

catalogue articles from those journals. Education is a different matter. *Many* journals are not peer reviewed, and ERIC catalogues those. Fortunately, ERIC also makes it simple to limit your search to peer-reviewed articles—you need merely to check a box. Doing so makes a big difference in the number of articles your search returns. For example, when I search on *"Orton-Gillingham"* (a method of reading instruction), I get thirty-nine article citations. When I limit my search to peer-reviewed articles, I get six citations. If I search on *"Bright Beginnings"* (a preschool curriculum), I get twelve articles. When I limit my search to peer-reviewed articles, I get one.

The Simplest View of Research Findings

If you take the simple measure of looking for research articles, you're way ahead of the game, and you haven't even read anything yet. The fact is that when most Persuaders say that there is scientific evidence supporting a Change, they are blowing smoke. There isn't any.

If you do find some articles on the Change, don't buy in just yet. You'll want to have a look at the content of those articles. Fortunately, both ERIC and PubMed list abstracts of all the articles they have catalogued. The abstract is a summary of the article, written by the authors. Your main purpose is, of course, to know whether or not the Change works, and that's typically pretty easy to discern from the abstract; that's what everyone wants to know, so it's very likely to be in the abstract.

Now, you can leave it there. You can just count the number of articles that conclude "the Change helped" or "the Change didn't help," and that's a start. But you're better off digging just a bit deeper by including some information that will qualify how you think about the results. To do so, you'll probably need the full article, not just the abstract. The full article is sometimes downloadable directly from PubMed or ERIC. If it's not, use a Web search engine (Google, Yahoo, and the like) to search for the name of the author. Researchers—especially those who are also college professors—frequently maintain personal Web sites from which you can download articles they have written. If not, you will likely find his or her e-mail address, and you can request a copy. This is not unusual or impolite. Researchers are used to it. And if there is more than one author listed, you can write to any of them.

A Nuanced View of Research Findings

Once you have the full article, what exactly do you want to know? I suggest that you create a scorecard (Table 7.1).

The authors will usually say plainly in the abstract whether or not the Change "worked." But the authors' definition of success may differ from yours. For example, at the start of this chapter I mentioned that the 2005 Brain Gym Web site listed some peer-reviewed research articles. True enough, but if you read the abstract of one of the listed articles, you'll see that the outcome the researchers measured was response time—that is, they measured how quickly subjects could press a button in response to a signal.[21] Subjects who underwent Brain Gym training were faster than those who had not undergone Brain Gym training. Unless your goal is to have students with really fast reactions, this article is not going to be relevant to your decision to use Brain Gym.

Another of the peer-reviewed articles that seems to support Brain Gym's effectiveness used a different outcome, one more commonly reported in education research.[22] The researchers report that the five students at a music conservatory rated Brain Gym as having had a positive effect on their playing. Participants also had a more positive attitude toward Brain Gym at the end of the experiment than at the start. But you want to know whether or not Brain Gym actually helps, not whether people *think* it does. And as we've seen, people who have invested their time in a Change are motivated to think that their time was well spent—that's cognitive dissonance at work. Thus you shouldn't be convinced by data showing that people liked a Change, or the close variant that is often reported: "94 percent of people who used this product said that they would recommend it to a friend!"

You should also make sure that there is a comparison group—in other words, there should be at least two types of students measured:

TABLE 7.1: A suggested "scorecard" to keep track of research findings.

	What Was Measured?	Comparison?	How Many Kids?	How Much Did It Help?
Article 1				
Article 2				
Article 3				

those who participated in the Change, and another group that did something else. Why? Well, suppose that I tell you I measured math problem-solving skills in ten third-grade classrooms, first in the autumn and then again in the spring. All the classrooms used Dan's SuperMath program, and scores on a standardized math test went from 69 percent in the autumn to 92 percent in the spring. Big improvement! But wouldn't we expect scores to be higher after a year of schooling? The real question is not whether third-graders are better at math in the spring than they were in the fall—we assume they will be. The question is whether Dan's SuperMath helps kids learn *more* math compared with whatever method is in place now. It seems pretty obvious when you spell it out, but it's surprising how often an article trumpets "Kids learned more!" without answering the question "Compared with what?"

The number of kids who were in the experiment also matters. Here's a simpleminded example. Suppose I wanted to know how friendly University of Virginia (UVa) students are. I stand on the main quad-rangle, stop a random undergraduate, and administer some test of personality, which we'll assume is a valid measure of friendliness. If I do this with, say, five students, do I have a good estimate of the friendliness of UVa undergraduates? Of course not. I tested only five, so I might have, by chance, selected five extroverts or five odd ducks, or whatever. But if I test a larger number of students, the odds get better and better that the group I'm testing is similar to UVa undergraduates as a whole. In extremis, if I tested all 14,297 of them, I'd know *exactly* how friendly the average UVa undergraduate is, at least according to the test I'm using. If I randomly select 14,000 out of the 14,297, I'm obviously still very close to the true average— I'm still testing most of them. How small can the number get and still allow me to have some confidence that my result is not quirky? It depends on several factors that are too technical to go into here, but a decent rule of thumb is that you'd like to see *at least* twenty kids who have been exposed to the Change and twenty who were not.

You will see plenty of peer-reviewed studies that test many fewer than that. Such studies *are* valuable, but for different reasons. There is almost always a trade-off between the number of people tested and the richness and detail of the measures used. Studies that involve hundreds of kids will probably use a paper-and-pencil test, and the experimenters will have no information about how the kids thought about the questions. When you see a study with six kids, the experimenters often have had long conversations with each child about the Change, multiple measures of the consequences of the Change, and so forth. This sort of study can be very useful to researchers, but is less useful to those who want to know if the Change reliably helps kids.

Finally, you want to pay attention to how much the Change helped. It's important to understand the logic behind the question "Did the Change make a difference?"—a question that you'll see in a moment is rather crude.

The statistical procedures used to answer that question have the following logic. I have two groups: one was exposed to the Change; the other was not. We'll call that the NoChange group. Let's say that the Change is supposed to help kids understand what they read. If the Change *doesn't* work, then both groups should score the same on a reading comprehension test at the end of the experiment. Now of course it's possible that the Change group will score higher just by chance. The test is not perfect, after all—it has some "static" in it, and maybe that will just happen to favor the Change group. Or maybe, even though I selected who was going to be in the Change and in the NoChange groups at random, the Change group happened to have a lot of kids who were good readers.

If the Change group scores a little higher than the NoChange group just by chance, I'll draw the wrong conclusion. I'll think that the reading program works. How can we protect ourselves from these possible chance occurrences? We say to ourselves, "Okay, maybe the Change group would, just by chance, do a little better on the reading comprehension test at the end of the experiment. But they would not do *a lot* better just by chance. So how about this: if they do a little better, I'll ignore it—that is, I'll say, 'The difference in scores may just have been due to chance, so I'm concluding that the Change didn't work.' But if there is a *big* difference between the two groups, then I will *have* to conclude that it couldn't be due to chance. The big difference in reading comprehension scores must be due to the Change."

So far, so good. But here's the complication. We just noted that how much "static" there is in a measure depends on how many people are in the group. If I test the friendliness of just five undergraduates,

I know that I might, by chance, have picked a quirky group, whereas if I test one hundred undergraduates, it's much less likely that the group is quirky. So let's apply that to my comparison of the Change and the NoChange groups. If each group has one hundred people in it, and I see that the reading comprehension scores of the two groups are different, shouldn't I be less worried that the difference is due to some quirk in one of my groups? And shouldn't I be more worried that the difference between the groups is a quirk if I have just five people in each group?

The answer is "Absolutely." And that factor is built into the statistical tests that almost everyone uses. As the number of people in each group increases, you set a lower and lower bar for how big the difference between the groups must be before you conclude "Wow, that difference is too big to have occurred by chance. The groups must be different, and that means the Change did something."

Statistical Versus Practical Significance

Here's why that matters for you. When you're looking through these articles, the natural thing to do is to mentally categorize each study as showing "the Change worked" or "the Change didn't work." That's fine, but note that "worked" really means that the authors were justified in concluding that "the difference between the Change and NoChange groups was so big that it was really unlikely to have happened by chance," and that conclusion actually depends on two factors: how big the difference was between the groups and how many people there were in each group. *So if there were lots and lots of people in the groups, a relatively modest difference in scores would still lead you to conclude that "the Change worked."*

Psychologists refer to this as the difference between "statistical significance" and "practical significance." Statistical significance means that you're justified in concluding that the difference between the Change and the NoChange groups is real, not a quirk due to chance. Practical significance refers to whether or not that difference is something you care about. As the name implies, that's a judgment call. For example, suppose the Change is a new method of teaching history, and at the end of a thirty-two-week program, kids in the Change group scored 1 percent better on a history test than kids in the NoChange group. If there were a lot of kids in each group, that difference might be statistically significant, but it's improbable that you'd think of it as practically significant. (Note that the opposite case is not possible. An experiment can't show a practically significant difference between the Change and the NoChange groups that isn't statistically significant.)

How can you judge whether or not a result is of practical significance? That can be hard to tell if you're not familiar with the measure. If it's a history test that the experimenters themselves created, it's hard to know what a 5 percent or a 15 percent improvement on the test means. If you can't get a good feel for whether or not the improvement is of practical significance, make a mental note of this fact and, if you have the opportunity, raise this point with the Persuader. You need to know in terms that are familiar to you how much your child or your students are supposed to improve.

Most important, you need to consider practical significance in light of your goals. A Change may offer a *guaranteed* improvement in, say, students' public speaking ability. The question is, How much do you need to invest in terms of time and resources to gain the guaranteed improvement? In education, a Change almost always carries an opportunity cost. That is, when you spend your time and energy on one thing, you necessarily have less time and energy for something else. So you need to decide whether this improvement in public speaking ability is going to be worth it. And that is a personal decision. The answer depends on your goals for education.

I've summarized the suggested steps for evaluating evidence in Table 7.2. As I did in Chapter Five, I strongly encourage you not only to carry out each action but to maintain a written record of the results.

We've been through three steps in our research shortcut: Strip and Flip it, Trace it, and Analyze it. Now it's time for the fourth and final step: making a decision.

TABLE 7.2: A summary of the actions suggested in this chapter.

Suggested Action	Why You're Doing This
Compare the Change's predicted effects to your experience; but bear in mind whether the outcomes you're thinking about are ambiguous, and ask other people whether they have the same impression.	Your own accumulated experience may be valuable to you, but it is subject to misinterpretation and memory biases.
Evaluate whether or not the Change could be considered a breakthrough.	If it seems revolutionary, it's probably wrong. Unheralded breakthroughs are exceedingly rare in science.
Imagine the opposite outcome for the Change that you predict.	Sometimes when you imagine ways that an unexpected outcome could happen, it's easier to see that your expectation was shortsighted. It's a way of counteracting the confirmation bias.
Ensure that the "evidence" is not just a fancy label.	We can be impressed by a technical-sounding term, but it may mean nothing more than the ordinary conversational term.
Ensure that bona fide evidence applies to the Change, not something related to the Change.	Good evidence for a phenomenon *related* to the Change will sometimes be cited as though it proves the change.
Ignore testimonials.	The person believes that the Change worked, but he or she could easily be mistaken. You can find someone to testify to just about anything.
Ask the Persuader for relevant research.	It's a starting point to get research articles, and it's useful to know whether the Persuader is aware of the research.
Look up research on the Internet.	The Persuader is not going to give you everything.
Evaluate what was measured, what was compared, how many kids were tested, and how much the Change helped.	The first two items get at how relevant the research really is to your interests. The second two items get at how important the results are.

8

Step Four: Should I Do It?

> The Owl of Minerva first takes flight only when the shades of night are gathering.
>
> *—G.W.F. Hegel[1]*

ecisions about education are seldom easy. The stakes are high, and the issues are complex. In addition, decisions are binary—you adopt a Change or you don't, even though you know that the effectiveness of a Change is best thought of in terms of probability. It's a bit like the weather: the forecast says that there is a 50 percent chance of rain, but you can't match your commitment to the probability by going on half a picnic. You have to go or stay home.

So how can you put together all of the information we've discussed? In this chapter, I'll briefly review the factors that I've suggested you consider, and I'll add a few nonscientific factors that I will argue are important. Finally, I'll suggest what may be the most important step you can take, should you adopt a change: acting like a scientist yourself.

Looking Back

Over the course of this book, I've posed a lot of questions and asked you to hunt down a lot of information. I've also asked you to write down your answers to these questions as you go. It's time to gather this information together in one place. The right column of

Table 8.1 lists the most important questions that I've suggested you pose. The left column ties these questions to the principles of good science (from Chapter Three) and the principles of effective application of science (from Chapter Four).

Table 8.1 ought to represent a review for you, but I do suggest that you take up these questions afresh. Although you considered these issues earlier, your opinion may have changed as you encountered new information or as you thought through the answer to another question. Once you have the answers to the questions in Table 8.1, then what? How do you knit this information together to come to a decision?

TABLE 8.1: The principles of good science and of good application of science (drawn from Chapters Three and Four), along with the questions suggested to evaluate the likely scientific integrity of a Change. This is a summary—a more complete treatment appears in this chapter and Chapters Five through Seven.

Property of Science or Its Application	Question to Ask Yourself
Property of science: Science is dynamic and self-correcting—it's not fixed; it is always advancing.	1. Is there new information in the Change, or is it something that you already know, presented in slick, technical-sounding language? 2. Is the theory strongly associated with one great individual? These may start as scientific theories, but they become frozen schools of thought.
Property of science: Science applies to the natural world and can generate predictions within the natural world.	3. Are you clear on the theory and clear on what the Change is supposed to make better?
Property of science: Science applies only to things measurable.	4. Will it be clear that the promised improvement has happened? Do I know how the improvement can be measured?
Property of science: Theories are cumulative.	5. Is the Change a retread of a bad idea that has been tried in the past? 6. Do the promised effects of the Change violate your experience and the experiences of others? 7. If the Change were successful, would that constitute a breakthrough?

(*continued*)

Property of Science or Its Application	Question to Ask Yourself
Property of science: Tests are empirical.	8. Are testimonials offered as evidence for the Change?
	9. When you examine what was measured, what was compared, how many kids were tested, and how much the Change helped, does the experimental evidence seem solid?
Property of science: Tests are public.	10. Can you access supporting evidence easily? The Persuader should provide it.
	11. Is the evidence peer reviewed?
Science application principle: The outer environment (classrooms and schools) is poorly understood, but is important to developing applied artifacts.	12. If you think there is reasonable scientific evidence supporting the Change, was the evidence collected in circumstances similar to yours?
Science application principle: Applied sciences are goal driven.	13. What *won't* get done if you take on the Change? Time and energy are scarce resources, so undertaking a Change almost always means *not* doing something else. Even if improvement were certain, you must evaluate whether the Change is worth the time and energy in light of your goals for schooling.
Science application principle: Many educational goals are ones for which we cannot get good feedback.	14. Do *you* have the resources and expertise to measure the expected outcome? (Question 4 asks whether it's measurable; it may be measurable by experts, but not in daily use by nonexperts.)
Science application principle: Evidence from basic science may be available, but it may be at a different level of analysis than the desired application.	15. How great is the distance between the intervention the Change proposes and the mind of the student? The greater the distance, the greater the likelihood that it won't work.
	16. Does the empirical evidence bear on the Change itself, or on the basic scientific assumptions of the Change? Good basic science can still lead to bad applications.

It's going to be a judgment call. Recall that in Chapter Three, I said that there are no hard-and-fast rules for deciding, "That theory must be wrong." A theory may be discarded because a new theory provides a better explanation of observed phenomena, because it is more consistent with other well-regarded theories, because it is simpler, or even because it is more readily comprehensible and easier to work with. So you ought to balance the answers to the questions in Table 8.1 one against the other. Any theory will have advantages and disadvantages, and how seriously you take the theory depends on some weighting of the two. But there is not a formula to do so. I can't tell you how to sum up all that you've learned about a Change and come to a decision. Still, I think that the answers from Table 8.1 vary in importance, and therefore in their implications. I suggest that they fall in four categories.

One set of questions I consider potential deal breakers; the wrong answer should be enough to make you end consideration of the Change. If the Change is something you already know, gilded with pretty language (question 1) . . . well, what's the point? There's no value added. If the Change is a failed idea, resurrected with new terminology and a new sales pitch (question 5), again, what's the point? If it has failed before, what reason is there to think that it will succeed this time? And if there's solid evidence that the Change doesn't work (question 9), forget about it. As Richard Feynman noted in the epigraph of Chapter Three, "If [an idea] disagrees with experiment, it's wrong."

In the second set of questions, a disappointing answer will not be as definitive, but might arouse your suspicions. If the theory represents a breakthrough solution to a historically difficult problem (question 7), or if the Persuader claims that supporting data exist, but somehow you aren't able to see the data (question 10), I'd be suspicious that the whole thing is hokum. If the theory makes a prediction that flagrantly violates common sense and there's no explanation as to why (question 6), the whole theory may not be hokum, but I'd at least be suspicious that part of it is wrong. And if the Change calls for modifications in practice that are quite distant from the student's mind (question 15)—a change in district management, for example—I'd be suspicious that the Change may not "trickle down" to impact student learning. Changes in district management might make the district more efficient or its workers happier—worthy goals—but it's less likely to make kids learn more math. So for this set of questions, disappointing answers ought to make you suspicious that the Change will not work as promised.

For the third set of questions, the wrong answer should not persuade you that the Change won't work; rather, it's a sign that there is not scientific evidence supporting the Change. If the theory is unclear (question 3) or if the predicted outcome is not measurable (question 4) or is difficult for practitioners to measure (question 14), it would be hard to know whether the scientific theory underlying the Change was right. If the Change is strongly associated with a single individual (question 2), it's unlikely that the Change has been subjected to serious criticism and review, a cornerstone of the scientific method. If the only "evidence" you're offered is testimonial (question 8) or is not peer reviewed (question 11), that's a sign that the idea has not been subjected to serious scientific study. And bear in mind that if the evidence you're offered pertains to basic scientific assumptions underlying the Change, that is not at all the same thing as scientific support for the suggested Change itself (question 16).

In the final set of questions, the answers may not persuade you that the Change is not scientifically based, but they might persuade you that the Change is not a good fit for you. If all of the evidence supporting the Change was collected under circumstances very different from yours—different-age kids, for example, or schools using a very different curriculum—you can't be sure that the Change will work under your circumstances (question 12). You will just have to guess, and it may not seem like a good risk to you. You may also be convinced that the Change is scientifically supported, but it addresses a goal that is not a priority for you (question 13).

So we have four families of questions. Some indicate that the Change won't work, some dictate suspicion that the Change won't work, and some don't tell you whether or not the Change will work, but indicate that scientific evidence on the question is lacking. The fourth category points to instances where the Change may have scientific support, yet you may not want to adopt it. This issue bears further discussion.

As I've said, I can't imagine adopting a Change that is *known* not to work. Why would you adopt a "perceptual motor" curriculum for kids with learning difficulties (which calls for a lot of visual training, balance, and body awareness) when it's *known* that it doesn't help academic skills?[2] But just because a Change has positive scientific proof doesn't mean that you'll adopt it. You can't implement every idea in education that has some scientific backing; there are simply too many of them. So on what basis do you select the ones that you'll use?

Science is very good for predicting what will happen; that's why I kept encouraging you to frame the promised Change as "If I do X, there is a Y percent chance that Z will happen." Predicting the likelihood of Z is what science is good for. Science is not, however, good for telling you how badly you want Z to happen, nor what you're willing to give up to see to it that Z happens, nor how Z may affect others if it happens. Other factors, such as perceived costs and benefits, are important in these evaluations (Table 8.2).

Then too, I could imagine choosing to implement a Change that does not have scientific backing. There are problems for which the data are pretty thin. Will my very shy child come out of his shell if I let him play a massively multiplayer online computer game? Where does a teacher start with a high school sophomore who is reading at a third-grade level? Will a project focusing on charity work foster a greater sense of community spirit in an eighth-grade classroom? Needless to say, I'm a big fan of applying scientific knowledge to education, but we have to be practical. Scientific evidence is sometimes unavailable, and we can't be frozen into inaction when that's so.

So to be clear, I see three categories into which the evidence for a particular Change might fall: evidence it doesn't work, evidence it works, or no clear evidence one way or the other. For the first, I cannot imagine a good argument for adopting the Change. For the latter two, I could imagine adopting or not adopting the Change, depending on your goals and resources. But whatever the status of the scientific evidence, there's always room for more. That's why, if you adopt a change, I urge you to collect your own data. It's time to be a scientist!

TABLE 8.2: An incomplete list of factors that may influence whether or not you adopt a Change, even if you conclude that it is scientifically sound.

Factor	Example
Implementing a Change likely incurs a cost in time, energy, or other resources. Even if you believe that the promised benefits will accrue, you must weigh them against the anticipated costs.	Reducing class size probably helps student achievement, but the benefit is modest.[3] Meanwhile, the cost is enormous because one not only needs more teachers (with salaries and benefits to be paid) but also more classrooms (increasing physical plant costs).
Any Change you adopt brings opportunity costs.	When you expend resources to do one thing, there is something that you can't do because you put your resources to the first thing. What potential benefit is lost by adopting a Change and not doing that something else?
A Change may work as described, but may also have negative side effects.	A friend of mine decided to homeschool her son. Her husband thought it was a bad idea, and it was the subject of several arguments, which ended when he said, "Fine, do it, but it's *your* thing. I'm staying out of it." My friend anticipated that homeschooling would be great for her son, but a strain on her marriage. She was right—her husband didn't stay out of it.
A Change may indirectly impact others.	A high school English teacher told me that when she had her kids putting on a play, they were so excited about it that they had a hard time settling down to their other work each day after rehearsal, a fact she learned from a colleague who had six of her students in his class the period after hers.

The Owl of Minerva

In 2005, I lay on a gurney, prepped by a nurse, waiting to be wheeled into the operating room. My surgeon approached me and asked me, "What's your name?" and then "Why are you in the hospital?" I've observed many neurological exams, and "Who are you" and "Where are you?" are standard questions to ask a patient if you think he might be demented. What was my surgeon getting at? I told her I was there to have a basal cell carcinoma (an easily treatable skin cancer) removed from my eyelid, whereupon she asked, "Which eye?" I pointed to my right, and she took out a fat purple marker and wrote "yes" on my right cheek and "no" on my left cheek. Then I got it. My surgeon was not ensuring that I knew who I was and what I was doing there. She was ensuring that *she* knew.

It was a few years later that I learned about physician Atul Gawande's research. Gawande examined the frequency with which avoidable errors are made in surgery: the surgeon "corrects" a bunion on the wrong foot, or a sponge is left *inside* a patient's body. No matter how skilled the surgeon, such oversights are possible, even inevitable, given the high cognitive load of surgery; there's just so much going on that even the ABCs of surgery might be overlooked. So how do you ensure that they are not overlooked?

Gawande took his inspiration from the way that pilots have dealt with this problem: they make extensive use of checklists. Like surgery, aviation calls for many steps that, although mundane, must be done right. For example, a checklist for the Jabiru J200 (a two-seater prop plane) calls for eighteen checks before the engine is started, three checks in the process of starting the engine, seven checks after the engine starts, and another fifty-one checks in various stages before takeoff.[4] Many of these are so obvious that they seem almost silly. Check that the door is closed. Check that the headset is plugged in.

Gawande created a checklist for surgeons, and these items too were startling in their simplicity. Items like "Are you sure you're performing the right operation on the right person?" "Are you sure enough blood is readily available?" "Is everyone on the surgical team clear on one another's role in the operation?" Indeed, the nineteen items on the checklist initially struck surgeons as "a little juvenile."[5] But a field test in eight hospitals showed that death rates dropped from 1.5 percent to 0.8 percent with the introduction of the checklist, and serious complications fell from 11.0 percent to 7.0 percent.[6]

You can probably see where I'm going with this. I'm about to suggest that you do something that may strike you as a little juvenile.

Let's start with the purpose. Step Four of our research shortcut is asking "Should I do it?" If the answer is no, then your job is finished. But if the answer is "Yes, I'm going to give it a try!" then there's a Step Five. At some point you should ask yourself, "Should I *keep* doing it?" When you make a change in your home, your classroom, or your school district that is meant to improve education, you want to know whether or not it works. If it works, you're going to keep doing it. If it doesn't work, you'll stop and try something else.

How will you know whether or not it's working? The epigraph of this chapter—"The Owl of Minerva takes first flight only when the shades of night are gathering"—provides a hint, though Hegel was referring to the field of history, not education. Minerva was the Roman goddess of wisdom, and she was often depicted with an owl, still a symbol of wisdom today. "Shades of night," or twilight, refers to the end of a historical era. So Hegel was saying that you can't assess a historical era with wisdom while you're in its midst. Only as the era is ending—twilight—can we hope to see it with clarity. So too, you cannot hope to see the consequences of a Change while you're in the middle of it. You need to evaluate it from some distance. You need a stark record of what has happened over the course of weeks or months. Then you need to compare that record to what you predicted would happen within that time frame. If the record differs from the prediction too much, you'll know it's time to quit.

This dictum makes good sense, given some of the mental biases we've discussed. For example, if you relied on casual observation to see how the Change was working, wouldn't the confirmation bias lead you to notice things that are consistent with this belief, and fail to notice things that are not? Wouldn't cognitive dissonance make you more likely to judge that the Change is working, because concluding that it is not forces you to face the fact that you've wasted your time and that of your child or your students? Yes, of course those would be dangers.

This problem—the likelihood that you won't change your evaluation of the Change—can be addressed in the same way it was addressed *before* you adopted the Change. You use the scientific method. People tend to emphasize objectivity as the cardinal feature of the scientific method, but objectivity is not the ultimate aim; the real goal is elasticity of mind. Science enables and impels us to change our beliefs.

If you're not a scientist, how can you turn yourself into one so that you can have more confidence in your judgment that the Change you've undertaken is working (or not)? Just as we did in evaluating scientific claims made by *other* people, we're going to be talking here about a cheat, a workaround, something that will approximate the value that a true scientific study of the Change would provide, without the necessary cost in cash, time, and expertise.

For inspiration we can again turn to the fundamentals of good science outlined in Chapter Four. Good science is empirical, measurable, and falsifiable. "Empirical" means that observation will form the backbone of your method. "Measurable" means that we want to be confident that those observations meaningfully measure whatever outcome you're interested in. And in this context, "falsifiable" means that although you make the decision to undertake the Change with full confidence that it will work, you also have clear in your mind what it will take to falsify this belief, what it will take to make you change your mind.

So here's where we get a little juvenile. Exhibit 8.1 shows a checklist, not unlike one that a pilot or a surgeon would use in that it lists steps that you know, on reflection, are important to take, but that you might forget.

We've covered the reasons behind most of the items on the checklist, but a few bear comment. Note that the 4th and 5th items ask you to measure outcomes that are not really the focus of your interest. That practice is quite common in behavioral research. You *think* you know what's going to happen, but if you end up surprised, you'd like to have some evidence relevant to the surprise. For example, suppose I adopt a Change that I expect will improve my child's performance in math. Could it also affect his *attitude* about math? That's not my intention, but it's at least plausible—so why not try to get some measure of that too, perhaps by noting the frequency with which he does his math homework without being asked? It's also worth thinking about unanticipated negative side

EXHIBIT 8.1: A Checklist to Be Completed Before You Adopt a Change

☐ The thing I'm hoping to change is _____.

☐ The way I can *see* that thing change (in other words, what I'm going to measure) is _____.

☐ I've measured it before I start the Change, and the level is _____.

☐ I'm also going to measure _____. It probably won't be helped by the Change, but you never know.

☐ The Change could have some negative effects. I'm most suspicious that it might influence _____. To be confident about whether or not it does, I'm going to measure _____.

☐ Here's how often I plan to collect the measurements, and the circumstances under which I'll do so: _____.

☐ My plan to keep these data organized is _____.

☐ The date by which I expect to see some benefit of the Change is _____.

☐ The size of the benefit I expect to see on that date is _____.

☐ If I don't observe the expected benefit on that date, my plan is to _____.

effects. If your son focuses on math, is it possible that he'll expend *less* effort on his other studies? Again, this is a plausible outcome, so it would be nice to have some data so that you can draw a conclusion with greater confidence.

Don't be put off by the items that ask about your plans for your data. Your plan needn't be elaborate, but it's worth thinking through how you're going to collect your data. Where will they be recorded, and when will you record them? Your planned measurement ought to be something that is highly relevant to what you expect to change, but it's also important that the measurement be practical—that is, something that you can observe without great difficulty, and on a regular schedule. For example, even if I think I can tell when my son is frustrated by his homework just by looking at his facial expression, am I really going to stare at him while he does his homework each day? It's also important that the timing be consistent. You can't figure that you'll make observations "when I think about it" because that can easily lead to unconscious bias—you're more likely to "think about it" when the data are turning out as you hope they will.

Looking Forward

The three centuries since the Enlightenment have brought unprecedented prosperity, health, and well-being to the average person on this planet. These blessings are not distributed equally around the globe, to be sure, but in my view new technologies are, overall, a boon. Medicine, agriculture, travel, communications, entertainment—it's difficult to think of a field that has gone untouched by advances in technology, and these advances are fueled by new discoveries of science.

That includes education. More is known than ever before about how children learn, about effective pedagogies, about learning disabilities and how to address them. That knowledge has been put to good use in curricula, lesson plans, instructional software, and other products and strategies that I have collectively called "Changes."

Advances in science have been used effectively to improve education. That's not the problem. The problem is recognizing the effective uses from the ineffective uses, because the advances have not meant a parallel decline in claptrap and out-and-out fraud. The scientist appears not to have more effective evidence than the charlatan because the charlatan not only trumpets "research" but probably does so more loudly than the scientist, who is trained to be cautious. And so virtually any idea can be supported by "data" of *some* sort. Education theorist E. D. Hirsch put it this way:

> The enormous problem faced in basing policy on research is that it is almost impossible to make educational policy that is not based on research. Almost every educational practice that has ever been pursued has been supported with data by somebody. I don't know a single failed policy, ranging from the naturalistic teaching of reading, to the open classroom, to the teaching of abstract set-theory in third-grade math that hasn't been research-based. Experts have advocated almost every conceivable practice short of inflicting permanent bodily harm.[7]

What's the solution? In the very short term, I wrote this book in the hope that it would help some people sort out the difference between science and sham. The idea that parents and teachers still have to fend for themselves, with the feeble help this book might provide, seems crazy to me. They should have reliable information as to whether a specific educational Change is known to work, just as there is reliable information available about the efficacy of medicine, the nutritional value of food, the safety of play equipment, and so forth.

Looking ahead to the next few years, I hold out the hope that an institution will step in to sort out the trustworthy educational applications from the junk science. As I mentioned in Chapter Four, many other fields that are informed by basic science—medicine, for example—do not require that practitioners sort through the basic scientific literature on their own. These practitioners band together and create institutions that take on the job. Teachers have already created these institutions: teachers' unions.* What remains is for the unions to see it as part of their mission to improve teachers'

---

* Some institutions—for example, the National Council of Teachers of Mathematics—do publish standards, directives, and general statements about what they take to be scientifically valid. They do not, however, evaluate existing Changes, and the truth is that these institutions lack the clout of the unions.

practice by providing authoritative information about the scientific reliability of various Changes. It would be highly appropriate for the evaluators in such an effort to come primarily from among the nation's teachers. I've emphasized that this evaluation job requires deep, specialized knowledge. I am confident that among the better than three million teachers in the United States, there are a sufficient number with the scientific chops and the desire to take on the job.

In the longer term, I hope for another change. People need to better understand what it means to know something scientifically, and what an application based on this knowledge is likely to do in education.

I've mentioned that nonscientists often incorrectly view science as static—as comprising laws and principles that are eternal, unchanging. Coupled with the static view is the belief that scientific knowledge is always deterministic; in other words, if you really *know* something scientifically, you can predict exactly what will happen—for example, that when I add water to sodium in a flask filled with chlorine gas, I'll see bright yellow flame, and that will happen each and every time. But in fact some scientific knowledge is probabilistic, not deterministic. For example, smoking cigarettes increases the probability of developing lung cancer, but it does not guarantee it.

The common belief that scientific knowledge is deterministic and absolute leads, I believe, to the perception that scientific knowledge tells you what you *have* to do—in other words, that a scientific approach to education would be highly restrictive to teachers. Scientists would (people believe) deduce the single best method of instruction and then expect all teachers to use it.

This perception is reinforced by the frequent comparison of education to medicine. There are some similarities between the two fields. In each case, practitioners are trained in basic science as well as in the particulars of practice during their apprenticeship. There is also a parallel in the sense that those in their charge (patients and students) know much less than they do and are relatively dependent on them. But there are vital differences between medicine and education that ought to color how we think about the application of science in each case.

In medicine, there is a single goal, shared by every patient and every doctor: good health, the definition of which is uncontroversial. In education, there is much greater diversity of goals, of what we hope children will get out of their schooling. In addition, the deterministic view of science is more often appropriate in medicine: if a child has strep throat, the doctor will administer an antibiotic, and the child is very likely to get better. In education, a strategy for the teaching of place value may have scientific backing, but that doesn't mean that it will work for each and every child.

I think architecture serves as a better comparison field than medicine does. Architects, like teachers, usually have multiple goals that they try to satisfy simultaneously. Safety is nonnegotiable, but architects may also be thinking to a greater or lesser extent about energy efficiency, aesthetics, functionality, and so on. In the same way, some goals for teachers are nonnegotiable—teaching kids to read, for example—but after that, the goals are likely to vary with the context. In addition, architects make use of scientific knowledge, notably principles of physics, and materials science. But this knowledge is certainly not prescriptive. It doesn't tell the architect what a building must look like. Rather, it sets boundary conditions for construction to ensure that the building will not fall down, that the floors can support sufficient weight, and so on.

In the same way, basic scientific knowledge about how kids learn, about how they interact, about how they respond to discipline—this knowledge ought to be seen as a boundary condition for teachers and parents, meaning that this knowledge sets boundaries that, if crossed, increase the probability of bad outcomes. Within these broad boundaries, parents and teachers pursue their goals.

Take as an example a scientific principle that I have emphasized elsewhere: factual knowledge is required for critical thinking.[8] That is, you can't teach kids to think critically about history or about science unless they are learning (or already know) facts about history and science. Oddly, some people take this principle as a directive to sit kids down and teach them lists of facts via teacher talk and textbooks. It's nothing of the kind. For one thing, any cognitive psychologist will tell you that a list is about the worst way to learn a bunch of facts—that it is much better to connect them into something meaningful. But what's more important is that the principle—gotta learn facts—says nothing about *how* they ought to be learned. It could be through teacher talk, a book, a project, a collaborative wiki, and so forth. The principle sets a boundary: if you try to get kids to think critically about history without their knowing any historical facts, you'll fail.

My hope is that in the future, the way that teachers and parents think about the relationship of science and education will change. Science will be seen not as a field that discovers "the right thing to do" but rather as the field that identifies a few must-haves (given typical goals), leaving multiple ways to "have" them, and identifies helpful tools to reach the goals that we select for education.[9]

I believe that the practice of education would be improved if better use were made of scientific advances, and I've named three changes I think would facilitate that: individuals who are better able to discern good science from bad, institutions that are willing to help individuals in that job, and a change of mind-set for all in how science relates to educational practice. Whether from some combination of these changes or from others, I hope the future brings a more fruitful use of scientific knowledge. Our knowledge of how children learn and grow, though imperfect, is far from negligible. We have, too, the knowledge to harness it in service of our education goals and to evaluate our efforts as we go, so that we're confident we are moving in the right direction. The question is whether we will do so. Will we continue to cheer on education reforms that sound right to us, convinced that the "evidence" supporting them must be strong only because we like the conclusion? Or will we cast a cold eye on our own beliefs, confident that, as Bacon said, by beginning with doubt, we will end with certainty? If we can do so, our children will be the richer for it.

Endnotes

Introduction

1. Polya, G. (1973). *How to solve it: A new aspect of mathematical method* (2nd ed.). Princeton, NJ: Princeton University Press, p. 113. (Original work published 1945)
2. For example, Boselie, F. (1984). The aesthetic attractivity of the golden section. *Psychological Research, 45,* 367–375; Boselie, F. (1997). The golden section and the shape of objects. *Empirical Studies of the Arts, 15,* 131–141.
3. Macrosson, W.D.K., & Strachan, G. C. (1997). The preference amongst product designers for the golden section in line partitioning. *Empirical Studies of the Arts, 15,* 153–163; Macrosson, W.D.K., & Stewart, P. E. (1997). The inclination of artists to partition line sections in the Golden Ratio. *Perceptual and Motor Skills, 84,* 707–713.
4. Olariu, A. (1999). Golden section and the art of painting. Available online at http://arxiv.org/PS_cache/physics/pdf/9908/9908036v1.pdf.
5. Clement Falbo had the simple idea of measuring a bunch of seashells. They do indeed form logarithmic spirals, but the ratios he observed of real seashells were not close to 1.6; they were all in a range of 1.24–1.43. Falbo, C. (2005). The Golden Ratio—a contrary viewpoint. *College Mathematics Journal, 36,* 123–134. Available online at www.sonoma.edu/math/faculty/falbo/cmj 123-134.
6. For an overview of problems, see Markowsky, G. (1992). Misconceptions about the Golden Ratio. *College Mathematics Journal, 23,* 2–19. Available online http://laptops.maine.edu/GoldenRatio.pdf.
7. Pashler, H., McDaniel, M., Rohrer, D., & Bjork, R. (2008). Learning styles: Concepts and evidence. *Psychological Science in the Public Interest, 9,* 106–119; Riener, C., & Willingham, D. T. (2010). The myth of learning styles. *Change, 42,* 32–35.
8. In fact, it had been proposed much earlier, but did not catch on until the 1920s. Mathews, M. M. (1966). *Teaching to read, historically considered.* Chicago: University of Chicago Press.
9. Notable were the "Dick and Jane" book series by William Gray (longtime dean of the University of Chicago Graduate School of Education) and Zerna

Sharp, published by Scott Foresman from the 1930s through the 1970s. They were often parodied for their repetitiveness, with page after page of text like "Oh see! Oh see Jane! Jane can run! Run, Jane, run!"

10. Balmuth, M. (1982). *The roots of phonics: A historical introduction*. New York: McGraw-Hill.

11. Flesch, R. (1955). *Why Johnny can't read*. New York: Harper.

12. For example, Bienvenu, H. J., & Martyn, K. A. (1956). Why can't Rudy read? *National Education Association Journal, 44*, 168–175; Betts, E. A. (1955). Teaching Johnny to read. *Saturday Review, 38*(31), 26–27; and Harris, A. J. (1956). Review of *Why Johnny Can't Read, Teachers College Record, 57*, 263. Flesch specifically singled out linguists and psychologists as worthy researchers of reading; education researchers were, he said, the problem. The review in the journal of the Linguistic Society of America was mostly favorable: Hall, R. A., Jr. (1956). Review of *Why Johnny Can't Read. Language, 32*, 310–313; but the review in *American Psychologist* less so: Carroll, J. B. (1956). The case of Dr. Flesch. *American Psychologist, 11*, 158–163.

13. Chall, J. S. (1967). *Learning to read: The great debate*. New York: McGraw-Hill.

14. It's probably more accurate to say it resurfaced with prominence in the 1980s. It never really disappeared. Prominent publications included Goodman, K. (1986). *What's whole in whole language*. Portsmouth, NH: Heinemann Educational Books; Smith, F. (1985). *Reading without nonsense*. New York: Teachers College Press.

15. National Institute of Child Health and Human Development. (2000). *Report of the National Reading Panel: Teaching children to read: An evidence-based assessment of the scientific literature on reading and its implications for reading instruction*. NIH publication no. 00-4754. Washington, DC: Government Printing Office.

16. Boulet, S. L., Boyle, C. A., & Schieve, L. A. (2009). Health care use and health and functional impact of developmental disabilities among US children, 1997–2005. *Archives of Pediatric & Adolescent Medicine, 163*, 19–26.

17. Bishop, D.V.M., Whitehouse, A.J.O., Watt, H. J., & Line, E. A. (2008). Autism and diagnostic substitution: Evidence from a study of adults with a history of developmental language disorder. *Developmental Medicine & Child Neurology, 50*, 341–345.

18. Centers for Disease Control. (2006). Prevalence of autism spectrum disorders—Autism and Developmental Disabilities Monitoring Network, United States, 2006. Available online at http://www.cdc.gov/mmwr/preview/mmwrhtml/ss5810a1.htm.

19. Shute, N. (2010, October). Desperate for an autism cure. *Scientific American*, pp. 80–85.

20. Vargas, D. L., Nascimbene, C., Krishnan, C., Zimmerman, A. W., & Pardo, C. A. (2005). Neuroglial activation and neuroinflammation in the brain of patients with autism. *Annals of Neurology, 57*, 67–81.

21. Neuroimmunopathology Laboratory. (n.d.). FAQs: The meaning of neuroinflammatory findings in autism. Available online at http://www.neuro.jhmi.edu/neuroimmunopath/autism_faqs.htm.

22. Search conducted October 14, 2010.

23. As of November 2011, the National Institutes of Health does not recommend the use of secretin to treat ASD. National Institute of Child Health and Human Development. (2011, November). Autism spectrum disorders (ASDs). Available online at http://www.nichd.nih.gov/health/topics/asd.cfm.

24. National Center for Education Statistics, U.S. Department of Education. (2010, November). Table 90: Number of public school districts and public and private elementary and secondary schools: Selected years, 1869–70 through 2008–09. *Digest of Education Statistics.* Available online at http://nces .ed.gov/programs/digest/d10/tables/dt10_090.asp.

Chapter One

1. Langer, E., Blank, A., & Chanowitz, B. (1978). The mindlessness of ostensibly thoughtful action: The role of "placebic" information in interpersonal interaction. *Journal of Personality and Social Psychology, 36,* 635–642.

2. James, W. (1890). *Psychology* (Vol. 1). New York: Henry Holt, p. 115.

3. Chartrand, T. L., Maddux, W. W., & Lakin, J. L. (2005). Beyond the perception-behavior link: The ubiquitous utility and motivational moderators of nonconscious mimicry. In R. Hassin, J. Uleman, & J. A. Bargh (Eds.), *The new unconscious* (pp. 334–361). New York: Oxford University Press.

4. 1 Corinthians 9: 2–22 (New International Version). Available online at http://www.biblegateway.com/passage/?search=1+Corinthians+9%3A19–23&version=NIV.

5. Johnston, L. (2002). Behavioral mimicry and stigmatization. *Social Cognition, 20,* 18–35.

6. There are two particularly prominent psychological models of how persuasion happens. Both have a conscious and an unconscious route. Petty, R. E., & Cacioppo, J. T. (1981). *Attitudes and persuasion: Classic and contemporary approaches.* Dubuque, IA: Brown; and Chaiken, S. (1987). The heuristic model of persuasion. In M. P. Zanna, J. M. Olson, & C. P. Herman (Eds.), *Social influence: The Ontario symposium* (Vol. 5, pp. 3–39). Hillsdale, NJ: Erlbaum.

7. Packard, V. (1957). *The hidden persuaders.* New York: McKay.

8. One recent example is Bullock, A. (2004). *The secret sales pitch: An overview of subliminal advertising.* San Jose, CA: Norwich.

9. Zajonc, R. B. (1968). Attitudinal effects of mere exposure. *Journal of Personality and Social Psychology Monograph Supplement, 9,* 1–27.

10. For example, Begg, I., Armour, V., & Kerr, T. (1985). On believing what we remember. *Canadian Journal of Behavioral Science, 17,* 199–214.

11. Bacon, F. T. (1979). Credibility of repeated statements: Memory for trivia. *Journal of Experimental Psychology: Human Learning and Memory, 5,* 2241–2252.

12. Begg, I. M., Anas, A., & Farinacci, S. (1992). Dissociation of processes in belief: Source recollection, statement familiarity, and the illusion of truth. *Journal of Experimental Psychology: General, 121,* 446–458.

13. For example, Petroshius, S. M., & Crocker, K. E. (1989). An empirical analysis of spokesperson characteristics on advertisement and product evaluations. *Journal of the Academy of Marketing Science, 17,* 217–225.

14. This phenomenon is observed not only in advertisements but in the media more generally. Perloff, R. M. The third-person effect: A critical review and synthesis. *Media Psychology, 1,* 353–378.

15. Stuart, E. W., Shimp, T. A., & Engle, R. W. (1987). Classical conditioning of consumer attitudes: Four experiments in an advertising context. *Journal of Consumer Research, 14,* 334–349.

16. Pendergast, M. (1993). *For God, country, and Coca-Cola.* New York: Basic Books.

17. Kelman, H. C. (1958). Compliance, identification, and internalization: Three processes of attitude change. *Journal of Conflict Resolution, 2,* 51–60.

18. DeBono, K. G., & Harnish, R. J. (1988). Source expertise, source attractiveness, and the processing of persuasive information: A functional approach. *Journal of Personality and Social Psychology, 55,* 541–546.

19. Curly Neal of the Three Stooges, from *Calling All Curs* (1938).

20. Yalch, R. F., & Elmore-Yalch, R. (1984). The effect of numbers on the route to persuasion. *Journal of Consumer Research, 11,* 522–527.

21. Abelson, R. P., Kinder, D. R., Peters, M. D., & Fiske, S. T. (1982). Affective and semantic components in political person perception. *Journal of Personality and Social Psychology, 84,* 18–28.

22. Bowman, N. A., & Bastedo, M. N. (2009). Getting on the front page: Organizational reputation, status signals, and the impact of the *U.S. News and World Report* on student decisions. *Research in Higher Education, 50,* 415–436. The effect may not hold for public institutions, however: Hemelt, S. W., & Marcotte, D. E. (2011). The impact of tuition increases on enrollment at public colleges and universities. *Educational Evaluation and Policy Analysis, 33,* 435–457.

23. Wason, P. C. (1960). On the failure to eliminate hypotheses in a conceptual task. *Quarterly Journal of Experimental Psychology, 12,* 129–140.

24. Snyder, M., & Swann, W. B., Jr. (1978). Hypothesis testing in social interaction. *Journal of Personality and Social Psychology, 36,* 1202–1212.

25. Elstein, A. S., & Schwarz, A. (2002). Clinical problem solving and diagnostic decision making: Selective review of the cognitive literature. *British Medical Journal, 324,* 729–732.

26. Krems, J. F., & Zierer, C. (1994). Are experts immune to cognitive bias? Dependence of "confirmation bias" on specialist knowledge. *Zeitschrift für Experimentelle und Angewandte Psychologie, 41,* 98–115.

27. Kelly, H. H. (1950). The warm-cold variable in first impressions of persons. *Journal of Personality, 18,* 431–440.

28. Snyder, M., & Cantor, N. (1979). Testing hypotheses about other people: The use of historical knowledge. *Journal of Experimental Social Psychology, 15,* 330–342.

29. Westen, D., Blagov, P. S., Harenski, K., Kilts, C., & Hamann, S. (2006). Neural bases of motivated reasoning: An fMRI study of emotional constraints on partisan political judgment in the 2004 U.S. presidential election. *Journal of Cognitive Neuroscience, 18,* 1947–1958.

30. Munro, G. D., Leary, S. P., & Lasane, T. P. (2004). Between a rock and a hard place: Biased assimilation of scientific information in the face of commitment. *North American Journal of Psychology, 6,* 431–444.

31. Taber, C. S., & Lodge, M. (2006). Motivated skepticism in the evaluation of political beliefs. *American Journal of Political Science, 50,* 755–769.

32. Cacioppo, J. T., & Petty, R. E. (1979). Effects of message repetition and position on cognitive responses, recall, and persuasion. *Journal of Personality and Social Psychology, 37,* 2181–2199.

33. Hafer, C. L., & Bègue, L. (2005). Experimental research on just-world theory: Problems, developments, and future challenges. *Psychological Bulletin, 131,* 128–167.

34. Feinberg, M., & Willer, R. (2011). Apocalypse soon? Dire messages reduce belief in global warming by contradicting just-world beliefs. *Psychological Science, 22,* 34–38.

35. For a different perspective on the adaptiveness of reasoning, see Mercier, H., & Sperber, D. (2011). Why do humans reason? Arguments for an argumentative theory. *Behavioral and Brain Sciences, 34,* 57–74.

36. Quine, W. V., & Ullian, J. S. (1970). *The web of belief.* New York: Random House.

37. Tolstoy, L. (1894). *The kingdom of God is within you* (C. Garnett, Trans.). New York: Cassell, p. 49. Available online at http://books.google.com/books?id=F00EAAAAYAAJ.

38. Cialdini, R. B., & Goldstein, N. J. (2004). Social influence: Compliance and conformity. *Annual Review of Psychology, 55,* 591–621.

39. Garrett, R. K., Nisbet, E. C., & Lynch, E. (2011). Undermining the corrective effects of media-based political fact checking. Paper presented at the annual conference of the National Communication Association, New Orleans, LA.

40. Haidt, J. (2001). The emotional dog and its rational tail: A social intuitionist approach to moral judgment. *Psychological Review, 108,* 814–834.

Chapter Two

1. Bacon, F. (2000). *The new organon* (Book 1, Aphorism 70; L. Jardine & M. Silverthorne, Eds.). Cambridge: Cambridge University Press. (Original work published 1620)

2. Stone, M.W.F. (2002). Aristotelianism and Scholasticism in early modern philosophy. In S. Nadler (Ed.), *A companion to early modern philosophy* (pp. 7–24). Malden, MA: Blackwell.

3. Wood, A. (1796). *The history and antiquities of the University of Oxford* (Book 1; J. Gutch, Trans.). Oxford: Oxford University Press, p. 226. Available online

at http://books.google.com/books?id=0gYVAAAAQAAJ&pg=PA226&lpg =PA226&dq#v=onepage&q&f=false.

4. Locke, J. (1899). An essay concerning human understanding (Book 4, chap. 17). Available online at http://etext.lib.virginia.edu/etcbin/toccer-new2?id=LocHuma.xml&images=images/modeng&data=/texts/english /modeng/parsed&tag=public&part=72&division=div2. (Original work published 1690)

5. Yellowstone Net. Geysers of Yellowstone—Old Faithful. http://www .yellowstone.net/geysers/geyser11.htm.

6. Locke, J. (1899). An essay concerning human understanding (Book 4, chap. 16). Available online at http://etext.lib.virginia.edu/etcbin/toccer-new2?id=LocHuma.xml&images=images/modeng&data=/texts/english /modeng/parsed&tag=public&part=71&division=div2. (Original work published 1690)

7. Many others have been called "the father of modern science," including Thales of Miletus (c. 624 BC–c. 546 BC), Democritus (c. 460 BC–c. 370 BC), ibn al-Haytham (965–1040), Roger Bacon (1214–1294), Leonardo da Vinci (1452–1519), and Galileo (1564–1642).

8. Gay, P. (1969). *The Enlightenment: An interpretation. From science to freedom.* New York: Norton, p. 137.

9. Gay, P. (1966). *Age of enlightenment.* New York: Time-Life.

10. Credited as *Astronomy,* a hand-colored engraving after a mezzotint by Richard Houston, c. 1750, Museum of the History of Science, Oxford.

11. Fairchild, H. N. (1931). *The Romantic quest.* New York: Columbia University Press.

12. Wordsworth, W. (1802). *Lyrical ballads.* London: Longman, pp. x–xi.

13. Trout, J. D. (2008). Seduction without cause: Uncovering explanatory neurophilia. *Trends in Cognitive Science, 12,* 281–282.

14. Weisberg, D. S., Keil, F. C., Goodstein, J., Rawson, E., & Gray, J. R. (2008). The seductive allure of neuroscientific explanations. *Journal of Cognitive Neuroscience, 20,* 470–477.

15. McCabe, D. P., & Castel, A. D. (2008). Seeing is believing: The effect of brain image on judgments of scientific reasoning. *Cognition, 107,* 343–352.

16. Ward, L. A., Cain, O. L, Mullally, R. A., Holliday, K. S., Wernahm, A.G.H., Baillie, P. D., et al. (2009). Health beliefs about bottled water: A qualitative study. *BMC Public Health, 9,* 196.

17. Newall, C. A., Anderson L. A., & Phillipson, J. D. (1996). *Herbal medicines. A guide for health-care professionals.* London: Pharmaceutical Press.

18. Klepser, T. B., Doucette, W. R., Horton, M. R., Buys, L. M., Ernst, M. E., Ford, J. K., et al. (2000). Assessment of patients' perceptions and beliefs regarding herbal therapies. *Pharmacotherapy, 20,* 83–87.

19. Neill, A. S. (1960) *Summerhill: A radical approach to child rearing.* New York: Hart; Holt, J. (1981). *Teach your own: A hopeful path for education.* New York: Random House.

Chapter Three

1. Feynman chaser—The key to science. [Video]. YouTube. http://www .youtube.com/watch?v=b240PGCMwV0.

2. Prasad, J. (1950). A comparative study of rumours and reports in earthquakes. *British Journal of Psychology, General, 41,* 129–144.

3. Festinger, L. (1957). *A theory of cognitive dissonance.* Evanston, IL: Row, Peterson.

4. Festinger, L., & Carlsmith, J. M. (1959). Cognitive consequences of forced compliance. *Journal of Abnormal and Social Psychology, 58,* 203–210.

5. Aronson, E. (1968). Dissonance theory: Progress and problems. In R. P. Abelson, E. Aronson, W. J. McGuire, T. M. Newcomb, M. U. Rosenberg, & P. H. Tannenbaum (Eds.), *Theories of cognitive consistency: A sourcebook* (pp. 5–28). Chicago: Rand McNally.

6. Carlsmith, J. M., Collins, B. E., & Helmreich, R. L. (1966). Studies in forced compliance: I. The effect of pressure for compliance on attitude change produced by face-to-face role playing and anonymous essay writing. *Journal of Personality and Social Psychology, 4,* 1–13.

7. Sagan, C. (1987). Keynote address to the Committee for the Scientific Investigation of Claims of the Paranormal (today known as the Committee for Skeptical Inquiry).

8. Hawking, S. (1988). *A brief history of time.* New York: Bantam.

9. Levy, F., & Murnane, R. J. (2004). *The new division of labor: How computers are creating the next job market.* Princeton, NJ: Princeton University Press.

10. Plucker, J. A., & Makel, M. C. (2010). Assessment of creativity. In R. J. Sternberg & J. C. Kaufman (Eds.), *The Cambridge handbook of creativity* (pp. 48–77). Cambridge: Cambridge University Press.

11. Cannon-Bowers, J. A., & Bowers, C. (2011). Team development and functioning. In S. Zednick (Ed.), *APA handbook of industrial and organizational psychology: Vol. 1. Building and developing the organization* (pp. 597–660). Washington, DC: American Psychological Association.

12. Popper, K. (1959) *The logic of scientific discovery.* New York: Basic Books.

13. I cannot find a source for this quotation. One author suggests that it is a paraphrase of things Einstein said in "Induction and Deduction," a paper published in 1919. Calaprice, A. (2011). *The ultimate quotable Einstein.* Princeton, NJ: Princeton University Press, p. 476.

14. Grosser, M. (1962). *The discovery of Neptune.* Cambridge, MA: Harvard University Press.

15. For example, Hoxby, C. M., Murarka, S., & Kang, J. (2009, September). How New York City's charter schools affect achievement. Cambridge, MA: New York City Charter Schools Evaluation Project. Available online at http:// www.vanderbilt.edu/schoolchoice/documents/092209_newsitem.pdf; Sass, T. (2006). Charter schools and student achievement in Florida. *Education Finance and Policy, 1,* 91–122.

16. For example, Bettinger, E. P. (2005). The effect of charter schools on charter students and public schools. *Economics of Education Review, 24,* 133–147; Bifulco, R., & Ladd, H. F. (2006). The impacts of charter schools on student achievement: Evidence from North Carolina. *Education Finance and Policy, 1,* 50–90; and Zimmer, R., Gill, B., Booker, K., Lavertu, S., & Witte, J. (2012). Examining charter student achievement effects across seven states. *Economics of Education Review, 31,* 213–224.

17. For example, Feyerabend, P. (1978). *Science in a free society.* London: New Left Books.

18. Ravitch, D. (2000). *Left back: A century of battles over school reform.* New York: Touchstone.

19. Ravitch, D. (2009). 21st century skills: An old familiar song. Available online at http://www.commoncore.org/_docs/diane.pdf.

20. Wilford, J. N. (1989, April 24). Fusion furor: Science's human face. *New York Times.* Available online at http://select.nytimes.com/gst/abstract.html?res=FA0716FE38580C778EDDAD0894D1484D81&pagewanted=2.

21. Browne, M. W. (1989, May 3). Physicists debunk claim of a new kind of fusion. *New York Times.* Available online at http://partners.nytimes.com/library/national/science/050399sci-cold-fusion.html.

22. Ibid.

23. For example, Kaptchuk, T. J. (2003). Effect of interpretive bias on research evidence. *British Medical Journal, 326,* 1453–1455; Mynatt, C. R., Doherty, M. E., & Tweney, R. D. (1977). Confirmation bias in a simulated research environment: An experimental study of scientific inference. *Quarterly Journal of Experimental Psychology, 29,* 85–95.

24. Feynman, R. P. (1985). *Surely you're joking, Mr. Feynman!* New York: Norton, p. 343.

25. Society of Clinical Psychology. (n.d.). Psychological problems and behavioral disorders. Available online at http://www.psychology.sunysb.edu/eklonsky-/division12/disorders.html.

26. Source: PubMed.gov, accessed June 10, 2011.

Chapter Four

1. Simon, H. A. (1996). *The sciences of the artificial* (3rd ed.). Cambridge, MA: MIT Press, p. 3.

2. Remarks by the president at the annual meeting of the National Academy of Sciences. (2009, April 27). Available online at http://www.whitehouse.gov/the-press-office/remarks-president-national-academy-sciences-annual-meeting.

3. National Science Board. (2010). Science and technology: Public attitudes and understanding. In *Science and engineering indicators 2010* (NSB 10-01). Arlington, VA: National Science Foundation. Available online at http://www.nsf.gov/statistics/seind10/c7/c7h.htm.

4. Ibid.

5. Bush, V. (1945, July 25). *Science: The endless frontier.* Washington, DC: U.S. Government Printing Office. Available online at http://www.nsf.gov/od /lpa/nsf50/vbush1945.htm. Roosevelt died before the report was completed. It was delivered to President Truman.

6. Solow, R. M. (1957). Technical change and the aggregate production function. *Review of Economics and Statistics, 39,* 312–320. For a more recent review, see Committee on Prospering in the Global Economy of the 21st Century. (2007). *Rising above the gathering storm: Energizing and employing America for a brighter economic future.* Washington, DC: National Academies Press. Available online at http://www.nap.edu/catalog.php?record_id=11463. There is also evidence that when the student population of a country is well trained in science, there is a substantial economic benefit; scientific knowledge makes for a high-quality labor force. See Hanushek, E. A., & Woessmann, L. (2010). The high cost of low educational performance: The long-run impact of improving PISA outcomes. Paris: OECD.

7. My discussion is based on Simon, 1996. Simon in fact uses the terms "Natural science" and "Artificial science," rather than basic and applied research, respectively. For the sake of clarity, I'll continue to use the latter set of terms.

8. Chua, A. (2011, January 8). Why Chinese mothers are superior. *Wall Street Journal.* Available online at http://online.wsj.com/article/SB1000142405274 8704111504576059713528698754.html.

9. Gardner, H. E. (1983). *Frames of mind.* New York: Basic Books. Prominent psychological theories arguing for multiple types of ability have been proposed by Louis Thurstone (1930s–1940s), Cyril Burt (1930s–1940s), Raymond Cattell (1940s–1950s), Joy Paul Guilford (1950s–1960s), and John Carroll (1990s). I discuss the differences between Gardner's theory and these others in my book *Why Don't Students Like School?*

10. The exact mechanisms by which even simple pointing movements are computed is a matter of some debate. See, for example, Meyer, D. E., Smith, J. E., & Wright, C. E. (1982). Models for the speed and accuracy of aimed movements. *Psychological Review, 89,* 449–482.

11. Society for Human Resource Management. (2010). *Workplace diversity practices: How has diversity and inclusion changed over time?* Available online at http://www.shrm .org/Research/SurveyFindings/Articles/Pages/WorkplaceDiversityPractices .aspx.

12. Those features have, indeed, been proposed as one characterization of an effective classroom. Pianta, R. C., La Paro, K. M., & Hamre, B. K. (2008). *Classroom assessment scoring system.* Baltimore: Brooks.

13. Bruner, J. (1960). *The process of education.* Cambridge, MA: Harvard University Press.

14. Schmidt, W., Wang, H. C., & McKnight, C. C. (2005). Curriculum coherence: An examination of U.S. mathematics and science content standards from an international perspective. *Journal of Curriculum Studies, 37,* 525–559.

15. Core Knowledge Foundation. (2010). *The core knowledge sequence: Content and skill guidelines for kindergarten–grade 8.* Charlottesville, VA: Core Knowledge

Foundation. Available online at http://www.coreknowledge.org/mimik /mimik_uploads/documents/480/CKFSequence_Rev.pdf.

16. For example, Van Dijk, T., & Kintsch, W. (1983). *Strategies of discourse comprehension.* New York: Academic Press.

17. For more on this, see Willingham, D. T. (2010, September 20). Left-right brain theory is bunk. Available online at http://voices.washingtonpost .com/answer-sheet/daniel-willingham/willingham-the-leftright-brain.html. See also this chapter by Mike Gazzaniga (one of the pioneers of this area of research) written *twenty-five years ago* in which he tries to calm down the hype: Gazzaniga, M. S. (1985). Left-brain, right-brain mania: A debunking. In *The social brain* (pp. 47–59). New York: Basic Books.

Chapter Five

1. From Blake, W. (1904). *Jerusalem* (E.R.D. MaClagan & A.G.B. Russell, Eds.). London: Bullen. Available online at http://books.google.com/books?id=kr M8AAAAYAAJ&printsec=frontcover&dq=william+blakepercent27s+jerusal em&hl=en&ei=GKTBTfzxFeX50gHP74m3Cg&sa=X&oi=book_result&ct =result&resnum=1&ved=0CDsQ6AEwAA#v=onepage&q&f=false.

2. Estimates vary, but the figures I've offered are in the ballpark. For example: U.S. soldiers experience increased rates of depression, PTSD on third, fourth tours in Iraq, study finds. (2008, March 10). *Medical News Today.* http:// www.medicalnewstoday.com/articles/99981.php.

3. Friedman, T. (2009, April 22). Swimming without a suit. *New York Times.* http://www.nytimes.com/2009/04/22/opinion/22friedman.html.

4. Coleridge, S. T. (1830). *On the constitution of the church and state.* London: Hurst, Chance & Co. Available online at http://books.google.com /books?id=_FTM_6q6G3gC&pg=PP15&dq=#v=onepage&q&f=false.

5. Gilovich, T. (1981). Seeing the past in the present: The effect of associations to familiar events on judgments and decisions. *Journal of Personality and Social Psychology, 40,* 797–808.

6. For example, Hamre, B. K., & Pianta, R. C. (2001). Early teacher-child relationships and the trajectory of children's school outcomes through eighth grade. *Child Development, 72,* 625–638.

7. Levin, I. P., & Gaeth, G. J. (1988). Framing of attribute information before and after consuming the product. *Journal of Consumer Research, 15,* 374–378.

8. For example, Davis, M. A., & Bobko, P. (1986). Contextual effects on escalation processes in public sector decision making. *Organizational Behavior and Human Decision Processes, 37,* 121–138; Dunegan, K. J. (1995). Image theory: Testing the role of image compatibility in progress decisions. *Organizational Behavior and Human Decision Processes, 62,* 79–86.

9. National Center for Education Statistics, U.S. Department of Education. (2010). *The Nation's Report Card: Civics 2010.* Available online at http://nces .ed.gov/nationsreportcard/pdf/main2010/2011466.pdf.

10. Barkley, R. A. (1998). *Attention-deficit hyperactivity disorder* (2nd ed.). New York: Guilford Press.

11. Tversky, A., & Kahneman, D. (1981). The framing of decisions and the psychology of choice. *Science, 211,* 453–458.

12. Gillen, J., Staarman, J. K., Littleton, K., Mercer, N., & Twiner, A. (2007). A "learning revolution"? Investigating pedagogic practice around interactive whiteboards in British primary classrooms. *Learning, Media, and Technology, 32,* 243–256.

13. Elements of this technique go back quite far. One of the more influential presentations is Allen, R. V., & Allen, C. (1969). *Language experiences in early childhood.* Chicago: Encyclopedia Britannica Educational Corporation.

14. McDaniel, M. A. (2007). Transfer: Rediscovering a central concept. In H. L. Roediger, Y. Dudai, & S. M. Fitzpatrick (Eds.), *Science of memory: Concepts* (pp. 267–270). Oxford: Oxford University Press.

15. For example, Ackerman, P. L., Beier, M. E., & Boyle, M. O. (2005). Working memory and intelligence: The same or different constructs? *Psychological Bulletin, 131,* 30–60.

16. For example, Ericsson, K. A., Chase, W. G., & Faloon, S. (1980). Acquisition of a memory skill. *Science, 208,* 1181–1182.

17. Klingberg, T. (2010). Training and plasticity of working memory. *Trends in Cognitive Sciences, 14,* 317–324.

18. For more on this, see Willingham, D. T. (2007, Summer). Critical thinking: Why is it so hard to teach? *American Educator,* pp. 8–19.

Chapter Six

1. Lazarus, D. (2002, March 10). If nothing else, man with past is persistent. *San Francisco Chronicle.* Available online at http://www.sfgate.com/cgi-bin/article.cgi?f=/c/a/2002/03/10/BU139492.DTL.

2. Dohrmann, B. J. (2005). *Whole brain learning.* Available online at http://www.superteaching.org/STMIND.htm.

3. Hannah, G. (2002, April 28). Bernhard Dohrmann. *Huntsville (AL) Times,* p. A9.

4. This figure is according to the Super Teaching purchase order: http://superteaching.org/CEO_ST_purchase_order_v4.pdf.

5. Mclaughlin, B. (2008, October 7). Learning at the speed of thought. *Huntsville (AL) Times,* p. 1A.

6. Ramhold, J. (2010, April 14). University dissolves "Super Teaching" partnership. *The Exponent.* http://exponent.uah.edu/?p=2538 (accessed July 17, 2011; this Web page is no longer available).

7. This blog entry is no longer available from the Flashpoint blog Web site (http://www.flashpointblog.com).

8. Shavers, A. (2009, October 21). Super Teaching: Learning at the speed of con. The Exponent. http://exponent.uah.edu/?p=1570 (accessed July 17, 2011; this Web page is no longer available).

9. Kolowich, S. (2010, May 27). University had short attention span for "Super Teaching." *USA Today.* http://www.usatoday.com/news/education/2010-05-27-IHE-Super-Teaching-U-Alabama27_ST_N.htm.

10. Hannah, G., & Lewin, G. S. (2002, April 28). "Can't fail" international success system based here has its skeptics. *Huntsville (AL) Times,* p. A1.

11. Kolowich, 2010.

12. Hendel, J. (2011, June 28). Can a dog still earn an MBA? *Fortune.* Available online at http://management.fortune.cnn.com/2011/06/28/can-a-dog-still-earn-an-mba/?section=magazines_fortune.

13. Lagemann, E. C. (2000). *An elusive science: The troubling history of education research.* Chicago: University of Chicago Press, p. 232.

14. Levine, A. (2007). *Educating researchers.* Educating Schools Project. Available online at http://edschools.org/EducatingResearchers/index.htm.

15. Gardner (1999) sought to correct this mistaken application of his theory (and others) in his book *Intelligence reframed: Multiple intelligences for the 21st century.* New York: Basic Books.

16. Schlessinger, L. C. (1974). Effects of insulin on 3-O-methylglucose transport in isolated rat adipocytes. *ProQuest Dissertations & Theses,* http://proquest.umi.com/pqdweb?did=761334421&sid=1&Fmt=1&clientId=8772&RQT=309&VName=PQD.

17. Dr. Laura. (n.d.). http://www.drlaura.com/g/About-Dr.-Laura/273.html.

18. Hemsley-Brown, J., & Sharp, C. (2003). The use of research to improve professional practice: A systematic review of the literature. *Oxford Review of Education, 29,* 449–470.

19. Shkedi, A. (1998). Teachers' attitudes towards research: A challenge for qualitative researchers. *Qualitative Studies in Education, 11,* 559–577.

20. Walton, D. (1997). *Appeal to expert opinion: Arguments from authority.* University Park: Pennsylvania University Press.

21. National Mathematics Advisory Panel. (2008). *Foundations for success: The final report of the National Mathematics Advisory Panel.* Washington, DC: U.S. Department of Education.

22. Kelly, A. E. (Ed.). (2008). Reflections on the US National Mathematics Advisory Panel Report [Special issue]. *Educational Researcher, 37*(9).

23. For example, Confrey, J. (2006). Comparing and contrasting the National Research Council Report *On Evaluating Curricular Effectiveness* with the What Works Clearinghouse Approach. *Educational Evaluation and Policy Analysis, 28,* 195–213.

Chapter Seven

1. Merton, R. K. (1973). *The sociology of science.* Chicago: University of Chicago Press.

2. All versions of the Brain Gym Web site were downloaded from the Wayback Machine (http://www.archive.org/web/web.php), which archives old versions of Web sites.

3. Chaker, A. M. (2005, April 5). Attention deficit gets new approach—as concerns rise on drugs used to treat the disorder, some try exercise regimen. *Wall Street Journal,* p. D4.

4. Hughes, J. (2002, September 7). Jane Hughes discovers how "Brain Gym" can help. *The Times Magazine,* pp. 64–65; Carlyle, R. (2002, February 7). Exercise your child's intelligence. *Daily Express,* p. 51.

5. Goldacre, B. (2006, March 18). Brain Gym exercises do pupils no favours. *Guardian,* p. 13.

6. Reported in Randerson, J. (2008 April 3). Experts dismiss educational claims of Brain Gym programme. *Guardian.* See also O'Sullivan, S. (2008, April 6). Brain Gym feels the heat of scientists. *Sunday Times,* p. 4.

7. Brain Gym claims to be withdrawn. (2008, April 5). *The Times of London,* p. 2.

8. Clark, L. (2009, December 19). Brain Gym for pupils pointless, admits Balls. *Daily Mail.* http://www.dailymail.co.uk/news/article-1237042/Brain-gym-pupils-pointless-admits-Balls.html.

9. Retrieved from http://braingym.org/ on August 9, 2011. The 2010 revision of the book *Brain Gym: Teacher's Edition* (Ventura, CA: Edu-Kinesthetics) still contains a lot of scientific inaccuracies about the mind.

10. Amethyst Initiative. (n.d.). Welcome to the Amethyst Initiative. http://www.amethystinitiative.org/.

11. Carpenter, C., & Dobkin, C. (2011). The minimum legal drinking age and public health. *Journal of Economic Perspectives, 25,* 133–156.

12. Watson offered his account of this competition in a controversial book: Watson, J. D. (1968). *The double helix: A personal account of the discovery of the structure of DNA.* New York: Atheneum.

13. There have been some studies that directly tested the efficacy of the Dore Program, and the results were published in professional journals. Reynolds, D., Nicolson, R. I., & Hambly, H. (2003). Evaluation of an exercised-based treatment for children with reading difficulties. *Dyslexia, 9,* 48–71; Reynolds, D., & Nicolson, R. I. (2007). Follow-up of an exercise-based treatment for children with reading difficulties. *Dyslexia, 13,* 78–96. These studies were later the subject of controversy, as a number of scientists stepped forward to question the research design. Bishop, D.V.M. (2008). Criteria for evaluating behavioural interventions for neurobehavioral disorders. *Journal of Pediatrics and Child Health, 44,* 520–521; McArthur, G. (2007). Test-retest effects in treatment studies of reading disability: The devil is in the detail. *Dyslexia, 13,* 240–252.

14. Rukeyser, M. (1968). *The speed of darkness.* New York: Random House.

15. Willingham, D. T. (2004, Summer). The privileged status of story. *American Educator,* pp. 43–45, 51–53.

16. Ayres, B. D., Jr. (1997, March 29). "Families learning of 39 cultists who died willingly." *New York Times.* Available online at http://www.nytimes.com/1997/03/29/us/families-learning-of-39-cultists-who-died-willingly.html.

17. "Witter: Elle Macpherson" (2010, May 30). *The Times of London.* http://women.timesonline.co.uk/tol/life_and_style/women/fashion/article7139977.ece?token=null&offset=12&page=2.

18. Zubieta, J.-K., Yau, W.-Y., Socct, D. J., & Stohler, C. S. (2006). Belief or need? Accounting for individual variations in the neurochemistry of the placebo effect. *Brain, Behavior, and Immunity, 20,* 15–26.

19. Sandler, A. D., & Bodfish, J. W. (2008). Open-label use of placebos in the treatment of ADHD: A pilot study. *Child: Care, Health and Development, 34,* 104–110.

20. Sandler, A. (2005). Placebo effects in developmental disabilities: Implications for research and practice. *Mental Retardation and Developmental Disabilities Research Reviews, 11,* 164–170.

21. Sifft, J. M., & Khalsa, G.C.K. (1991). Effect of educational kinesiology upon simple response times and choice response times. *Perceptual and Motor Skills, 73,* 1011–1015.

22. Moore, H., & Hibbert, F. (2005). Mind boggling! Considering the possibilities of Brain Gym in learning to play an instrument. *British Journal of Music Education, 22,* 249–267.

Chapter Eight

1. Hegel, G.W.F. (1896). *Elements of the philosophy of right* (S. W. Dyde, Trans.). London: George Bell & Sons. (Original work published 1820)

2. Kavale, K., & Mattson, P. D. (1983). "One jumped off the balance beam": Meta-analysis of perceptual-motor training. *Journal of Learning Disabilities, 16,* 165–173.

3. Hattie, J. (2009). *Visible learning.* London: Routledge.

4. This checklist came from http://freechecklists.net, a site that features checklists for specific aircraft, submitted by pilots.

5. Reinberg, S. (2009, January 14). Surgeon's checklist saves lives. *U.S. News and World Report.* Available online at http://health.usnews.com /health-news/managing-your-healthcare/treatment/articles/2009/01/14 /surgeons-checklist-saves-lives.

6. Haynes, A. B., Weiser, T. G., Berry, W. R., Lipsitz, S. R., Breizat, A.-H. S., Dellinger, E. P., et al. (2009). A surgical safety checklist to reduce morbidity and mortality in a global population. *New England Journal of Medicine, 360,* 491–499.

7. Hirsch, E. D., Jr. (1997, April 10). Address to the California State Board of Education. Available online at http://www.coreknowledge.org/mimik /mimik_uploads/documents/5/AddCASTB.pdf.

8. Willingham, D. T. (2009). *Why don't students like school?* San Francisco: Jossey-Bass.

9. For example, Willingham, D. T., & Daniel, D. (2012). Beyond differentiation: Teaching to what learners have in common. *Educational Leadership, 69,* 16–21.

Name Index

A

Aarts, H., 33
Abelson, R. P., 45
Ackerman, P. L., 161
Adank, P., 33
Alba, J., 6–7
Allen, C., 157
Allen, R. V., 157
Amethyst Initiative, 187
Anas, A., 36
Anderson, L. A., 74
Aquinas, T., 61
Aristotle, 61, 169
Aronson, E., 85
Ayres, B. D. Jr., 194

B

Bacon, F., 57, 61, 64–65, 68, 222
Baillie, P. D., 74
Balmuth, M., 14
Bargh, J. A., 33
Barkley, R. A., 149
Bastedo, M. N., 45
Bedford, F. L., 87
Begg, I., 36
Bègue, L., 49
Beier, M. E., 161
Bekkering, H., 33
Berry, W. R., 214
Bettinger, E. P., 94

Betts, E. A., 15
Bible Gateway, 34
Bienvenu, H. J., 15
Bifulco, R., 94
Bishop, D.V.M., 42, 194
Bjork, R., 13
Blagov, P. S., 48
Blake, W., 135
Blank, A., 31
Bobko, P., 148
Boselie, F., 11
Boulet, S. L., 41
Bowers, C., 91
Bowman, N. A., 45
Boyle, C. A., 41
Boyle, M. O., 161
Breizat, A.-H.S., 214
Browne, M. W., 101, 102
Bruner, J., 124
Bullock, A., 35
Bush, G. W., 180–181
Bush, V., 109–110
Buys, L. M., 74

C

Cacioppo, J. T., 34, 48
Cain, O. L., 74
Cannon-Bowers, J. A., 91
Cantor, N., 47
Carlsmith, J. M., 83, 85–86

Carpenter, C., 187
Carroll, J. B., 15
Castel, A. D., 73
Center for Disease Control, 42
Chaker, A. M., 184
Chall, J., 15–16
Chall, J. S., 38
Chanowitz, B., 31
Chartrand, T. L., 33
Chase, W. G., 161
Chua, A., 113–114
Cialdini, R. B., 51
Clark, L., 184
Coleridge, S. T., 143
Collins, B. E., 85
Confrey, J., 181
Crocker, K. E., 38

D
Daniel, D., 38, 222
Daniel, M. H., 53
Davis, M. A., 148
DeBono, K. G., 42
Dellinger, E. P., 214
Descartes, R., 62–65
Detterman, D. K., 53
Dewey, J., 88
Dijksterhuis, A., 33
Dobkin, C., 187
Doherty, M. E., 102
Dohrmann, B., 167–169, 176
Dohrmann, H. J., 168
Dole, R., 140
Doucette, W. R., 74
Dukakis, M., 140
Durand, A., 69

E
Elmore-Yalch, R., 45
Elstein, A. S., 46

Engle, R. W., 40
Ericsson, K. A., 161
Ernst, M. E., 74

F
Fairchild, H. N., 68
Falbo, C., 11
Faloon, S., 161
Farinacci, S., 36
Federer, R., 175
Feinberg, M., 49
Festinger, L., 82–83, 84
Feyerabend, P., 95
Feynman, R. P., 81, 96, 102, 210
Fibonacci, L., 6
Fiske, S. T, 45
Fleischmann, M., 100–102
Flesch, R., 15
Ford, J. K., 74
Friedman, T. L., 140

G
Gaeth, G. J., 148
Galileo (Galilei), 65
Gardner, D., 180
Gardner, H. E., 115, 174–175
Garrett, R. K., 55
Gawande, A., 214
Gay, P., 65, 66
Gazzaniga, M. S., 126
George III (England), 66
Gillen, J., 156
Gilovich, T., 144
Goldacre, B., 184
Goldstein, N. J., 51
Goodman, K., 39
Gore, A., 140
Gray, J. R., 73
Gray, W., 14
Grosser, M., 94

H

Hafer, C. L., 49
Hagoort, P., 33
Haidt, J., 56
Haldane, J.B.S., 93
Hall, R. A. Jr., 15
Hamann, S., 48
Hambly, H., 194
Hamre, B. K., 120, 146
Hannah, G., 168, 169
Harenski, K., 48
Harnish, R. J., 42
Harriss, A. J., 15
Hattie, J., 213
Hawking, S., 89
Haynes, A. B., 214
Hegel, G.W.F., 207, 215
Helmreich, R. L., 85
Hemsley-Brown, J., 177
Hendel, J., 172
Herman, P., 34
Hibbert, F., 200
Hirsch, E. D. Jr., 218, 219
Hitler, A., 144
Hoffman, J., 70
Holliday, K. S., 74
Holt, J., 75
Horton, M. R., 74
Hoxby, C. M., 94
Hughes, J., 184
Hume, D., 65
Hussein, S., 143–144

J

James, W., 33
Jardine, L., 61
Jefferson, T., 167
John V (Portugal), 66
Johnston, I., 34

K

Kahneman, D., 149
Kang, J., 94
Kaptchuk, T. J., 102
Kavale, K., 212
Keats, J., 8
Keil, F. C., 73
Kelly, A. E., 181
Kelly, H. H., 46
Kelman, H. C., 42
Kepler, J., 65
Kerry, J., 47–48
Khalsa, G.C.K., 200
Kilts, C., 48
Kinder, D. R., 45
Kintsch, W., 126
Klepser, T. B., 74
Klingberg, T., 161
Koch, E., 117
Koehler, J. J., 48
Kolowich, S., 168, 169
Krems, J. F., 46
Krishnan, C., 45

L

La Paro, K. M., 120
Ladd, H. F., 94
Lagemann, E. C., 172
Lakin, J. L., 33
Langer, E., 31–32
Lasane, T. P., 48
Lazarus, D., 167
Leary, S. P., 48
Levin, I. P., 148
Levine, A., 172
Levy, F., 91
Lillard, A., 86
Line, E. A., 42
Lipsitz, S. R., 214
Littleton, K., 156

Lloyd, J. W., 123
Locke, J., 63–65
Lodge, M., 48
Lynch, E., 55

M
MacDaniel, M., 13
Macpherson, E., 194
Macrosson, W.D.K., 11
Maddux, W. W., 33
Mahoney, M. J., 48
Makel, M. C., 91
Markowsky, G., 11
Martyn, K. A., 15
Mathews, M. M., 13
Mattson, P. D., 212
McCabe, D. P., 73
McDaniel, M. A., 160
McKnight, C. C., 125
Mclaughlin, B., 168
Mercer, N., 156
Mercier, H., 50
Merton, R. K., 183
Miller, M., 141
Mondale, W., 140
Montessori, M., 86
Moore, H., 200
Mullally, R. A., 74
Munro, G. D., 48
Murarka, S., 94
Murnane, R. J., 91
Mynatt, C. R., 102

N
Nascimbene, C., 45
Neill, A. S., 75
Newall, C. A., 74
Newton, I., 65, 68, 86
Nicolson, R. I., 194
Nisbet, E. C., 55
Nisbett, R. E., 53

O
Obama, B., 107, 141
Olariu, A., 11
Olson, J. M., 34

P
Packard, V., 35
Pardo, C. A., 45
Pashler, H., 13
Patton, G., 117
Pendergast, M., 41
Perloff, R. M., 39
Peters, M. D., 45
Petroshius, S. M., 38
Petty, R. E., 34, 48
Phillipson, J. D., 74
Piaget, J., 86–87
Pianta, R. C., 120, 146
Planck, M., 89
Plucker, J. A., 91
Polya, G., 1
Pons, S., 100–102
Popper, K., 92
Prasad, J., 82
PubMed.gov, 105

Q
Quine, W. V., 50

R
Ramhold, J., 168
Randerson, J., 184
Rauf, F. A., 55
Ravitch, D., 16, 95, 96
Rawson, E., 73
Reagan, R., 140
Reinberg, S., 214
Reynolds, D., 194
Riener, C., 13, 37
Rohrer, D., 13
Roosevelt, F. D., 109

Rostand, J., 114
Rukeyser, M., 194

S
Sagan, C., 87
Sandler, A., 195
Schieve, L. A., 41
Schlessinger, L. C., 175–176
Schmidt, W., 125
Schwarz, A., 46
Sharp, C., 177
Shavers, A., 168
Shimp, T. A., 40
Shkedi, A., 177
Shute, N., 43
Sifft, J. M., 200
Silverthorne, M., 61
Simon, H. A., 107, 111–113
Snyder, M., 46, 47
Socct, D. J., 195
Solow, R. M., 109
Sperber, D., 50
Staarman, J. K., 156
Steward, J. P., 25
Stewart, P. E., 11
Stohler, C. S., 195
Stone, M.W.F., 61
Strachan, G. C., 11
Stuart, E. W., 40
Swann, W. B. Jr., 46
Swift, J., 31

T
Taber, C. S., 48
Theus, K. T., 35
Thorndike, E. L., 160
Times of London, The, 184, 194
Tolstoy, L., 50
Trout, J. D., 71
Tversky, A., 149
Tweney, R. D., 102
Twiner, A., 156

U
Ullian, J. S., 50

V
Van Dijk, T., 126
Vargas, D. L., 45
Voltaire, 65
Vygotsky, L. S., 86–87

W
Wagner, R., 70
Walton, D., 178
Wang, H. C., 125
Ward, L. A., 74
Wason, P. C., 46
Watson, J. D., 191
Watt, H. J., 42
Weisberg, D. S., 73
Weiser, T. G., 214
Wernahm, A.G.H., 74
Westen, D., 48
Whitehouse, A.J.O., 42
Wilford, J. N., 101
Willer, R., 49
Willingham, D. T., 13, 37, 123, 126, 161, 171, 194, 221, 222
Wood, A., 61
Woodworth, R. S., 160
Wordsworth, W., 57, 58, 68–69, 70

Y
Yalch, R. F., 43
Yau, W.-Y., 195
Yellowstone Net, 64

Z
Zajonc, R. B., 36
Zanna, M. P., 34
Zierer, C., 46
Zimmerman, A. W., 45
Zubieta, J.-K., 195

Subject Index

A

Abstract, defined, 199

Academic institutions, Persuader's affiliations with, 171

Accelerated Reader program, 197

Accuracy, and beliefs, 50–51

Alabama, University of (Huntsville), business relationship with Dohrmann, 168–169

American Educational Research Association (AERA), 181

American Physical Society, 104

Analysis, levels of, 120–126

Analyze it process, 183–205; Brain Gym, 183–185, 200; breakthroughs, 190–191; double-checking experience, 188–190; evidence, evaluation of, 191–196; misremembering experiences, 186–187; research studies, finding/interpreting, 196–205; testimonials, 194–196; use of term, 26–27; using experience, 185–191

Applied research, 109–110

Applied science: artifacts, 112; goal of, 114; relationship between basic science and, 109–112

Architects, multiple goals of, 221

Astrological theory, failings of, 95

Attractive people, and unconscious persuasion, 38–39

Authority: believing someone based on, 170; conflicting authorities, 176–178; failure of, 169–171; marginally useful guides, 171–173; misapplied scientific expertise, 175–176; misunderstood claims, 174–175; situations in which arguments can go wrong, 178; useless guides, 173–174; What Works Clearinghouse (WWC), 181; work in educational research, 178–182

Autism spectrum disorder (ASD), 17–21; behavioral therapy for, 17, 17–18; fringe treatments, 18–19; immunoglobulin, 18

Autopilot, 42–43; and engagement in complex behaviors, 32–33

B

Background, judging, 176

Basic mental process, using Latin to train with content-free exercises, 160–161

Basic research, 109–110

Basic science: artifacts, 112; how to use/respond to facts from, 115; levels of analysis, 120–126; outer environment, 119–120; relationship between applied science and, 109–112

Basic scientific knowledge, drawing on, 113–127

Belief: and emotions, 54–56; fuel for, 1–2; motivation for, 50–51; and science, 57–79; and self-identity, 51–52; and social ties, 53–54; and values, 52–53; as a web, 50

Benefit vs. belief, 194–195

Best Evidence Encyclopedia, 181

Bias, 57–58; confirmation, 46–49, 102; in messages, 2

Birth order, impact of, 91–92

Body Heat (movie), 100

Brain, and TV watching, 73–74

Brain-based education products, 73

Brain games software packages, 160

Brain Gym, 183–185; adoption of, 185; Brain Gym Journal, 184; support of effectiveness of, 200; training, 200; unsubstantiated scientific claims, 184–185; Web searches, 184; Web site, 183–184, 200

Breakthroughs, 190–191

Bright Beginnings, 199

C

Carnegie Corporation, 15

Carryover effects in repeated testing, 99

Chain of influence in education, 155–156

Change, See also Persuader: amounting to classroom micromanagement, 157; breakthroughs, 190–191; chain of influence, 156; defined, 136; effectiveness of, 207; evaluating, 158; extravagant claims about, 159–160; failure of, 210; lacking evidence to support it, 168–169; of placing an interactive whiteboard in a classroom, 156; promising to improve a skill, 163; promising to remediate a problem, 163–164; research based, 196; urging project learning/group learning, 156–157; using your experience, 185–191; without scientific backing, 212

Charter schools, public schools compared to, 94

Christian scriptures, and wisdom, 60–61

Cluster sampling, 98

Coca-Cola: New Coke, 41; taste-test experiments, 41

Cognitive dissonance theory, 82–83, 159; core of, 82; criticism of, 85

Comparison groups, 200–201

Complex behaviors, and consciousness, 33

Confirmation bias, 46–49, 102

Convenience sampling, 98

Core Knowledge Foundation, 126

Correlation vs. causation, 98

Credibility, and familiarity, 36

Critical thinking: applying a strategy, 162–163; and factual knowledge or information, 221–222; and subject matter, 161–162

D

Decision maker: acting as, 27–28; posing questions to, 27

Deism, 68

Differential attrition rates between groups, 97

Disputations, 61

Dissonance, and conflict, 85–86

Do-it-yourself School mission statement, 116

Dore Program, 197; logic behind, 193–194

Doubt, 62

Dr. Laura Program, 175–176

E

Education: and advances in science, 218; chain of influence in, 155–156; comparison to architecture, 221; comparison to medicine, 220–221; decisions, 207; and delivery of information, 145; and government regulations, 94–95; and scientific advances, 218, 222

Education decisions, 207

Education Resources Information Center, 197

Education system, levels of, 23

Educational research: basing policy on, 219; criticism of, 172–173; personal Web sites for download of articles written, 199; settled truth, 180; skill of, 180; suggestions, interpretation by parents / teachers, 180; suspicion of, 177

Educational research study problems: carryover effects in repeated testing, 99; cluster sampling, 98; convenience sampling, 98; correlation vs. causation, 98; differential attrition rates between groups, 97; experimenter expectancy effects, 97; haphazard sampling, 98; nonrepresentative volunteers, 98; purposive sampling, 98; quota sampling, 98; random sampling, 98; regression toward the mean, 99; Simpson's paradox, 97; stratified sampling, 98

Educational researchers, compared to fields of trustworthy experts, 178–179

Educational programs, with Romantic sensibility and Enlightenment-style scientific proof, 78–79

Edwards' syndrome, 16

Emile (Rousseau), 75

Emotional conditioning, 39–41

Emotions, and beliefs, 50, 54–56

Empirical nature of good science, 216

Enlightenment: and the intellectual elite, 67; peripheral cues, 78

Enlightenment thinking: divine nature, 68; and first meta-belief, 58–59; on knowledge, 62; meta-beliefs, 71–72; nature as a mechanism, 67–68; nature's closeness to the divine, 68; pervasiveness of, 67–68; Voltaire on, 65

Epic skyscraper (Miami FL), 128–129

ERIC, 198–199; downloading articles from, 199

Ethicology, 88–89

Evaluation of research, See Research-based studies: attention, 43–44; bias, 45–50;

confirmation bias, 46–49; stereotypes, 47; strength of an argument, 45–50; stumbling blocks, 43–50

Evidence: evaluation of, 191–196; scientific, 12, 24–25; in sixteenth-century European culture, 59–60; testimonials, 194–196

Expectations, 159

Experience: being misled by, 186–187; breakthroughs, 190–191; double-checking, 188–190; misremembering, 186–187; using, 185–191

Experiment on a Bird in the Air Pump (Wright), 67

Experimenter expectancy effects, 97

F

Factcheck.org, 55

Factual knowledge, and critical thinking, 221–222

False beliefs, protecting ourselves from, 57–58

Falsifiable nature, of good science, 217

Familiarity, 36–37; and credibility, 36

Feedback, 117–119, 126, 164; and complex actions, 118; in education research, 118–119; functions of, 117; providing information for ongoing correction, 117–118

Fibonacci arc, 6–8

Fibonacci sequence, 6–7

Flashpoint blog Web site, 168

Flip it process: combining framing effects, 149–152; common

neuroscientific claims stripped, 154; old/familiar claims, 153; outcomes, 146–148; suggested steps, 164–165; use of term, 26; vague claims, 153–166; what you're to do, 148–149; writing down thoughts about action steps, 165–166

freechecklists.net, 214

Fusion vs. fission, at nuclear power plants, 100–102

G

Galileo Gambit, 173–174

Golden Ratio, 2–11; in classical architecture, 3; dimensions of books/magazines corresponding to, 9–10; interpretation of the aesthetic value of, 8; invalidity of, 11; observed in nature as a spiral, 6; persuasion, connection to, 8, 11; and ratios of body parts, 5–6; rectangles, 11; in Western art, 4

Good observation in science, 89–91

Good science, 88; cumulative nature of, 95; empirical nature of, 216; falsifiable nature of, 217; measurability of, 216; principles of, 103–104, 208–209

Google, 197–198; searching for author name on, 199

Government agencies, affiliations with, and Persuaders, 171

H

Haphazard sampling, 98

healthfinder.gov, 104

Heaven's Gate religious cult, 194
Herbal remedies, 74
Hidden persuaders, identification
    of, 2–11
Hidden potential/power, and the
    Romantic period, 69–70, 76
Homeopathy, 72–73
Homosexuality, beliefs about
    (example), 55–56
Honda, dating-investment strategy
    in advertisement, 38–39

I
Ignored messages, influence of, 2
Imaginary Invalid, The (Molière),
    192
Imitation of behaviors, and social
    interactions, 33–34
Impromptu, in music, 69
Inner environment, 120, 126, 127
Interactive whiteboard, defined,
    156
Intuition, 69

J
Johns Hopkins University School
    of Education, Best Evidence
    Encyclopedia, 181
Just-world belief, 49

K
Kindred Spirits (Durand), 69

L
Language Experience technique,
    157
Latin, difficulty in learning,
    160–161
Learning styles: child vs. adult
    reading styles, 13–14; main cost
    of, 13; theories of, 12–13

Left Back (Ravitch), 16
Leonard and Gertrude (Pestalozzi),
    75
Levels of analysis, 120–126; con-
    tent knowledge, 125–126; and
    educational psychology, 125;
    evaluating an education product
    claim, 125–126; false claims,
    126; practice, importance to
    learning, 125
Life Adjusting Movement, 96
Life Success Academy, Super
    Teaching program, 168–169

M
Math curricula, factors to equate
    when comparing, 163
Measurability: of good science,
    216; and scientific investigation,
    91
Measurement, importance of,
    89–91
Medical News Today, 139
Medieval thought, 62
Memorization, and reading, 14
Meta-analyses, and homeopathic
    remedies, 72
Meta-beliefs, 49–50, 58–59,
    65–66; and catchphrases, 59;
    "natural is good," 74–75; per-
    sonal experience, 58; reasoned
    thought and scientific method,
    58; in today's education, 71–79;
    and worldview, 59
Mimicking of behaviors, and social
    interactions, 33–34
Mixed data, 94
Multiple intelligences theory
    (Gardner), 115, 174–175
Music Man, The (musical), 159

N

National Academy of Sciences, 107
National Center for Education
    Statistics, 46, 149
National Council of Teachers of
    Mathematics, 219
National Institute of Child Health
    and Human Development, 40
National Institutes of Health, 46,
    197
National Mathematics Advisory
    Panel, 180–181
National Science Board, 107, 108
Neptune, discovery of planet, 94
Neuroimmunopathology
    Laboratory, 45
Neurophilia, 73
New Organon, The (Jardine/
    Silverthorne), 61
No Child Left Behind Act (2002),
    71
Nonrepresentative volunteers, 98

O

Obsolete industries, 145
"Ode on a Grecian Urn" (Keats), 8
Old Faithful geyser (Yellowstone
    National Park), 64
Orton-Gillingham, 199
Outer environment, 119–120, 126,
    127
Owl of Minerva, 213–215
Oxford University, decree regard-
    ing Aristotle, 61

P

Pavlov's conditioning experiments,
    39–40
Peer review, 101, 198; and
    science, 102

Pegboard experiment (Festinger),
    84–85, 159
Penicillin, 108–109
Peripheral cues, 43, 45, 57, 146;
    to boost credibility of education
    programs, 57–59, 75, 78–79
Personal experience,
    understanding the world
    through, 58
Persuader, See also Change: ask-
    ing to explaining a Change,
    192; citation of research papers,
    193; confusion of label with
    proof, 192–193; creden-
    tials, trustworthiness of, 170,
    173–174; defined, 136; degrees,
    171–172; desire to appear
    authoritative, 146; in education,
    140–141; experience of, 169;
    flipping claims of, 149; fram-
    ing by, 148; Galileo Gambit,
    173–174; pressing to explain a
    Change, 192; promises regard-
    ing Change, 158–159, 164;
    requesting report data from,
    196; and risks, 152; targeting of
    teachers, 141–142; ways sought
    to establish authority, 171
Persuasion: connection to Golden
    Ratio, 8, 11; and educational
    intervention, 23–24; and
    similarity, 34; unconscious,
    34–43
Phonics, 16
Placebos: effect, 194–195; and
    improved symptoms of ADHD/
    autism, 195
Poetry, 68–69
Policy, basing on research, 219
Politifact, 55
Ponte Fabricio, 130

Popular media, and Persuaders, 171

Principia (Newton), 65

Problem solving: deep structure of problem, making apparent, 162; and subject matter, 161–162

Prominent companies, affiliations with, and Persuaders, 171

Publications/public speaking, and Persuaders, 171

PubMed, 105, 197–199; downloading articles from, 199; peer review, 198–199

Purposive sampling, 98

Q

Questions, for decision making, 28

Quota sampling, 98

R

Race to the Top initiative (2009), 155

Random sampling, 98

Reading Wars, 16

Reason, understanding the world through, 58

Regression toward the mean, 99

Report data, requesting from a Persuader, 196

Research-based studies, 19–27; car purchase process (example), 21–23; evaluation of an idea's scientific merit, 25–27; and previous research results, 21; quality of research, evaluation of, 20–21; shortcuts to getting the job done, 21–23; subject distinctions, 21; weaknesses/ strengths in, 100

Research based, use of term, 19

Research findings: comparison groups, 200–201; experiment participants, number of, 201–203; nuanced view of, 200–203; simplest view of, 199; statistical vs. practical significance, 203–205

Research shortcut, 25

Research studies, finding/interpreting, 196–205

Research, where to find, 197

Romantic period, 58, 67–71, 75; children's natural propensity to learn, 75–76; child's propensity to learn crushed by school routine (meta-belief), 75–76; differences in motivation while, 77; emotion, 68–69; emphasis on the individual, 76–77; hidden potential/power, 69–70, 76; mechanistic view of the universe, 68; meta-beliefs, 73–75; "natural is good" meta-belief, 74–75; nature, 73–74; negative side of schooling, 75; peripheral cues, 78; and reason, 68; reverence for nature, 75; romantic impulse, 67–71; spontaneity in, 69–70; view of nature, 68

Royal Society of London motto, 167, 177–178

S

Sampling, types of, 98

Schooling: goals of, 113–117, 119, 126; unfounded beliefs related to, 12; and values, 119

Science, See also Applied science; Basic science; Good science; Science Cycle: Americans' view of, 107–108; and belief, 57–79; and education goals, 116–117; how it works, 83–88; how to use, 107–132; and peer review, 102; safeguarding, 102–105

Science Cycle, 83–88, 92–93; Test phase, 127–128

Scientific consensus views, 104

Scientific evidence, 212; absence of, 12; laypeople's view of, 24–25

Scientific expertise, misapplied, 175–176

Scientific findings, and the classroom, 25

Scientific knowledge, 212; drawing on, 113–127; static view of, 220; using to improved education, 86

Scientific method: as a cycle, 85–86; cyclical nature of, 86–87; ethicology, 88–89; inappropriate areas for, 89; and objectivity, 216; putting human experience into an experimental context, 186; testing a theory, 96–102

Scientific research: Americans' view of, 107–109; federal expenditures on, 108

Scientific theory: provisional nature of, 86; and use of scientific knowledge to improve education, 86

Secretary's Commission on Achieving Necessary Skills (SCANS), 96

Secretin, defined, 20

Self-actualization, 115

Self-concept, and beliefs, 51–52

Semiotics, 9

Similar-to-me effect, 42

Similarity, and persuasion, 34

Simon the Scientist/Billy the Believer, 170, 174, 176, 182

Simpson's paradox, 97

Singapore Math, 197–198

Social interactions, and thought, 31–32

Social pleasantries, 34

Social proof, 37–38

Social ties, and beliefs, 53–54

Society for Human Resource Management, 118

Society of Clinical Psychology, 104

Spiral curriculum, 124–125

Spirals in plants, 8–9

Spontaneity, 69–70

Stratified sampling, 98

Strip it process: analogies, creating, 143–146; claims the Persuader is "like you," 142–143; emotion, 139–142; suggested steps, 164–165; use of term, 25–26; writing down thoughts about action steps, 165–166

Subliminal persuasion, 34–35

Success, defining signs of, 158–159

Summa Theologia (Aquinas), 61

Summary volumes of research, 105

Summerhill: A Radical Approach to Child Rearing (Neill), 75

Super Teaching program, Life Success Academy, 168–169

Supernatural, use of term, 88–89

Surgeon's checklist (Gawande), 214

Systematic manipulation, outside of our control, 2

T

"Tables Turned" (Wordsworth), 70

Teach Your Own: A Hopeful Path for Education (Neill), 75

Teachers, nonnegotiable goals for, 221

Technical jargon, 72

Temperature, significance of red and blue to, 9

Testimonials, 194–196

Theory, discarding of, 210

Trace it process, 167–182; authority, failure of, 169–178; conflicting authorities, 176–177; educational research and authority, 178–182; marginally useful guides, 171–173; misapplied scientific expertise, 175–176; misunderstood claims, 174–175; Super Teaching program, 168–169; use of term, 26; useless guides, 173–174; What Works Clearinghouse (WWC), 181

Treatise of Human Nature (Hume), 65

Trisomy 18, 16

Trust, similar-to-me effect, 42

Trustworthiness, of messages, 2

Twenty-first-century skills movement, 95

U

Unconscious persuasion, 34–43, 41; and attractive people, 38–39; emotional conditioning, 39–41; familiarity, 36; meta-beliefs, 49–50; and people we perceive to be similar to us, 42; social proof, 37

Underpants Gnomes (South Park), 110–111, 113, 120

Uranus, irregularities in orbit of, 94

U.S. Department of Education, What Works Clearinghouse (WWC), 181

U.S. National Library of Medicine, 197

U.S. Office of Scientific Research and Development, 108

V

Vague claims, 153–166

Values, and beliefs, 51–53

W

Wayback Machine, 183

What Works Clearinghouse (WWC), 181

Whole-language reading, 15–16, 95

Whole-word reading, 15

"Why Chinese Mothers Are Superior" (Chua), 113–114

Why Johnny Can't Read, 15

Wisdom, and Christian scriptures, 60–61

Working memory: inability to train, 161; large, and tests of reasoning, 160–161

Y

Yahoo, 197; searching for author name on, 199

Credit Lines

Figure I.1 Rectangle: © Daniel Willingham

Figure I.2 Parthenon: Nevena Kozekova © Fotolia; Pyramid of Giza: © Dmitry Pichugin, Fotolia.com

Figure I.3 Violin: © Eric Monaton Fotolia; Mona Lisa © Wikimedia Commons/Musée du Louvre; The Last Supper: © Wikimedia Commons

Figure I.4a Leonardo da Vinci, Vitruvian Man © Wikimedia Commons; Human arm: © Alx, Fotolia.com

Figure I.5 Jessica Alba © Helga Esteb / Shutterstock.com

Figure I.6 Fibonacci arc: © Daniel Willingham

Figure I.7 Nautilus Shell: © JoinGate–123RF; Sunflower Center © Mike Kosiusko; Romanesco © Tamara Kulikova, Fotolia.com

Figure I.8 Rubber plant © Tamara Kulikova, Fotolia.com

Figure I.9a *The Ultimate Dog Treat Cookbook: Homemade Goodies for Man's Best Friend*; Liz Palika; Copyright © 2005 by Wiley Publishing, Inc.; Reprinted with permission of John Wiley & Sons, Inc.

Figure I.9b *Teaching with Fire: Poetry that Sustains the Courage to Teach*; Sam M. Intrator, Megan Scribner; Copyright © 2003 by Center for Teacher Formation; Reprinted with permission of John Wiley & Sons, Inc.

Figure I.9c *Why Don't Students Like School? A Cognitive Scientist Answers Questions About How the Mind Works and What It Means for the Classroom*; Daniel T. Willingham; Copyright © 2009 by Daniel T. Willingham; Reprinted with permission of John Wiley & Sons, Inc.

Figure I.10 From the *New England Primer: A Reprint of the Earliest Known Edition*. P. L. Ford, Editor. Dodd, Mead & Company, 1899.

Figure 1.1 Car model © Doan Vien Che, via Flickr.com

Exhibit 6.3 When authorities conflict © Daniel Willingham

Exhibit 6.4 How authority can go wrong © Daniel Willingham

Exhibit 6.5 How authority works © Daniel Willingham

Chapter Seven feature Logic behind the Dore claim © Daniel Willingham

Figure 7.1 The problem with testimonials © Daniel Willingham

Table 7.1 Research scorecard © Daniel Willingham

Exhibit 8.1 Checklist © Daniel Willingham